Old Age and the Search for Security

INTERDISCIPLINARY STUDIES IN HISTORY

Harvey J. Graff, *General Editor*

OLD AGE AND THE SEARCH FOR SECURITY

An American Social History

Carole Haber and Brian Gratton

Indiana University Press

Bloomington and Indianapolis

The paper used in this publication meets the minimum
requirements of American National Standard for Information
Sciences—Permanence of Paper for Printed Library Materials, ANSI
Z39.48–1984.

⊗™
Manufactured in the United States of America

Library of Congress Cataloging-in-Publication Data

Haber, Carole, date.
Old age and the search for security: an American social
history / Carole Haber and Brian Gratton.
p.   cm.—(Interdisciplinary studies in history)
Includes bibliographical references and index.
ISBN 0-253-32691-5 (alk. paper).—ISBN 0-253-20836-X (pbk. :
alk. paper)
1. Old age—United States—History. 2. Aged—United
States—Economic conditions. 3. Aged—United States—Social
conditions. 4. Social Security—United States.
I. Gratton, Brian. II. Title. III. Series.
HQ1064.U5H183   1993
305.26′0973—dc20
93-12258

1 2 3 4 5 99 98 97 96 95 94

*To Bernice and Stanley Haber, who never had
the chance to grow old. (C. H.)*

To Janet Gould: El amor no tiene edad. (B. G.)

Contents

Tables and Figures

Preface

DURING THE PAST two decades, scholars have established the conceptual and empirical foundations of the history of old age. In this book, we hope to provide a framework upon which a more complete history can now be built. To accomplish this task, we have drawn on the findings of the extant literature as well as on our own research. In this synthesis of secondary and primary evidence, we rely on a variety of disciplines in order to present a *social* history, that is, a conceptualization of the lives of the American elderly in the broad sense. We present a series of studies exploring the historical paths taken by Americans in their search for a secure and satisfying old age. Along several major lines of inquiry—the family, wealth and welfare, work and retirement, the institution, and advice—we trace the experience of old age from the colonial period to the present and seek to understand the differences in such experience by reason of race, gender, class, and region.

Although we are deeply impressed by the contributions made by scholars from several fields, the current literature is marked by dispute within disciplines and disharmony across them. Reflecting its origins in multidisciplinary social gerontology and the divisive impact of the debates over Social Security in the 1980s, the historiography of old age resembles an unassembled jigsaw puzzle. Individual pieces seem sharp and clear, yet these fragments have not been placed in relationship to one another. Scattered through a wide number of monographs, dissertations, and articles, they form no coherent picture. While historians, historical sociologists, and historical economists have examined attitudes, political events, or social and economic theory, few have attempted to construct a usable past that resolves the controversies within disciplines and harmonizes the dissonance among them. Throughout much of the work, as well, no effort has been made to compose a history that considers both cultural attitudes and structural factors.

To create a framework that uses these diverse findings, we have first identified the principal themes that have dominated the literature of the several disciplines. In the introduction, we review the existing scholarship, describing its achievements and limitations and isolating the issues that continue to attract the energy of scholars and the attention of readers. As we shall see, numerous debates separate the work of historians, economists, and sociologists. Early scholars had been content to draw on highly deterministic models and paradigms; later studies revealed that the history of old age may be far more complex and less linear than these early models suggested.

In chapter 1, we then explore the family life of the old. In the colonial era, as in the present day, the family relationships of the elderly have been central to the experience of old age. Nonetheless, a substantial body of work shows that the family life of the elderly changed dramatically across time; where once most elderly persons lived with their children in nuclear families, most now reside only with their spouse or alone. The explanation for these evolving patterns remains a matter of debate. Several historians cite the role culture has played in family dynamics; other researchers emphasize the importance of economics or demographics. Yet, few scholars have devoted great attention to the diversity in family life according to race, gender, class, and region. A mature history of the elderly in the family requires an explanation of broad structural change as well as a sensitivity to differences among individuals.

As family has provided a central focus for many of the studies of old age, so too has the economic status of the old. Scholars have assumed that at least since the rise of an industrial society, the elderly have comprised an extremely impoverished population. As a result, most twentieth-century studies of the elderly concentrate on welfare programs designed to protect them. In chapter 2, we present evidence on both the poverty and the wealth of the elderly and challenge the supposition that being old meant being impoverished. Rather, we find that aged men and women have always experienced a wide range of economic possibilities. Individuals of great affluence as well as those of extreme need can consistently be found among the aged population. The discovery that many older people may have been in good economic circumstances and that their well-being improved during the industrial era leads us to explore why welfare programs based on age have been so common in American history.

Chapter 3 considers another issue germane to the economic condition of older men and women: work and retirement patterns. The conventional belief that the aged were driven relentlessly from the industrial labor market has recently been subject to a series of effective criticisms. A new model explaining the work patterns of the elderly, however, has not yet emerged. Scholars debate when and why the elderly withdrew from employment and turned to retirement. This controversy exposes an important disharmony: cultural historians observe strong evidence of ageism and disparagement of older workers in the same period when some historical economists report stable or improving labor force conditions for older men. In this debate, scholars' varied perceptions of the industrial period's impact on the elderly lead to diverse explanations for Social Security and its effects on work and retirement.

A similar discordance attends accounts of aged inmates in the poorhouse and the nursing home, which have been, as chapter 4 suggests, crucial metaphors in Americans' conceptualization of old age. Early twentieth-century advocates for state pensions argued that almshouses played an ominous and ever-growing role in the lives of the old. As a result, they demanded that the state step in to eradicate the institution. As we shall see, however, the threat of the almshouse was clearly exaggerated. Despite statistics that seemed to prove the elderly were increasingly vulnerable to institutionalization, the proportion of aged inmates in asylum remained remarkably stable. Nonetheless, perceptions of institutionalization figured greatly in the political struggle for Social Security and have since been a dominant issue in old-age politics.

The institution and other age-based welfare measures dictated roles for the old and provided a discourse through which the aging process has been interpreted. Since the colonial period, a variety of experts have offered advice to the elderly on both the meaning of old age and the proper behavior for those in the last stage of life. In chapter 5, we examine these ideals and the interpretation of old age on which they were based and find that prescriptive advice never operated outside the realm of structural change. As the roles of the old were transformed in the family and the workplace, cultural beliefs about old age and the value of senescence became radically altered as well.

In the conclusion, chapter 6, we weave the chronicles of family, wealth, work, institutionalization, and advice into a reinterpretation of old age in the United States. This history differs significantly from conventional accounts. Although impoverished and deserted elderly individuals have certainly existed in the nation's past, they hardly made up a majority of the old and should not be the dominant image in their history. We offer a new history of the American elderly that explains both the increasing economic well-being of the old and the formation of policies that placed the elderly at the center of the welfare state.

Throughout this study, we consistently rely upon a three-part periodization. The first major shift in the history of old age occurred in the mid-nineteenth century as the United States was transformed from a preindustrial to an industrial society. A second major shift then occurred in the mid-twentieth century with the creation and implementation of Social Security. In each of these three historical stages—the preindustrial, industrial, and Social Security eras—the families of the old, their work, wealth, institutionalization, and advice reflected the economic and social context of the era. None of these turning points, however, represents a total transformation. At no time did cultural standards, family patterns, or the social and economic status of the aged undergo a complete break with the past. Yet the conditions inherent in these periods still had a pronounced influence on most aspects of aging; they provide the most useful temporal structure for the history of old age in the United States. Irregular in timing and uneven in effects, the eras can nonetheless be identified distinctly in each of the main lines of scholarly inquiry.

The periodization, however, provides no simple ascension or declension in the history of the American elderly. As a group, the old have reflected the diversity of the population from which they sprang. Age alone has never defined their status; like persons of every age, they represent their gender, race, ethnicity, and class as well. Moreover, we argue that a profound dissonance existed between the cultural and the political history of the industrial period, on one hand, and its economic and familial history on the other. In the late nineteenth and early twentieth century, cultural and political declarations about old age revealed an unmistakable decline in status. In their advice to the elderly, experts voiced an increasing intolerance for aging; politicians and welfare advocates assumed that state policies were required to rescue the elderly from disease and dependence. In contrast, by the first decades of the twentieth century, a significant proportion of the elderly experienced stable or rising standards of work and well-being, increased affluence, and a reduction in familial tensions. For the first time, their work and family patterns met longstanding expectations of what comprised a "good old age."

In this history of old age, we have attempted to be sensitive to complexity and dissonance. We know that we have failed to capture that history whole. Indeed, we have written this book in part to encourage future scholarship and to engage the continued interest of readers in a subject filled with contradiction and difficulty. Part of that complexity lies in the great variety of social, economic, and personal conditions encountered by elderly Americans and the diverse strategies they employed to achieve a secure old age. In each of the studies of the elderly, we find that there never was one old age in the United States; a number of patterns and possibilities always existed.

As no singular old age ever existed, neither has a separate and segregated senescence been common. Despite policies and programs that have tended to define old age as distinct, the old have remained part of a familial and communal system, with enduring relationships to the young and middle-aged. Indeed, an essential unity exists in the shared experience of the life cycle; all persons see the future in the elders. The history of old age is therefore a subject replete with opportunity for understanding not only one group but Americans as a whole.

This book explores the work of a vigorous scholarly community; we have been fortunate to depend upon its members as colleagues, friends, and critics. The simple list that follows does an injustice to their contributions, but through it we wish to express our debt and gratitude: W. Andrew Achenbaum, Thomas Cole, Nancy Folbre, Janet Gould, William Graebner, Jay Gubrium, Rodney Ito II, Elizabeth Kogen, Jon Moen, John Myles, Michael Nash, Jill Quadagno, Margaret Rose, Frances M. Rotondo, Peter Stearns, David D. Van Tassel, Robert Whaples, and the students of HIS382. We also thank our editors, Harvey Graff and Robert Sloan.

We have been fortunate in receiving financial support from a variety of sources. Brian Gratton gratefully acknowledges research assistance from a Rockefeller Residency in Humanities at the Reuther Library; an NEH/Mellon Advanced Research Fellowship at the Hagley Library; a research grant from the American Philosophical Society; Lubin-Winant Research Fellowship, Franklin and Eleanor Roosevelt Institute; Hoover Library Grant-in-Aid; Rockefeller Archive Center Research Grant; Truman Library Research Grant; NEH Travel to Collections Grant; and a Wood Fellowship, College of Physicians of Philadelphia. Arizona State University made several generous awards, including a travel grant, a Research Assistantship Award from the Graduate College, a Faculty-Grant-in-Aid for Research, and College of Liberal Arts and Sciences Summer and Mini-Grants. Carole Haber would additionally like to thank the Southern Regional Educational Board, the University of North Carolina at Charlotte Foundation, and the administration of University of North Carolina at Charlotte for a Reassignment of Duties Leave.

The vices and virtues of the book we share in equally; the order of authorship follows the arrangements we made with Indiana University Press and Harvey J. Graff, General Editor of the Interdisciplinary Studies in History Series. Although each of us has been primarily responsible for certain sections, we struggled earnestly over every draft and revision, seeking a truly collaborative presentation. Years ago, we followed Roscommon's adage to choose an author as one chooses a friend; his principle has made coauthorship an adventurous and rewarding journey.

Old Age and the Search for Security

Introduction

Historians and the History of Old Age in America

U NTIL THE MID-1970S, scholars expressed little interest in the history of old age. Before then, social scientists looked back with a certain nostalgia to a "premodern" period. They assumed that industrial society had degraded and impoverished the aged, causing the old to become the natural clients of the welfare state. For their part, historians seemed oblivious to the possibility that the study of the elderly might illuminate historical periods or invigorate research on leading historical issues. Even the studies of the "new" social historians focused almost entirely upon the activities of the young and the middle-aged.

The contrast with scholarly activity over the past two decades could not be more marked. Among sociologists, debate over the origins of the Social Security Act has emerged as a leading issue in the discipline and has renewed interest in both Marxian and Weberian theory. Anthropologists conceive of age and age systems as complex and important to the understanding of culture. Historical economists have been attentive to age and life-course phenomena. Uneasy with causally derived statistical series on work and retirement, they studied labor force participation rates in the nineteenth and early twentieth centuries, examined savings patterns that might influence work and retirement, and tested life-cycle theory in the career patterns of workers.

Among historians, interest in the elderly has grown markedly as well. In the mid-1970s, articles on the history of aging first began to appear in major journals, conferences were held on the influence of age in United States history, and several monographs reviewed the history of the American elderly. This initial enthusiasm has been followed by fifteen years of sustained attention to questions about the role and image of old age in the past. In this introduction, we trace the evolution of scholarly inquiry into old age and focus on key issues in the literature that have provoked considerable debate. Such controversy is, in a sense, ironic. Before recent research efforts, the chronicle could be presented in broad and clear strokes: the once-venerated position of the old had eroded with the advent of the modern era. The old had little hope of retaining power or respect in the urban-industrial world. Current work has clearly complicated the narrative. The outlines of the new history are no longer so indisputable or precise; nor has a firm replacement for conventional theory been established. Instead, dialogue continues on the place of older men and women in American history.

The Conventional View: Modernization Theory

Lacking a historical perspective, scholars interested in aging first relied upon a broad sociological model that asserted that the old once reigned as the most valuable members of their communities. They held complete power in their families, ruled unchallenged over councils of government, and prescribed social values through their religious and cultural authority. Then, modernization theorists continued, a radical transformation occurred. The status of the old fell sharply; they became outcasts in societies that celebrated youth and vitality.[1]

According to the thesis, the high status of the old in the past rested on four seemingly obvious factors.[2] First, as patriarchs in extended families, the elderly presided over large kinship networks. Their children and grandchildren rarely failed to show them the deference their great age commanded. Second, in an agricultural society, the elderly's control of land ensured that they retained not only the respect of their kin but the dependence of their offspring as well. Their heirs would not challenge the authority of their elders if such behavior led to disinheritance and poverty. Third, given the economic organization of society, the old, despite advancing age, retained their productivity. On the farm, age-based retirement was rare; the elderly generally remained active until debilitating illness or death intervened. And fourth, the knowledge and skills of the old provided them with continued prestige. Traditionally the source of valuable information, they played essential parts in the community.

All this changed, according to modernization theorists, with the advent of industrialization and urbanization. In the factory and the office, the old neither controlled the young nor retained economic independence. The advent of the wage economy marked the decline of their self-sufficiency. Furthermore, the demographic changes that led to the modern family meant the end of their patriarchal power. Now members of small nuclear families, they spent their final years in the "empty nest," apart from their grown children. Finally, professionalization and the growth of literacy made the skills of the old seem useless and outdated. With urban and industrial growth, modernization theorists concluded, the status of the old sharply declined; they seemed useless and irrelevant in modern society and inevitably became the recipients of welfare and Social Security programs.[3]

In many gerontological textbooks, a related historical theory often accompanied the "great transformation" model: given the assumed dramatic break in experience, the elderly of today are devoid of any relevant past. According to this thesis, their lives bear little resemblance to the experiences of the old in other eras. In part, this assumption was drawn from the historical narrative sketched by modernization theorists. If the elderly of a century or two ago were uniformly respected, their past experience bore little relationship to the problems of today's aged population.

The assertion of the unique and ahistorical nature of the lives of the contemporary elderly was based on an additional belief as well. Scholars have assumed that before recent times the old were not only too secure but also too rare to attract much concern. As the author of one recent college-level text stated, "In the past, the aged received little attention from writers, poets, philosophers, or scientists because they were so few in number."[4] As a result, contemporary old-age policies must have few meaningful antecedents. In much of the current gerontological literature, issues such as nursing homes, pension plans, and geriatric medicine are often discussed as if they were born full-grown, the result of extremely recent demographic and economic realities.

The Challenge to Modernization Theory

A small group of scholars has now challenged both the grand theory of transformation and its attendant ahistoricism. In the first phase of this challenge, historians focused on the "culture" of growing old. They examined the history of Americans' attitudes toward old age, the apparent growth of negative beliefs about senescence, and the factors that led to this "ageism." In their research, scholars shared several of the most important concerns of contemporary social theorists. As they explored the question of a premodern gerontocracy, their work also reflected the central importance of modernization theory. In conferences and publications, they focused on whether the elderly ever ruled as the most powerful members of society. And if so, they pondered when and why the elders fell from such exalted heights.

Much of this research led historians to critical assessments of modernization theorists' view of the roles and status of the premodern elderly. Yet, while historians rejected the notion of the exalted status of the colonial old, they generally accepted the second part of modernization theory. They assumed that by the early twentieth century, old age had become an economically and socially disadvantaged stage of existence. As one historian remarked, "The main lines of change in modern America were full of trial and trouble for the aged."[5] In part, this conclusion relied on evidence gathered by turn-of-the-century experts on aging and Progressive Era reformers who together sought to establish public old-age pensions. The advocates for the elderly maintained that the future of the once-powerful and respected old had become increasingly dim. In the modern world, the elderly no longer had a vital function in their families or in the productive world.

The second phase of historical inquiry subjected this claim to scrutiny. The next wave of articles and monographs critically examined the pessimistic evaluation of the social and economic circumstance of old age in modern industrial society. Turning from broad questions of culture, historians explored the actual work, family, and residence patterns of the elderly. Their conclusions, as we shall see, often differed sharply from both the assertions of reform-minded experts and the conventional modernization theory dominant in the social sciences. During the industrial era, the majority of the old did not fit the model predicted by advocates of ominous modernization; their lives were hardly uniformly impoverished and useless. Even in highly urbanized areas, large numbers of aged persons maintained a vigorous work life and retained considerable independence and authority in their households. Nor did age alone determine the character of their existences. In family relationships, economic status, work patterns, and even the meaning given to the last stage, old age was marked by wide diversity.

This critical reassessment of the lives of the elderly led historians, sociologists, economists, and other social scientists into a third phase of research. If the depiction of the old as completely diseased and dependent was not entirely valid, then the establishment of programs to assist the old was not easily explained. Welfare programs could not be seen simply as a reaction to steadily growing poverty; institutions did not serve only to shelter large numbers of isolated elders. Rather, historical research began to focus on the specific nature of economic and familial life for the aged: their ability to work, the savings they accumulated, the household and familial arrangements they made. Other scholars looked at policy as the product of forces largely independent of the aged themselves, finding it in the machinations of capitalists, the rise of labor unions, or the inner workings of the state.

The First Phase

Scholars have long had reason to question at least part of the modernization thesis. Research on the structure of households in both seventeenth-century England and colonial America demonstrated the fallacy of the belief that the old had once compelled respect through their dominance over large kinship groups. As Lawrence Stone, Peter Laslett, John Demos, and others have shown, the family of the seventeenth century was clearly nuclear in structure.[6] For the most part, only two generations—parents and unmarried children—resided together. In England and Wales, from the late sixteenth century until the first decade of the twentieth century, households contained, on average, about 4.75 persons, only slightly larger than the average household in the industrial era. In western Europe and the United States, at least, few households exhibited the classic structure implied by modernization theory in which an aging patriarch presided over several generations of kin.[7]

Beginning in the late 1970s, new historical research specifically on aging further undermined modernization theory. Advocates of modernization had tied respect of the old firmly to agrarian economies and linked decline in status to the advent of urban and industrial change. In the first major study of the history of aging, David Hackett Fischer directly attacked this assumption. In *Growing Old in America*, Fischer argued that industrialization and economic growth were not central factors in transforming the history of the American elderly. Rather, the key to that history lay in changing cultural beliefs. Religion, political theory, and philosophy, far more than economics, determined the nature and timing of the elderly's loss of status. Indeed, the fundamental shift in their position occurred almost a century before industrialization.

Despite Fischer's sharp disagreement with the modernization thesis, his study did not completely depart from the traditional model. According to the author, a time had occurred when the elderly comprised the most powerful group in society. During the colonial period, Fischer contended, a gerontocracy had clearly existed; the old, rather than the young or middle-aged, regulated social norms and behaviors. For Fischer, evidence of the age-based hierarchy was everywhere apparent: contemporary fashion placed gray wigs and stooped shoulders even on the young; artists painted family portraits in which the eldest member was displayed most prominently; meetinghouses were arranged so that the old received the best front-row pews; and census reports indicated that individuals reported themselves to be older than they actually were.

Between 1770 and 1820, Fischer argued, new cultural paradigms emerged, despite the absence of significant economic changes. With the revolutionary generation, the elderly were removed from positions of authority. Their gray hair, bent posture, and advanced years became symbols of decay rather than honor. The United States presented itself to the world as a young republic founded on revolutionary ideas. In such a society, the old had little place. Their outdated skills and conservative ideas were now viewed as standing in the way of growth and progress. According to Fischer, modernization played little role in shaping the nation's treatment of the old. Urban and industrial development occurred well after the noted "deep change" in cultural attitudes. Republican principles of equality and liberty served to displace the virtues of old age. With people of any age free and equal, there was little reason to conform to the hierarchy of age. A once firmly established colonial gerontocracy gave way to a system that favored youth; U.S. society moved inexorably toward gerontophobia.

Numerous scholars soon challenged Fischer's central assertion. Subsequent research questioned the existence of the hierarchy of age in the colonial period. Fischer had argued that the old were the most important members of the social order; without question, they had dictated the roles, behavior, and status of the young. In fact, a number of historians asked, was there ever really a time when old age was celebrated as the most glorious and powerful stage of existence?

The answer was ambiguous; even in the colonial period, wide variation appeared in society's treatment of elderly persons. In "Old Age in Early New England," John Demos argued that the old had often commanded great respect in early America.[8] Ministers routinely admonished the young to honor aged men and women whose long lives and accumulated wisdom were signs of God's great favor. Demos found, however, that the high status of the elderly generally arose not out of cultural prescriptions for deference but from specific economic and demographic factors. As Philip Greven and others have shown, many elderly individuals clearly profited from the landholding system. In early America, fathers generally held on to their estates—and the respect of their offspring—until their deaths. In their refusal to deed assets to their kin *inter vivos*, they guaranteed their exalted position.[9] Aged individuals often continued to work and to control their unmarried children until death. As a result, in their final years, the elderly generally retained both considerable wealth and self-sufficiency.

Old age in early New England, however, was not always a time of honor and privilege. According to Demos, even in the seventeenth century senescence was often portrayed in harsh and unrelenting terms. The same ministers who spoke of the noble qualities of age did not fail to consider its negative characteristics. The elderly were depicted as "touchy, peevish, angry, and forward"; they were found to be "hard to please, and . . . full of complaints of the present times."[10] Although no laws dictated the elderly's retirement, those who remained too long in positions of power were apt to feel the resentment of would-be successors. Children coveted the land of their fathers; aspiring middle-aged leaders jealously eyed the power of aging magistrates, jurists, and ministers.[11] "To summarize," Demos wrote, " . . . the position of the elderly in early New England was sociologically advantageous, but psychologically disadvantageous. Their control of important resources seemed to command honor and respect, but not affection or sympathetic understanding."[12] According to Demos, the hierarchy of age described by Fischer appeared to be based more on power and property than on harmonic society wide consensus.

Daniel Scott Smith, in "Old Age and the 'Great Transformation': A New England Case Study," largely confirmed Demos's conclusions.[13] Smith found that honor for old persons was based on their ability to perform needed services. The elderly's past roles, ascribed powers, or prescriptive ideals meant little in the day-to-day assessment of their worth. In contrast to Fischer, Smith suggested that in the eighteenth century, middle-aged men, rather than the elderly, exerted unchallenged authority in society. It was they who possessed the wealth of the community, ruled over the councils of government, and controlled the unmarried children in their households. Aged individuals who refused to cede their position to the next generation often found themselves targets for intergenerational conflict and social disapprobation.

Smith contended, however, that while the old were not always the most powerful members of society, they nevertheless occupied a unique place in the culture. Especially in the seventeenth century, community values protected the elderly; they were considered religious symbols of God's benevolence and the possessors of essential wisdom. Although hardly established as a "golden age" for the elderly, early colonial society did recognize that great age often brought valued assets and indispensable knowledge. Yet, as Smith explained, this was an especially fragile hierarchy. By the late eighteenth century, an increasing scarcity in land served to deprive the old of their economic power over the young. As a result, he concluded, "the older matrix of values sustaining respect for the aged withered."[14]

The work of Demos, Smith, and others therefore raised serious questions about Fischer's simple gerontocracy.[15] Even in the early seventeenth century, they maintained, the actual position of the old seemed insecure. If the elderly continued to control family, assets, or desired position, they might provoke hostility from the young; if they retired, they were likely to be judged to have outlived their usefulness. And for those who faced old age alone and poor, the last years often brought scorn rather than the admiration of the culture. Elderly persons who failed to possess valued assets quickly learned that age alone brought few rewards. Such poverty-stricken individuals were placed at the rear of the meetinghouse and greeted with disrespect; their physical ailments and weaknesses invoked only communitywide contempt.

Nonetheless, aging in colonial America did appear different from the experience of growing old in later periods.[16] Among historians there was a general consensus that in the seventeenth and early eighteenth century, the elderly often exerted power, while the young were admonished to show them respect. Cultural prescriptions and the economic organization of agricultural society combined to ensure the prestige as well as the social integration of a sizable proportion of the elderly members of society.

Despite disagreement over the existence of a gerontocracy, Fischer's study presented an early agenda for historians and generated an important new construct for the study of the history of old age. Fischer maintained that at least for the history of the old, the nation's political and intellectual philosophy was far more influential than economics or demographics. In his view, throughout American history, cultural beliefs rather than urbanization or industrialization determined the social worth of all aged individuals.[17]

The next history of the nation's aged, W. Andrew Achenbaum's *Old Age in the New Land*, clearly endorsed the new axiom. "Ideas about the worth and function of the elderly," Achenbaum wrote, "have a life of their own: the unprecedented denigration of older Americans arose independently of the most observable changes in their actual status."[18] Again the forces of modernization were found to have little effect upon perceptions of old age. Instead, negative attitudes toward the old arose independently of social conditions and were the driving force in shaping the elderly's history.

Fischer and Achenbaum, however, disagreed on one key issue: their studies presented radically different periodizations. While Fischer saw veneration for the old dissipating in the American Revolution, Achenbaum found evidence of respect for the aged in the early republic. During the first half of the nineteenth century, he argued, the old continued to be held in veneration as symbols of longevity and guardians of virtue. New ideas of liberty and equality made little impact on their status. Only after the Civil War, Achenbaum stressed, did the elderly begin to lose the power and honor they once had possessed. In this period, negative views of the aged became prominent in middle-class literature. As the mortality rates among the young declined, death came to seem the province of only the old. Characterized as diseased and dependent, the old faced mandatory retirement and age limits. Government and private employers, even advocates for the old, described them as useless and outdated and as obstacles to the efficiency of the workplace.

While Fischer and Achenbaum disagreed over the timing of this "deep change," they both concluded that by the early twentieth century respect for old age had turned into unrelenting ageism. The elderly were, as a group, demeaned for their numerous years and derided for the physical decline that often accompanied old age. This conclusion led inevitably to a second major problem in the historiography of aging: what in the nature of U.S. society or in old age itself had caused the dramatic fall from grace, and how could the creation and widespread acceptance of such ageism be explained?

Thomas Cole's work provided one answer. According to Cole, a distinctive antagonism to old age arose with the development of nineteenth-century middle-class culture, based especially on new religious convictions. The culture's central beliefs in activity, vitality, and self-control devalued the worth of the old. The elderly's once-honored wisdom and skill were now judged to be of little use. Their habits were old-fashioned, their ideas simply obstacles to progress. Moreover, the physical signs of age had clearly become distasteful. Gray hair and wrinkles—once badges of honor and respect—had evolved into unwanted reminders of inevitable decay and death.[19]

For Cole, the Second Great Awakening played an especially crucial role in the transformation of these cultural beliefs. In the second quarter of the nineteenth century, religion, once the foundation on which a hierarchy of age had been built, became the basis for those who advocated reform and change. From their pulpits, evangelical ministers stressed the importance of youth. In adolescence, possibilities were limitless and salvation lay close at hand. For the old, however, little solace could be extended; the time for redemption had long passed. In delineating the new belief system, Cole emphasized that it was more than simply a revolt of children against their fathers or a rejection of hierarchy during a revolutionary age. "If old age in America had only suffered the usual misfortune of being identified with an old order," Cole wrote, "the impact might have been short-lived. But old age not only symbolized the eighteenth-century world of patriarchy and hierarchical authority, it also represented an embarrassment to the new morality of self control." The elderly, who seemingly had little future in which to progress, had become irrelevant to the culture of self-improvement. In the bourgeois world of civilized morality, he explained, the old came to signify "dependence, disease, failure and sin."

In *Beyond Sixty-Five*, Carole Haber found a similar characterization of old age evolving in nineteenth-century America. For Haber, however, the source for these stereotypes lay most evidently in the ideas of doctors, social workers, statisticians, and businessmen who came to categorize and treat all elderly individuals as members of a uniquely needy group. Employing an increasingly popular medical model of aging, these professional groups depicted advanced age itself as a progressive and inevitable disease. Newly described changes in physiology and anatomy of the old meant the elderly could no longer be seen as older versions of younger people; instead, they were categorically different. Their advanced age could be taken as a reliable sign that they required professional care, retirement, and segregation.

In the late nineteenth century, according to Haber, this model of aging was institutionalized in the programs and policies that were established to assist the elderly. The founders of nursing homes, mandatory retirement programs, and geriatric medicine all shared the belief that old age was a time of particular disease and dependence. In their view, all old men and women would eventually become both physically and mentally senile. There was little reason to hope that they could remain active in the industrialized world.

In contrast to Achenbaum, Haber did not find that such ideas had lives of their own.[20] Instead, in her study, as in the work of Michel Dahlin, the negative characterization of the old grew directly out of the daily experience of the professional groups that dealt with the elderly.[21] Largely urban in their orientation but deeply concerned about the negative effects of the industrial society in which they lived, these new professionals and social reformers per-

ceived radical changes in the fate of the old. In the almshouse rosters, outdoor relief rolls, and hospital wards, they discovered an aged population separated from kinship networks and incapable of work. The presence of such
aged individuals and the squalid conditions in which they lived seemed an
affront to a rich nation and an indictment of the heartless effects of the new
industrial society. From this evidence, social analysts concluded that structural poverty was gathering all the aged into its grasp. Experts on the elderly,
such as Edward T. Devine, Abraham Epstein, I. M. Rubinow, and Lee Welling Squier, had little doubt that the old in modern society were to be relegated to "the industrial scrap heap."[22]

This negative perception of the status and future of the elderly led social
advocates to argue that specific bureaucratic responses were required in the
face of the elderly's deteriorating physical, economic, and social conditions.
In stressing the need for state pensions, old-age homes, and "familylike"
almshouses, they characterized old age as a time of complete dependence.[23]
Yet despite this broad depiction, all old people were not treated the same.
Cultural attitudes and biases still influenced the institutional solutions to the
perceived helplessness of old age. Private old-age homes were established primarily for native-born women and public almshouses for immigrant men; in
the large cities of the South, segregated, poorly maintained institutions
housed the most unfortunate of elderly blacks.[24]

In the initial wave of historical work, attitudes and ageism—themes gerontologists know well—dictated research and debate among scholars. Fischer,
Achenbaum, Demos, Cole, Haber, and others generally emphasized the importance cultural beliefs played in determining the experience of aging. Historians largely agreed with Fischer's account of the relatively high status of
many of the old, while disagreeing about its extent, strength, or duration.
They concurred that the elderly had suffered significant declines in status but
disputed the exact timing of the transition from one era to the other. An
argument over periodization then led to the second phase in historical research. If cultural change could be located at different points in time, perhaps
it was a less than reliable indicator of status. Several works had noted the
part economics and demographics played in influencing the status of the old,
and these hints raised curiosity about the actual circumstance of older persons. Were contemporary experts' perceptions of degradation valid? Had industrialization diminished the worth of the elderly and reduced old age to
nothing more than a social problem requiring serious intervention?

The Second Phase

In an attempt to answer these questions, scholars turned from cultural
evidence to economic and social data. According to their findings, both the

early social analysts and the later modernization theorists seriously overestimated the negative effects of industrialization. By accepting contemporaries'
accounts uncritically, the first histories had simply repeated this error. Examining the actual employment, residential, and family status of the old, researchers concluded that in the late nineteenth and early twentieth centuries,
the old did not undergo a dramatic and revolutionary displacement in the
home and the workplace. Despite the harsh judgments by reformers such as
Epstein and Rubinow, the elderly were neither uniformly deserted by their
children nor relegated to obsolescence.

Historical research on the economic and social conditions of the old in
the late nineteenth century, in fact, revealed family and employment patterns
far different from those depicted by contemporary social advocates. With urbanization and industrialization, the lives of the old did not change abruptly;
they did not suddenly find themselves outcasts in the modernizing world.
According to Howard P. Chudacoff and Tamara K. Hareven, in the second
half of the nineteenth century, few dramatic transitions occurred in the final
stage of life. The central demarcations of old age—loss of control over children, household, and employment—never occurred for a majority of old persons. Even in the industrial city of the late nineteenth century, most older
men remained employed and heads of their households.[25]

Moreover, Chudacoff and Hareven argued that the family and household
relationships of most elderly persons changed little with advancing age. The
old rarely experienced the empty nest syndrome common today; most spent
the majority of their lives with at least one child in the home. Such co-residence may in fact have actually grown along with urban and industrial
growth. Drawing on Michael Anderson's findings for British cities, Chudacoff and Hareven argued that the economic transformation of the late nineteenth century increased the likelihood that the old would live in an extended
family. Especially in cities where a shortage of housing existed, the old maintained a desired commodity: a relatively inexpensive place to reside. The
young, in search of affordable living space or care for their children, turned
to homes of their elders. As a result, intergenerational exchange of valuable
resources created strong familial ties. While agreeing that complex households
increased in number during the industrial period, Steven Ruggles argued that
the need for space did not in fact determine patterns of co-residence. Rather,
only by the second half of the nineteenth century had the U.S. population
matured to a point where a large proportion of families had the potential to
form complex households.[26]

While challenging the notion that aged individuals in the industrial era
became isolated, the discovery of complex family structures in the late nineteenth century also revealed that the elderly made up an extremely diverse
segment of the population; they followed no single residential, familial, or

employment pattern. Although a majority of men continued to labor, a minority searched futilely for work while others were able to retire comfortably on their savings. Although most continued to live with their spouse and children, others resided alone, and a small number were forced to seek institutional refuge. Through a study of the 1900 census, Daniel Scott Smith found that the elderly adopted a wide variety of living arrangements. For some, especially widows, aging did bring sharp changes in family structure; not all retained the patterns of their middle age. Although most old, married, and employed men continued to head their households, the death of a spouse or long-term unemployment often meant that new strategies had to be devised.[27] The life of a widowed elderly women was typically quite different from that of her married male counterpart. Her gender and marital status— not simply her age—cast the mold of her final days. Other factors apart from age also influenced household characteristics. Thomas A. Arcury, Hal S. Barron, N. Sue Weiler, and others found that differences in race, ethnicity, and class had independent effects.[28]

The family that historians recovered from the past, therefore, was not one in which old people found themselves isolated and severed from kinship networks, nor one in which old age itself was the dominant factor shaping residential arrangements. Their findings showed that the stark pronouncements of the demise of the elderly's family life had been greatly exaggerated. Did similar hyperbole then exist in the grim portrayal of the older worker? Was industrialization the chief agent that led to the elimination of the old from the labor market and caused the elderly to rely upon state and federal assistance?

Historians have offered a wide variety of responses to these questions. In *Growing Old in America*, Fischer categorically rejected industrialization as the central factor; the trend toward the displacement of the old, he argued, began between 1790 and 1820, well *before* industrialization.[29] Achenbaum also rejected industrialization as a key determinant, stating that the displacement of older workers became most apparent well after the economic transformation of the United States. He found no decline in labor force activity during the dramatic industrialization of the nineteenth century. He argued that 1900 marked the beginning of the withdrawal of older men from work.[30] Had economic change been the primary factor in displacing the aged, Achenbaum reasoned, a larger proportion of the old would have left the labor force in the mid–nineteenth century. Achenbaum declared that ageism, not urban or industrial growth, was the key element in the decline of the elderly worker. In contrast, William Graebner linked the segregation of the aged to late-nineteenth-century managerial practice. The rise of large-scale industrial capitalism, he argued, led to the origins of "forced" retirement. Graebner asserted, however, that the consequences of such practices were not fully realized until the 1930s, and then only under the aegis of the federal government.[31]

More recent historical research has suggested that industrialization had a far different impact. Roger Ransom and Richard Sutch maintained that late-nineteenth-century census takers grossly exaggerated the number of active aged workers by including men who were permanently unemployed.[32] Providing new estimates, Ransom and Sutch suggested that very high levels of retirement—or, more accurately, withdrawal from the labor force—could be observed as early as 1870. The level of labor-force participation for the old then remained essentially unchanged between 1870 and 1930. Moreover, this level was considerably lower than that cited by earlier studies, in part owing to the continued difficulties of older job seekers in labor markets. Ransom and Sutch, in fact, argued that trends toward a more industrial labor force during this period suggest that the labor-force participation rates of industrial workers may actually have been increasing in the early twentieth century.

Although several scholars raised objections to this new labor-force series, Brian Gratton also challenged the widely accepted belief that elderly men experienced a slow and steady withdrawal from the labor market after 1890. In his study of early-twentieth-century Boston, Gratton argued that rates of activity among elderly men remained relatively unchanged throughout the first decades of the century. Moreover, Gratton contended that few workers, or even nonworkers, suffered from overt ageism; for the most part, age discrimination in employment was more assumed (and discussed) than real. To a great degree, he argued, the absence of elderly workers in many occupations followed from their entry into traditional occupational categories in their youth. Over time, "modern" occupational titles, which were supposedly closed to the old, displayed increasing proportions of older workers.

In subsequent articles, Gratton contended that dramatic change in the work lives of older men did not occur until the enactment of Social Security in 1935. Before then, labor-force rates were somewhat lower in industrial areas, in part because urban wealth allowed retirement and in part because of the negative effects traditionally attributed to industrialization. But high levels of withdrawal from work were also evident in certain agricultural states and depended greatly on the economic organization, wealth, and racial and ethnic characteristics of various state populations. After 1935, however, a striking change occurred in labor-force participation: retirement drew older workers of every type out of the labor market. The catalyst causing mass retirement of the old, Gratton argued, was not age discrimination or industrialization but the enactment and dissemination of Social Security. By 1950, even the modest benefits of the welfare system induced aging workers to retire. With the subsequent liberalization of the program and the rise of private pensions, the trend toward retirement of the old increased in speed and magnitude.

Such findings sparked a series of new inquiries into the position of the older (usually male) worker and the economic status of the aged. Some researchers confirmed, some modified, and some rejected the initial conclusions, but all brought new attention to the complex effects of industrialization and economic growth. In the work, the focus upon the relationship between age and industrialization was significantly altered. Factors such as age discrimination and attitudinal forces became far less dominant. Aside from broad statements in the contemporary press or the declarations of advocates for public pensions, little evidence existed that industrial employers ever fired large numbers of elderly workers. New emphasis was given instead to the idea that industrialization might have had positive consequences for the old or that previously unexplored factors, such as Civil War pensions, had a significant impact upon the economic condition of the old.[33]

The Third Phase

The reassessment of the impact of industrialization posed new problems and offered stimulating new opportunities for historians of aging. Before this reconsideration, both the timing and the widespread acceptance of old-age welfare policies had been easily explained. In the preindustrial era, the elderly were too few in number, too powerful, and too immersed in family support systems to require substantial public assistance. By the late nineteenth century, however, they began to face isolation, declining employment opportunities, and steadily growing ageism. In the Great Depression, the elderly's poverty-stricken state could no longer be ignored. The enactment of Social Security was an understandable and seemingly inevitable step. The second phase of research, which examined the actual social and economic experience of the old, raised questions about this simple explanation. If, as recent research implied, industrialization did not have uniformly negative consequences, what then accounted for the creation and national acceptance of the welfare state?

No issue in the history of aging raised greater controversy among historians and social scientists. The U.S. welfare model clearly stood apart from its European counterparts. In terms of both its late acceptance and its reliance upon the contributions of workers, it seemed to be "exceptional" among Western industrial societies. Even before focusing on Social Security itself, however, historians had demonstrated that support of the elderly had been a longstanding tradition, deeply enmeshed in recurrent debates over the nature and impact of poor-relief systems. Since the colonial period, relief policies reflected cultural beliefs about the worthiness of the old, the extent of their poverty, and the best forms of welfare. Elderly individuals—especially aged women—were consistently viewed as the appropriate recipients of relief and formed a significant proportion of the "worthy" and dependent population.

In the colonial period, however, as Rothman, Quadagno, and others

found, the elderly were rarely held as a distinctive class.[34] Grouped with orphans, the insane, and the handicapped, the nature of their relief was based
on their inability to support themselves and their ties to the community. For
those who were local residents, town officials allotted outdoor relief or, in
rare cases, a place in the almshouse. For those who did not belong to the
community, however, age awarded few benefits. Like paupers far younger,
they would be "warned out" of the community, forced to wander from town
to town in search of assistance.

In the nineteenth century, new policies and programs were developed
that separated the old from other needy groups and defined their worthiness
not by their community status but by their age. The relatively small number
of elderly paupers did not deter benevolent groups, businesses, and municipalities from establishing age-based programs. In old-age homes, pension programs, and burgeoning almshouses, advanced years defined the old as
unproductive and needy and awarded them distinctive treatment. Yet, as historians have demonstrated, such policies did not simply grant all old people
the same care. Blacks rarely received the same treatment as whites; women
were often granted different forms of support from their male counterparts.
Historians concurred, however, that even before Social Security, old age had
become clearly recognized as a social problem.[35]

These findings, combined in some accounts with a growing appreciation
of the profound implications of economic growth, led scholars to attempt
new explanations of the origins of Social Security. The first histories—especially those of Fischer and Achenbaum—followed the traditional interpretation that Social Security was a benevolent response on the part of
policymakers to increasing unemployment and poverty among the old.[36] In
William Graebner's view, however, Social Security rested on the state's ability
to use mandatory retirement as a labor-control technique. Relying on management practices that arose at the turn of the century, New Deal policymakers hoped to provide work for the young by retiring the competing
elderly. In contrast to Achenbaum, Graebner argued that the needs of the
elderly were never the primary concern of policymakers. First and foremost,
New Dealers sought to bring recovery and reform to a severely troubled
economy.[37]

In *The Transformation of Old Age Security*, Jill Quadagno extended Graebner's argument concerning Social Security's labor management functions
while attempting to explain the exceptionalism of the U.S. welfare state. According to Quadagno, the delayed establishment of Social Security was due
to three critical factors: the failure of unions in the United States to organize
mass-production workers, the strength of capitalists in the private sector, and
the power of southern legislators in Congress. Moreover, even during the
Great Depression, these forces sustained the conservative nature of U.S. wel-

fare. Business leaders and southern planters combined to determine the provisions of Social Security, rewarding specific groups with government-supported retirement while assuring the protracted employment of others. Even today, she concluded, such policies continue to influence the welfare state and the nature of support for the elderly.[38]

Quadagno's explanation led to renewed interest among sociologists in Marxist explanations for the state. Rather than adopting the perspective of Marx, however, Theda Skocpol and various co-authors offered a Weberian analysis of the exceptionalism and origins of U.S. welfare. Skocpol and others proposed that the "state," by which they usually meant the federal government, was an independent actor in history.[39] Civic-minded middle-class reformers, politicians, and eventually bureaucrats first opposed and then molded Social Security to their own ends. In this explanation, the working class played only a minor part and capitalists lost as often as they won. Most important, cliques of experts and government officials comprised an ominously autonomous State, which steered welfare onto its conservative moorings.

Having begun as a relatively simple foray into a neglected area of social history, research into the history of old age has become a complex field of inquiry. For some, the scholarship commands attention because of the story itself. What really happened to the aged in the past? What caused changes in their circumstances? What periodization best explains their history? For others, research on the aged constitutes a window into other issues—the labor markets of previous eras, the family and household relationships of all Americans, the origins and structure of the welfare state.

Each approach poses intriguing challenges. Clearly, the experiences of the old in the past have differed sharply from the assumptions drawn from modernization theory. In seventeenth- and eighteenth-century America, the elderly did not rule over extended families; their power and prestige came from control over their own land, wealth, and immediate offspring. Nor did industrialization and urbanization cause the old to be suddenly displaced and abandoned. Furthermore, the history of Social Security can no longer be seen as a simple and direct charitable response to the impoverishment of old people. Finally, the elderly have never comprised a unified group whose great age alone dictated the course of their lives. Their history has varied with their race, gender, region, class, and ethnicity.

The findings of this historical research have significant meaning for gerontologists. The present-day condition of the old can no longer be explained by reference to a one-dimensional past. The premodern period was not golden or uniform; neither industrialization nor ageism led directly to the elderly's current status. Indeed, Social Security—usually seen as a *reaction to* industrialization or ageism—may in fact have been the major *cause* of modern conditions.

Scholars have shown, too, that the lives of the contemporary old have deep historical precedents. Past generations of elderly people were neither invisible nor invulnerable. Well before the advent of the urban and industrial world, disrespect for the elderly and ageist assumptions existed. Some elderly individuals were displaced from positions of authority while others, especially women, had to confront and overcome abrupt changes and poverty in late life. Although many like to contrast the "good old days" with present conditions, the gender, race, and ethnicity of the poverty-stricken elderly of past eras bear a striking resemblance to the characteristics of those impoverished today. So too do the attributes of the present-day rich elderly parallel those of the past. Moreover, old-age homes, geriatric medicine, and welfare policies were not the creation of the mid–twentieth century but must be understood in terms of their eighteenth- and nineteenth-century antecedents.

For historians, this new research demonstrates that the elderly did not simply play a secondary role in the past; to assume so is to be shaped by present-day biases that discount the contributions of the old. Despite their small numbers, the elderly represented a significant part of the adult population and an even more important proportion of those holding wealth, resources, and power. They played a crucial part in the transformation of work, family, and welfare in the United States. Across centuries, both their power and their poverty provoked critical historical responses.

Yet, while this research has revealed that many assumptions about the history of aging are false, it also has left significant questions unanswered and has failed to make important links among the various phases of inquiry. To accomplish these tasks, historians need to resolve a number of central issues. Although scholars have traced the evolution of cultural biases against the elderly in the course of the nineteenth century, the impact of ageism has yet to be measured. Although cultural sentiments against the old certainly began to be visibly apparent by the mid–nineteenth century, the effects of such beliefs on employment and residential patterns remain unclear. Did feelings against the elderly actually limit their opportunities and life-styles or were such beliefs simply a convenient and consistently invoked rationale for otherwise-determined behavior? Moreover, how can such sentiments and perceptions be explained? If the old did not undergo a dramatic decline in economic status, why were the old suddenly portrayed as dependent and impoverished? How, indeed, do attitudes connect to the social and economic conditions of growing old?

The evolution of culture requires that we understand economic and demographic conditions more precisely. Traditionally, the history of the old has been described as a continuous descent of the elderly from veneration and usefulness into modern obsolencence. According to this characterization, only the welfare state saved the elderly from complete isolation and impoverishment. Historians, however, must examine the actual family situations of the old as they changed through time, as well as the diversity in those patterns according to class, ethnicity, region, and gender. They need to be attentive not only to the welfare advocates' description of destitute old age but to objective measurements of their economic conditions as well. By examining the activities of the elderly in the work force and their control over income and wealth, a far more complex characterization of the history of old age emerges. At the heart of this inquiry is the question: did industrialization undermine the elderly, or was it a positive force which improved their lot and raised their expectations about what constituted a "good old age."

As historians reexamine the economic status of the old, they need to explain the impetus behind social measures developed "for" the elderly. Ranging from outdoor relief and almshouse residency through Social Security, these measures often came to characterize old age and inspired a language through which aging could be interpreted. Need alone cannot explain the rise of the policies; authorities clearly exaggerated poverty. What, then, led to programs that defined old age as a time of dependence and disability? If a large proportion of the old did not experience a steady decline in employment and wealth, how can we explain the creation of a welfare state that made old-age poverty a national concern?

These inquiries depend on an understanding of the historical experience of aging from the perspective of both cultural prescriptions and actual expectations. Often the elderly of the past appear to be little more than puppets controlled by economic forces or passive patients waiting to be treated by ever-growing numbers of professionals. Yet the old have clearly determined their own history and have sought to control their destinies.[40] This interpretation has generally been more complex than the social scientist's rendition of economic or social status and the historian's description of welfare policy or family relationships. Why, for example, did even middle-class aged individuals repeatedly express a fear of encroaching poverty and institutionalization? What once led generations of aged individuals to see great meaning in growing old while another cohort dreaded the passing of the decades?

In the chapters that follow, we attempt to address each of these issues. By looking at family, wealth, work, institutionalization, and advice, we endeavor to create a new and more complex social history of the elderly in the United States. This history underscores the diversity found in the lives of the old. The experiences of the elderly were not simply a function of growing old; they were rooted in the entire life course. We begin, therefore, by placing the aged in their own families. Here, across the preindustrial, industrial, and Social Security periods, Americans of all ages gave meaning to the last stage of life. Through their kinship relationships and family obligations, they effectively fashioned the nature of their old age.

1

The Families of the Old

THROUGHOUT AMERICAN HISTORY, the family has been central to the lives of elderly. Before recent decades, most aged persons lived out their days surrounded by kinship members. In their last years, the majority of older people remained in their own households, accompanied by their spouse and maturing children. Even aged spinsters and elderly bachelors often found shelter in the homes—and family networks—of their relatives or neighbors. Such household arrangements reflected economic and demographic constraints as well as cultural expectations. Until the mid–nineteenth century, few individuals lived beyond the maturity of all their children; even as they approached old age, they often remained responsible for adolescent offspring. Moreover, the family served as a source of economic and emotional support. Before the establishment of Social Security, only the most impoverished and isolated looked to private or public charity. Most needy individuals maintained kinship networks that provided for their financial needs.

In recent decades, however, the family life of the elderly has taken on a radically new form. Increases in longevity have had a dramatic impact upon the daily experiences of the old. In contrast to the preindustrial period, the elderly are likely to live long enough to become intimately acquainted with several generations of family members. They are apt to survive well into the middle age of their children, who routinely leave parental households to establish their own homes. No longer surrounded by growing offspring, the old now live alone or with their spouse in the empty nest household.

This modern household structure has provoked considerable anxiety among contemporary social analysts about the place of the elderly in the family. Pointing to the fact that a large proportion of older people live apart from their kin, critics charge that the American family has lost its traditional integrity and compassion. The existence of large numbers of solitary elders, these critics claim, is proof that family members exhibit far less respect and concern for their aging kin than they once displayed.

Such charges are hardly new.[1] Since the industrial era, social analysts have focused on the apparent decline in status of the elderly as conclusive evidence of the deterioration of the modern family. According to their narratives, in the classical family of Western nostalgia, the rural elderly presided over complex, extended households full of generations of attentive and loving kin.[2] In modern times, however, these families' ties have been broken. No longer honored or respected, the elderly have been deserted by their kin, left alone to fend for themselves.

As we have seen, however, the traditional view of the family has been challenged by recent historical studies. Across American history, most households have been "nuclear," composed only of husband, wife, and children; few were extended to include grandparents, grandchildren, or other relatives or nonkin.[3] In many eras, demographic conditions made it unlikely that three-generational households could ever be formed. Although the complex household did exist in the preindustrial period (perhaps more commonly than revisionists have claimed), it never was the predominant form.

Moreover, the current highly isolated arrangements of the old cannot be labeled a sign of loathing for the elderly. Recent studies have found that intergenerational exchange between the aged and their children continues to be extremely important and vibrant. Indeed, scholars have characterized their findings of interdependence and intimacy as a modified form of the "extended" family, even if three generations rarely choose to live in the same house.[4]

Given these apparently contradictory findings, the family history of the elderly demands a new and careful treatment.[5] In the pages that follow, we suggest that demography, economics, and cultural expectations created a dynamic history of the elderly in their families. In the preindustrial era, most aged persons resided with their children in nuclear households. Rarely did they live to see all their children grown and married. Often depending on economic strategies that encouraged co-residence with maturing children, they relied on both cultural expectations and promises of inheritance to insure the children's continued assistance. In the industrial era, the family structure of the old became increasingly complex. Many Americans still employed family-based economic strategies. But economic growth and especially demographic change broadened familial possibilities. Race, class, ethnicity, and gender influenced the establishment of a variety of household structures. Moreover, as we shall see, the elderly's family varied according to locale. On the farm, in the city, and in the small villages of the United States, the elderly established distinctive types of households. In the village of the industrial era, in fact, large numbers followed a strikingly "modern" family structure. Living alone or simply with their spouse, they created the empty nest household.

As today, however, this arrangement did not necessarily reflect desertion by kin. Instead, during the industrial era, many older people finally had the financial capability to establish a long-preferred model of separate rather than extended or complex households. While popular beliefs consistently emphasized the importance of assisting needy family members, U.S. cultural admonitions have also stressed the primacy of the distinct nuclear family.[6] As we shall see, throughout the elderly's family history, two cultural paradigms have played a key part in influencing household structure. On one hand, families have continuously attempted to meet kinship responsibility; on the other, they have striven to maintain autonomous living. Individual strategies for fulfilling these ideals have been influenced by economic, demographic, and regional constraints. In the industrial era, for example, farmers and urban workers often extended their households to care for their aged kin. In contrast, retired village couples, as well as the increasingly affluent middle class, resided in nuclear households yet were able to retain intimate intergenerational contact. (See illustration, 'Family Circle.')

In recent decades, the ideal of autonomous living has become a widely shared reality. For the first time, guaranteed Social Security benefits, growth in real income, and increased longevity have made it possible for most older Americans, especially elderly women, to establish separate households while maintaining a close and rewarding family life. In the past, few could achieve these aspirations; only today have economic and demographic conditions supported the dual realization of intimacy at a distance. Rather than being scorned by their kin, the old may in fact be experiencing the most satisfying chapter in the long history of their family relationships.

Preindustrial America

In the seventeenth century, individuals generally lived their entire life spans as members of family households. Few, whether young or old, resided alone. For individuals in colonial America, the family played a multitude of roles. Within the household, families educated their children, taught vocations to adolescents, provided the needy with welfare, and worked together to meet basic necessities.[7]

The multiple roles of the family were dictated by pressing economic realities. In a preindustrial agrarian system, the family served as the basic unit for production. The old as well as the young contributed to the economic well-being of the kinship group. No well-established lines marked the point at which the elderly ceased to be contributing family members. Nor did sharp demographic boundaries distinguish the last stages of life for an elderly family member. Until the mid–nineteenth century, the average age at which women bore their last child was near forty. Well into old age, therefore, men and women remained active parents whose transition to old age was quite ambiguous. Retirement at a fixed age was uncommon; few distinctive exits marked aging adults as having completed one stage of life and begun another. Most aged persons did not experience the empty nest in which all the children had grown and departed. Few were ever simply grandparents without

Table 1.1 Demographic Life Cycle in America, 1650–1950

	1650	1700	1750	1800	1850	1890	1950
Men							
Mean age at:							
First marriage	24	25	26	25	26	26	23
Last birth	42	42	43	42	37	37	29
Last child comes of age	63	63	64	63	58	57	50
Last child marries	65	64	66	67	61	59	50
Death	52	52	c.52	c.56	62	66	77
Women							
Mean age at:							
Menarche	n.a.	n.a.	n.a.	15.2	14.6	14.2	12.8
First marriage	20	21	23	22	24	23	20
Last birth	38	38	39	39	35	32	26
Last child comes of age	59	59	60	60	56	53	47
Last child marries	60	61	63	64	59	56	48
Death	c.50	c.50	c.50	c.56	61	71	81

Source: David Hackett Fischer, *Growing Old in America*.

parental responsibilities of their own. Quite commonly, as table 1.1 suggests, the elderly's youngest children and oldest grandchildren would be of the same age. Having become parents in middle age, older people had adolescents of their own in the home.[8]

The demographic structure of the family, therefore, supported the elderly's roles as parents, household heads, and active family members. In seventeenth-century America, however, the patriarchal power of the old hardly extended beyond the immediate nuclear family of parents and children; the old rarely ruled over extended households with multiple generations of kin. Few such families existed because, quite simply, not enough people survived to experience the maturity and marriage of all their children. As a result, the early colonial family was generally nuclear in form: an elderly couple resided with their unmarried offspring. If younger heads of household included others in their homes, they were likely to have children, servants, or apprentices under their roof rather than their elderly parents. In Bristol, Rhode Island, in 1689, extended households accounted for the living arrangements of only 3 percent of the population; in 1698 in Bedford, New York, only 6 percent.[9]

Few married elderly Americans appeared to have sought refuge in the residences of their young, or themselves provided shelter to numerous generations of married children and grandchildren. Instead, they remained in their own homes, supported by the presence—and labor—of at least one younger family member. The status of the aging couple was linked to their persisting functions and responsibilities as parents and household heads in a nuclear household.

Legal and cultural prescription also dictated that the young would not desert the home of their aging parents. From birth, children were taught to respect their parents. Biblical injunctions and community laws warned that insolence or neglect would be treated harshly. In colonial Massachusetts, adolescents over the age of sixteen could by law be put to death for striking or cursing their parents. Although it is unclear whether anyone ever actually met this dire end, the command to "honor thy father and mother" was taken quite seriously.[10] The magistrates of communities did not hesitate to interfere in family matters when they felt the children were not properly treating their elders or providing their basic necessities.[11] In 1690, for example, the selectmen of Boston warned James Barbor that unless he cared more properly for his father, "you may expect wee shall; prosecute the Law upon you [*sic*]." Nor did religious leaders shun the tasks of castigating their congregations if they failed to meet their filial obligations. "Children," thundered Reverend Samuel Willard, "that have been the Charge of the Parents, to bring them up to be capable of doing something, should not presently, in hope of doing better from themselves, desert their helpless Parents, as thinking it now time to look to themselves, and left them [to] shift as they can."[12]

But it was not only religious and legal decrees that held the family of the old together. Aged landholders often maintained their control of the young through significant economic power that diminished little with advancing years. As we discuss in chapter 2, male heads of household rarely disposed of their property before their deaths. The continued possession of land and assets assured the status of the aging couple in the family. They controlled their children and guaranteed their enduring support by holding out the promise of valued estates.[13]

Custom and inheritance patterns dictated that at least one child remain with the aging couple. Generally, this individual would not marry and sire a new generation while in the home of the old. Rather, in return for the homestead or a larger portion of the estate upon the death of the parents, an individual—whatever his or her age—remained a "child," providing aging parents with labor and support. Only upon the death of the landholder would the child become an adult and be financially able to begin a family of his or her own.[14]

For elderly widows, the ownership of land also ensured a continued role in the family. In colonial wills, an elderly man often listed the care that was to be bestowed upon his widow and the assets that, upon his death, would become her possessions. This list could be as broad as simply giving her one-third of the assets (the "widow's share") or as specific as the names of cows and sheep she was to receive and the room in the home in which she was to sleep. Children were often warned that failure to respect and esteem the wife would mean the loss of the homestead or the forfeiture of valued and hard-earned possessions.[15]

Colonial wills often granted power to the widows by making them guardians of the children and trustees of the estate. Despite the numerous barriers in the seventeenth century to women's legal equality, these documents could bestow considerable power upon an elderly widow. Once granted the control of children or land, she, like men, could threaten her children with grave consequences if they were to desert her. Even the woman who was granted only the traditional "widow's third" was given the opportunity to control some assets—and exert some power—over her kin in her old age. Offspring who one day looked forward to the possession of her realty or the financial gain from its sale would be likely to treat her with continuing respect.[16]

Every colonial widow, however, did not find authority and prosperity in her family relationships. While some clearly retained influence over their offspring and even added materially to their husbands' estates, others experienced considerable hardship in their final days. Richer men often dictated precise wills that reduced a widow's expected share in favor of certain children. Granting only a portion of the assets to the widow, such documents clearly limited the woman's authority among her kin. Moreover, if the will stipulated, as many did, that she would lose the assigned assets upon remarriage, her power was further constricted. To a great degree, therefore, the detailed bequest marked a significant reversal in the family hierarchy; relegated to specific rooms and possessions, she relinquished the status of household head to her adult children.[17]

The living arrangements of widows, in fact, were markedly different from those of their married counterparts. While few elderly couples lived with their married children and their offspring, the widowed old—both male and female—often resided with the young. In late-seventeenth-century Bedford, New York, for example, two of the town's six elderly citizens lived in extended households. Both aged individuals had experienced the death of their spouse; in their last years, they sought shelter in homes headed by their adult children.[18]

Yet, while cultural and legal admonitions assumed that the family would support such needy relatives, the existence of three generations within the home did not always lead to harmonious kinship relations. Although ministers warned their congregations to respect and shelter their aged mothers, they cautioned that power now rested with the new generation. Aging adults who interfered with the upbringing of their grandchildren were sure to do the youngsters irreparable harm. Some middle-aged adults simply avoided the problems of the extended family by boarding their elderly relations in the homes of others, assuming only a financial responsibility for them. Even the most resourceful of mothers, like the admirable midwife Martha Ballard, found children disrespectful and selfish, unwilling to make a parent's old age more comfortable. Such behavior led Ballard to remark bitterly that her children ought to "Consider they may be old and receiv like Treatment. [*sic*] "[19]

Not all elderly individuals, of course, had children to provide them with the necessary labor or to contribute to their support. While colonial New England society encouraged all to wed, some men and women remained unmarried; others failed to reproduce the requisite offspring; many experienced the early death or desertion of their spouse and children. Even these persons, however, generally did not reside alone. Communities quickly placed elderly spinsters and bachelors, as well as widows and widowers, in the homes of neighbors and kin or assigned others to live with them.[20] Able and propertied aging women became the proprietors of boarding houses. Such establishments provided them both an acceptable kinship structure and a necessary source of financial support. Those physically unable to operate such institutions often became boarders themselves.[21]

Yet even in colonial America, demographic and economic realities tended at times to challenge the traditional family support and authority of the old. Especially in seventeenth-century New England, individuals often lived to great age. In Plymouth Colony, 68 percent of all twenty-year-olds reached at least their sixtieth birthday; in Ipswich, Massachusetts, the proportion rose to 72 percent. While adult mortality in the South was higher, by the mid–eighteenth century the chance of obtaining advanced age had become far greater even in this region. Such extensive life spans may have led to significant strains within the family: children who remained in the household, waiting for their parents to die and pass on the estate, found their stay far longer than anticipated.[22]

Moreover, across the eighteenth century, the division of land reduced the size and potential of estates; the portion that the elderly adult could promise the young—or use to ensure authority—became greatly diminished. By the eighteenth century, elderly couples often deeded the land to their children before their deaths. No longer able to dictate the continued labor or residence of the young, the aged came to rely on financial assets and annual rents to support their own final days.[23] Widows, too, may have been less able to exert power within the family. Unlike their counterparts a century earlier, they were not always named in the will as the guardians of their children or the executrixes of their husbands' estates. Especially among richer households, the widows' power was often shared by kin, acquaintances, or court-appointed representatives.[24]

Such changes may account for the growing concern of ministers and magistrates over the plight of their communities' aged widows. In the eighteenth century, customary forms of family support for the old met the needs of most and provided considerable power to some. But for a small and increasingly visible minority, the system did not operate successfully. As we discuss in chapter 4, large cities such as Boston, Philadelphia, New York, and Charleston established poorhouses that offered shelter to poverty-stricken and dependent elderly; within these asylums the aged poor and debilitated often made up a quarter of the inmate population. Yet the founders of these institutions viewed the establishments within the traditional system of family welfare. The asylums now provided the needy with the "kin" that they were obviously lacking.[25] In the industrial era, this institutional response would become increasingly important. Yet even in this later period, for the great majority of the old the family remained the most important resource against an impoverished, debilitated, or simply solitary old age.

The Industrial Era

As the colonial family of the elderly does not meet the extended, patriarchal profile projected by a sentimental and nostalgic view of the past, their household and family patterns in the industrial era did not follow a simple pattern of degeneration. According to the early-twentieth-century advocates for the elderly as well as some modern-day scholars, industrialization disrupted "traditional" family relationships and severed the old from their kin. All alone in the city, the elderly experienced isolation and impoverishment. Only on the farm, individuals such as Abraham Epstein and Isaac Rubinow declared, could the old retain the stable and supportive familial relationships that ensured continued financial and emotional support.

Historical evidence, however, tells a far more intricate and varied tale. Beginning in the mid–nineteenth century, wide-scale demographic changes dramatically affected the nature of the U.S. population and broadened the possible combinations of family patterns. Declines in mortality, both for infants and for women at childbirth, meant that a larger proportion of individuals survived to old age. Earlier marriages and earlier ages for childbearing increased the probability that three generations of family members would be alive simultaneously. In the midst of the industrial transformation, many more families had the opportunity to create three-generational arrangements.[26]

Such residences, however, remained the exception rather than the rule. In the late nineteenth and early twentieth centuries, they comprised perhaps one-fifth of all U.S. households. By 1900, 70 percent of all individuals age sixty and over lived as the head of the household or the spouse of the head;

22 percent, most of whom were older women, resided as a relative to the householder; and only 8 percent lived outside the family, often with a nonrelative, as a boarder in a lodging house, or as an inmate of an institution.[27]

For those who did live in complex households, such arrangements generally did not rely on sheer sentiment. Complex structure was very strongly related to the particular economic circumstances faced by elderly individuals and their families. As chapter 2 will demonstrate, complex family relationships were often founded on economic agreements. For many older people, a prosperous old age depended on the continued contribution of offspring to family resources. Reliance on the wages of children, the pressing dependency of the sick or incapacitated elderly, and cultural norms that demanded that children assist their aging kin meant that the elderly rarely lived alone. While few aging married couples extended their households to include subfamilies, their homes commonly included an adult child, an arrangement that could be considered only technically "nuclear."[28] Among the elderly, older women without spouses were the most likely to live in households extended to three generations. In the homes of their married children, such women took their place as dependents of the younger generation.

For the middle class, economic considerations determined whether their household structure would be extended. With increasing assets, relatively affluent individuals were able to provide for their relatives, even if they did not contribute to the family's resources. Such limited prosperity allowed both the elderly and the nonelderly to shelter their dependent kin and apportion their resources efficiently. For every class, complex structures surely were as much a product of necessity as of desire. In organizing their families, Americans found themselves torn between two important and quite contradictory values. While they clearly believed that family members had a duty to support each other, they also saw the small nuclear family as the ideal household. For those who opened their homes to their kin as well as for those who chose to live in nuclear families, the ideal of familial responsibility often came into conflict with a parallel belief in separate households.

The Public Use Sample of the 1900 U.S. Census allows us to examine the diverse arrangements of the industrial period and especially to assess the effects of gender, race, and ethnicity. It reveals as well that household structure was determined according to the location of the older people's residences. Three very different and highly significant locales existed: farm, village, and city. In 1900, 38 percent of Americans aged sixty and over lived on farms. Another 25 percent lived in nonurban areas with fewer than 2,500 residents, although they did not reside on farms. This group we shall refer to as village residents. The remaining 37 percent lived in larger towns and cities. The most important distinctions in these settings are displayed in table 1.2. As the subsequent discussion reveals, no continuum in family circum-

Table 1.2 Household Characteristics by Locale for Males and Females
Aged Sixty and Over, 1900

	Farm		Village		City	
	M(%)	F(%)	M(%)	F(%)	M(%)	F(%)
Relationship to household head:						
Head	82	13	74	32	77	30
Wife		44		36		31
Parent	13	36	6	18	11	25
Other relative ·	4	6	2	5	2	4
Nonrelative	2	1	18	9	10	10
Extended household						
Yes	41	61	26	42	31	47
Up to parents	12	29	6	14	10	21
Down to child	19	16	13	16	14	13

Source: Public Use Sample of the 1900 U.S. Census.

stances carried from farm to village to city. The farm offered no special refuge for the elderly; the city rarely marked the dissolution of kinship alliances. By contrast, the village was hardly an interim step, but appears almost modern in its familial structure.

Old Folks on the Farm

The farm family of the nineteenth century evokes an image of old people gently rocking on well-worn porches, surrounded by extensive generations of loving and supportive kin. In reality, the final days of the aged—especially those of widowed farm women—may have been quite different. Gender, marital status, and economic standing controlled farm-family experience. The myth of the extended farm household had some validity for the wealthy, married, and native-born. Aging male farmers generally retained the role of household head. Their valued property encouraged younger members to remain in the household and provide their assistance. At the turn of the century in a rural county of Kentucky, for example, a great majority of old men remained married, gainfully occupied, and heads of their households. Two-thirds of the Kentucky aged, in fact, continued to have children living in their homes. Moreover, their families had become increasingly complex; more than half of the men aged sixty-five to seventy-four resided with the family of one of their children or lived with a secondary, nonrelated individual in their households.[29]

Poorer families, however, exhibited different patterns of family structure.

The less affluent struggled as hired hands and subsistence farmers; they were far less likely to own valuable property. Additional family members did not necessarily contribute to their financial well-being or allow for an adequate distribution of limited resources. Rather, such extended support networks existed generally among individuals of moderate wealth. They, rather than the poor, possessed the ability to offer support and shelter to dependent relatives and the capacity to use extra hands efficiently. Among elderly farmers in mid-nineteenth-century Erie County, New York, the richer the farm, the more likely it had an extended family; the value of the estate predicted household structure.[30]

These findings reveal the importance of both economics and demography. In contrast to the relatively attenuated colonial family, extended and complex households arose in the industrial era partly because they were finally demographically possible: earlier ages of marriage along with a decline in adult mortality meant that three generations more often existed simultaneously. Moreover, relative economic success permitted the elderly to support nonproductive kin. On the large farm, landholders were able both to sustain additional family members and to hold out the promise of estates to kin in exchange for their labor and assistance.

But census records also suggest that the elderly on the nineteenth-century farm had begun to accept a significant change in their roles and responsibilities. Sheltered within a multi-generational home, the old traded the status of household head for sustenance and gradual retirement. In the farm regions of nineteenth- and early-twentieth-century America, households that included aging parents and adult children had more sons in residence than did urban households, where adult daughters predominated.[31] When older men gave up headship, their male heirs took over the operation of their valuable farms. In contrast to inheritance patterns of colonial America, the transmission of authority may even have occurred while the older farmers were still active and registered as the heads of household. Although their property still served as a vehicle for support in old age, nineteenth-century farmers did not necessarily wait for death or extreme debility to cede control.[32]

Such significant shifts of power were often spelled out in deeds that legalized the transfer of land from one generation to another. These settlements were based on strict guarantees that ensured continued care of the elderly. Children promised that in return for ownership of the family farm, they would provide room, board, clothing, and medical attention to their aging parents and assure them of a proper burial. The new complex families that were formed, therefore, were based on a well-defined understanding of transformed functions and obligations.[33]

Such patterns, however, were not universal. Like the poorer native-born elderly, aging farmers of foreign birth had less access to arrangments based on wealth and were less often found in their children's households. Foreigners were, in fact, the least likely of any group to live in extended households. Their housing arrangements were complex, however, in that they relied on the continued presence of an adult child. In contrast to 65 percent of the native-born heads of farm households, 75 percent of foreign-born male farmers still had a child present in the home. The continued status of the old as household head may be due to ethnic and cultural norms—as its consistency among locales suggests—but it also reflects economic demands. The foreign born were among the poorest of all white farmers. Having fewer resources by which to attract and retain kin outside the nuclear family, the elderly depended upon the willingness of children to remain unmarried and continue to assist them.[34]

The households of African Americans varied still more dramatically from their white counterparts, whether rich or poor. Over 45 percent of aged black men on farms lived in extended households, in contrast to only 37 percent of aged foreign-born men. One-third of these African-American households were extended to younger generations. Thus, unlike native-born white farmers who sacrificed headship, the kinship networks of African Americans tended to be extended *down*, with men heading households well into old age, at rates higher than any other group.[35] Having little wealth to offer their children, who had few assets to offer them in return, black men and women rarely had adult children in their homes or lived as dependents in their offsprings' households.[36] But because of a need for laborers, aged blacks extended their households to include a wide variety of individuals: grandchildren, nieces, nephews, other kin, and even nonrelated persons who might be described as fictive kin. The sharecropping system in southern states, where 90 percent of all African Americans lived in 1900, explains the unique family arrangements of elderly blacks. Contractual, noncash tenancy demanded that older men be able to deliver a large labor force to the landholder.[37]

The most significant difference among farm families, however, was related to gender. For most aged male farmers, the land continued to provide authority, or at least support; for elderly farm widows, however, power quickly passed to the next generation. The widow who acted as head of household was extremely rare.[38] In contrast to their counterparts in both villages and urban areas, farm widows were least likely to exert the power and responsibilities inherent in managing the estate. One consequence was that fewer aged women than men lived in farm households—only 35 percent of the elderly female population, in contrast to 41 percent of all aged men. If a widow continued to live on the farm, she usually assumed the part of a dependent, reliant on the support of the next generation. Although a widow was as likely as other women to have children present in her home, she was far less likely to be considered the head of household. As table 1.2 shows, while 25 percent of aged urban women and 18 percent of aged female villagers endured the status of dependent ("parent"), 36 percent of all aged farm women spent their last years as dependents in the household of kin. Once widowed, they either left the farm or passed their final years as the mother or mother-in-law in the homes of middle-aged landholders.

Village America

Not all Americans had to choose between the farm and the city. The village provided an alternative, one with important implications for life in old age. Village residents had diverse roots; a middle class of merchants, teachers, industrialists, businessmen, and professionals was joined by employees of rural firms, railroad workers, independent mechanics, and farm laborers living away from the farm. In addition, during the nineteenth century, an increasing number of farmers chose to sell or rent their property and settle down to the gentler life of the village.

The decision of elderly farmers to liquidate their estates and to provide for their own retirement marked a significant change in inheritance patterns. In the early colonial period, elderly farmers often held onto their land until death, assuring themselves of continued power. Members of later generations often deeded the land to their children, continuing to live in the established homestead and legally guaranteeing themselves the support of their offspring. In the late nineteenth century, however, aging farmers with sufficient property began simply to sell or rent their land, utilizing the funds to support themselves. Dependence on the benevolence—or the control—of their children was replaced by establishing their own retirement capital.

In Bucks County, Pennsylvania, for example, a significant evolution in inheritance patterns occurred in the course of two centuries. During the colonial period, 87 percent of all testators passed their farm or other businesses to their heirs; in the 1790s, the proportion had fallen to 71 percent. By 1890, a dramatic change had taken place. Only a little more than a third of all who made out a will bequeathed the property to their offspring.[39]

The conversion of estates, the creation of a retirement "nest egg," and the movement of village youth into the cities help to explain the distinct household structure of the village elderly. Half of all the male heads of village households lived without offspring in their homes, as opposed to one-third in other locations. Even in extreme old age, therefore, they retained their independence as household heads and resided either with their wives or alone. And if they lived with children, they generally did not relinquish their position of authority. If their households were extended, they tended to be extended down. Table 1.2 shows that only 6 percent of all aged village men (in contrast to 11 percent in cities and 13 percent on farms) lived as parent to the household head.

Nor was the role of household head in small communities limited to males. While farm widows appeared to have had a difficult time retaining authority, in rural nonfarm settings more than two-thirds of all women aged sixty and over were listed by census takers as either married to the household head (36 percent) or themselves head of the household (32 percent). On the farm, only 57 percent of all aged women maintained these statuses; in the city, the proportion was 61 percent. For elderly village women, even widowhood did not necessarily lead to dependence. In the village, 56 percent of widows were able to retain their authority as household heads, in contrast to 48 percent in the city, and a mere 24 percent on the farm.

The comparative autonomy of village women was a result of both their relative affluence—they had retained property or retired on their assets—and the shortage of children upon whom they could rely. In contrast to their counterparts on farms and in cities, they were least likely to have a child present. Table 1.2 indicates that 18 percent of all older women in villages lived in households in which they were the mother or mother-in-law of the household head, half the farm rate. In the small village rather than the farm or even the city, elderly women often lived as self-reliant individuals.

For both elderly men and women, therefore, the village seems to have offered an unusually independent, stable, and, by household standards, isolated experience. Unlike the farm, and, to a lesser degree, the urban dwelling, the village home did not represent a valued economic asset. Not expecting to inherit a farm or to share valued urban real estate, the children of the elderly had little reason to co-reside with their parents; they searched for opportunities elsewhere. But the village also offered elderly individuals a new opportunity to establish independent households. Especially for the native-born white elderly, the autonomous village household may have provided a setting for self-sufficiency, achieved through years of economic planning. This setting may also have been the primary residential choice of Civil War veterans, whose receipt of a regular, guaranteed income in old age allowed them to retire.[40] Able to afford to live by themselves, they chose to retain the position of household head and, within the individual household at least, did not rely on co-residence with generations of offspring. Such kinship arrangements, however, did not mean that the village elderly had severed all ties with their families or did not consider them important to their own well-being.[41] Rather, village household structure reveals that when economic circumstances permitted, these elderly individuals preferred to live in separate households.

Urban America

In the village, the households of the elderly began to take on a compact, relatively isolated shape. This rural structure has largely been ignored in the modern indictment of familial irresponsibility. Traditionally the city has been blamed for the solitude and isolation of the elderly. Here, critics assumed, the family life of the old was torn apart. Deserted by children who joined the incessant migration of workers from place to place or who, lured by high wages, left the household and began their own families, the old spent their last years with little family contact. Urbanization supposedly transformed a vibrant intergenerational life into an isolated and solitary experience.

In reality, the family life of the urban aged in the industrial era bore little similarity to this depiction. Historians have often found that urbanization *increased* the likelihood that the old would live with their children. In key cities of Massachusetts, for example, urban growth strengthened rather than weakened ties among generations. Between 1860 and 1880 in Salem, Lawrence, and Lynn, the percentage of the elderly who headed households inhabited by adult children increased. Moreover, a higher proportion of urban elders lived with their children than did elders in nonurban areas of Essex County. Similarly, in early-twentieth-century New York, a majority of the urban old lived with their children, while only a minority of rural elderly did so.[42]

The urban environment affected the structure of the household in another important way. As table 1.2 reveals, only 11 percent of urban men aged sixty and over lived as dependents in their children's home, a rate slightly lower than that of men living on the farm. The city offered aging men who experienced the death of a spouse a variety of strategies for remaining in control of the home. Some took in boarders; others, more affluent, hired servants. Wealth in the city, like prosperity on the farm, allowed older men and women to bring more kin into their households. In 1900, the wealthier of the elderly—defined as those with servants—were more likely than the poor to reside with at least one child.[43] Their relative affluence often allowed them the privilege of both paid help and the continued residence of their offspring.

For women, urban family life also differed significantly from that of the farm or village. Upon the death of their husbands, widows did not necessarily forfeit authority and become dependents in the homes of the children, a common fate for farm women. Rather, towns and cities provided many elderly women with the means by which to remain heads of households. In contrast especially to the farm, which many widows abandoned, urban areas attracted large numbers of widowed women in search of economic independence. As a result, a larger percentage of older women than men lived in towns and cities. Whether native-born white, foreign-born white, or African American, such women discovered that the urban environment provided a better arena than the farm for finding employment and remaining in control of the household.[44] In 1900, only 29 percent of all city women lived as dependents in households, compared to 42 percent of aged women on farms. Nearly half of the urban widows remained heads of their households.

Many of these independent women relied on the wealth accumulated by themselves and their husbands; in native-born white households, they often resided with a servant. Other women managed to support themselves and maintain their independence through the operation of boarding and lodging houses. In 1900, 15 percent of widows who remained heads of households ran such establishments. For these individuals, their residences not only represented a place for them to live but also provided a highly valuable asset. In the mid-nineteenth century, boarding houses played a significant part in the life cycle of many city dwellers. For young migrants, they provided a suitable shelter; for the old they offered a source of needed revenue. As children matured and left the house, vacant rooms could be turned to economic gain. Especially for women approaching old age, therefore, managing a boarding house constituted a viable and legitimate occupation and gave them a way to retain their autonomy.[45]

As with farm dwellers, ownership of a home represented a substantial economic asset for the urban elderly, but its effects on household structure were significantly different. In the city, ownership of a dwelling did not lead automatically to the transferral of power to the next generation. When farm families included three generations, they tended to be extended *up*; middle-aged males had taken control of the land, and with it, the dominant role in the family. In contrast, urban families often continued to be headed by the old. Table 1.2 shows that 14 percent of the households in which urban aged men lived extended down to a younger generation, while only 10 percent were extended up to the aged. In addition, urban elderly commonly lived with adult daughters rather than with sons. Young women remained in the households of their parents or, if another family lived with the old, it was their daughters' husbands and children.[46] Most commonly, urban households headed by the aged were not extended but complex in structure: adult children—usually female—remained in their aged parents' home.

In urban settings, complex relationships came to serve critical functions for both the old and their children. As we will discuss in chapter 3, the elderly and their children employed numerous family strategies to deal with the demands of urban, industrialized society. The establishment of complex families brought measurable benefits to both generations: highly desirable living space could be shared and income combined. Moreover, in cities, where the elderly were far more likely to own property than the young, the adult children sought lodging in homes already established by the older generation.[47]

As in the countryside, however, complex structures were not products of impoverishment. Rather, they were formed by those who could afford to live together and pool their resources; the poorest of the old had the least opportunity to sustain independent, complex households. Middle-class older people had the resources necessary to support additional kin; working-class elders had the greatest reason to encourage adult children to remain unmarried and contribute to the family income. Daniel Scott Smith's study of the 1900 census showed that complex families were more often formed by middle-class persons.[48] In 1900, while 68 percent of all urban middle-class individuals aged 55 and older resided with at least one child, the percentage among the urban working class was only 61.[49] Richer people had the resources—especially the ownership of a home—necessary to bring others into their households. The actions of the most affluent may have been charitably inspired; for those of lesser means, the arrangement was a way of using resources in realty to combine income and reduce per capita expenditures. The elderly were more likely to possess the assets necessary to achieve these objectives.[50]

Despite differences in household arrangements—by locale, class, and gender—the most striking feature at the turn of the century was an increasing complexity in household structure and higher rates of extension. To some degree, the appearance of large numbers of such households in the nineteenth century was the result of broad demographic change; for the first time, a large number of Americans survived long enough to reside in multigenerational households. Except in the village, where independent households were most likely, the particular form of household varied greatly: many elderly individuals lived in homes with downward extension; other households were extended up; some aged resided with distant kin, fictive kin, or even unrelated individuals. But the result for elderly people outside the village was clear: most individuals shared a dwelling with other individuals; few resided alone or even with their spouse in the empty nest household.[51]

The Decline of Complex Households

Although the demographic conditions upon which these new household structures were built did not dissipate, the tendency toward extended and complex forms quickly eroded after 1900. By the second decade of the twentieth century, the likelihood that members of the middle class would extend their households to accommodate kin began to weaken. For the first time, a considerable proportion of middle-class children and their elders established separate residences.[52] Between 1900 and 1940, the proportion of men aged sixty-five and over who lived as dependents in their children's home declined from 16 percent to 11 percent; for women the percentage fell from 34 to 23.[53] While this decline may have reflected a cultural shift marking a deterioration of the desire of generations to live together, the discovery that prosperous village elders had previously established autonomous households challenges the theory of the creation of a new cultural preference. The decrease in residential dependency may instead have been based on rising opportunities that allowed a significant numbers of Americans to realize a longstanding ideal of autonomous living. Rather than exposing neglect on the part of the young or a sudden dislike of their elders, such living arrangements were largely the result of economic prosperity. Increased wages and additional wealth allowed some families to achieve an ideal of separate dwellings. Among the more prosperous families, elderly individuals could amass sufficient wealth in the course of a lifetime to live independently, without depending on their children's support. As in the villages of the nineteenth century, assets in the form of pensions, investments, or savings accounts provided these persons with the option of living without their relatives. By 1915, in fact, a new pattern began to emerge: fewer middle-class families formed complex household's while in the working-class, extension and modification became more common.[54]

One explanation may be found in the economic conditions of industrialization. The average income levels of the working class rose to the standards that the middle class had achieved decades before. As a result, the more prosperous workers secured wealth sufficient to provide housing and support for relatives, although inadquate for separate residences.[55] The "luxury" of kinship co-residence, once only available to the middle class, now became a pattern among laborers. Moreover, the additional high wages of family members increased the financial well-being of the group. In 1880 in Erie County, New York, for instance, the inclusion of extended family among the unskilled generally diminished family wealth. By 1915, this loss of average income was no longer the case. The extended family, in fact, was likely to signal an improvement in the economic status of the unskilled worker.[56]

The middle class, on the other hand, now began to follow a different pattern. Before 1900, even white-collar workers were impoverished by present-day standards. Despite their comparatively higher economic status, they were often unable to establish separate living quarters for aged relatives. In the twentieth century, however, their increased well-being allowed them to live independently. This strategy was not entirely new; it had long been followed by the upper class and the fortunate elderly who resided in U.S. villages.

The growing isolation of the middle-class household not only reflected its superior economic basis but was supported as well by evolving cultural expectations. In the mid-nineteenth century, middle-class sentiment proclaimed the family to be the foundation of all social order, responsible for the development of an individual's personality, values, and character.[57] Few questioned that the family was ultimately accountable for the support of its members. The care of the dependent relative, and especially the widowed mother, was a moral obligation that went beyond economic considerations.[58] In dealing with their own families as well in defining the correct welfare policy for the poor, the nineteenth-century middle class continually espoused the primary importance of family responsibility.

Despite such beliefs, as in the preindustrial era, co-residence with an elderly relative did not always imply peaceful coexistence, nor the absence of an alternative vision of what might be better. Within complex households, the lines of authority often led to conflict and dissension.[59] In the mid–nineteenth century, Julia and Bildad Merrill, Jr., of Utica, New York, moved into the household of Bildad's elderly parents. Faced with growing disability, Bildad Merrill, Sr., and his wife, Nancy, traded their independence for the support of the younger generation. Yet this economic strategy did not translate into harmonious relations; the elderly couple found it difficult to relinquish their authority to their offspring. Both mother and daughter-in-law claimed command over the servants and preeminence with the children. Ultimately, their dispute led to an outbreak of violence between the two women and an ignominious church trial. After public apologies and resolutions, they returned to share the same abode—and many of the same generational tensions.[60]

The Merrills' household arrangements reflected their emerging middle-class status. Their relative level of affluence allowed them to support the elderly in times of need and to sustain the belief that the family was fulfilling one of its primary responsibilities. For such individuals, the neglect of relatives would have been a sure sign of little breeding or refinement; to share possessions and space was part of the cultural code of the bourgeoisie. Like the Merrills, therefore, few middle-class individuals would have questioned the necessity of assisting kin, if such assistance was required. Before the advent of the welfare state, resorting to public welfare was viewed as ultimate failure; the family rather than the state was responsible for the well-being of its relatives.[61]

Such beliefs, however, were not immune to demographic pressures. Although widows with small families could expect to live with their offspring in old age, they were not as confident of co-residence as their counterparts with many children. In 1910, 63 percent of all white widows over the age of sixty-five who had only one surviving child lived with that offspring. For those with five or more offspring, co-residence reached 85 percent.[62]

But it was not only the elderly who experienced the changing demographics of the family in the United States. The decline in family size also placed greater burdens on the children, presenting a much larger share of them with often-difficult living arrangements. In large families, children had a relatively low expectation of co-residence with an aging mother; in contrast, an only child had little hope of avoiding the complex household. As the number of offspring decreased, the risk for the existing children increased, and the predicament of how to provide for the needs of the elderly parent was shared by more Americans.[63] The aged could not select the most congenial environment; nor could the children decide which of several siblings might bear primary responsibility for aging parents. Especially for urban daughters, care of the old became an obligation they were increasingly likely to face as they themselves entered middle age. (See illustration, 'Daughters of the Elderly.')

Given the decline in the number of siblings, such middle-aged women often found themselves forced to choose between two powerful and enduring norms. On one hand, they had a preference for separate residences—a desire shared by both young and old. On the other, they continued to be committed to the support of needy aged parents. Thus, while the decline in family size did not lead to the abandonment of the old, it raised the potential for even greater tensions within the family group. In the early 1930s, an anonymous female writer recalled the problems of three-generational households. "When I was a child," she wrote,

> I took it for granted that a grandmother or grandfather should live in the house of nearly everyone of my playmates. Soon I came to take it for granted, also, that these houses should be full of friction. The association of grandparents with friction took such a hold in my mind that I called myself lucky because my own were dead![64]

Despite her antagonism to such residence patterns, in adulthood the author found herself with little choice but to take her aging mother into the household. The results, she reported, were disastrous. "Harmony is gone. Rest has vanished." Her daily routine, the lives of her children, and the stability of her marriage, she asserted, had been reduced to sheer chaos. Nor, she argued, was she alone. Numerous friends and acquaintances similarly reported the demise of their family and social life upon the residence of an aging parent. "The intrusion," she argued, "is probably a common cause of divorce, and most certainly of marital unhappiness and problems in children."

The anonymous author's complaints reflected her struggle between opposing values and norms. Her conviction that her elderly mother could not be abandoned conflicted with her strong desire to reside only with her husband and children. Although she felt obligated to open her home to her widowed mother, she strongly objected to the situation. "So strong is the tradition," she wrote, "so strong the sense of duty which we carry on for generation to generation," that she found herself with little choice. The only happy families, she concluded, were those who were financially secure enough to allow aging parent and adult children to live in separate residences.

The author's expressed desire for different dwellings hardly marked her as unique. Even in eighteenth-century England, elderly individuals who were financially able chose to live apart from their offspring. Wealth allowed both the old and their adult children the luxury of separate dwellings.[65] By the twentieth century, this preference—clearly visible in the nineteenth-century village, in the Merrills' conflicts, in the unhappiness of the magazine writer, and, perhaps most apparent, in the continuing effort of older Americans to remain heads of households—began to find expression as a "modern" cultural prescription. While the ideology of supporting the old was never rejected, twentieth-century social critics and advocates of proper family behavior began to stress the centrality of the small private household.

According to their recommendations, few institutions better served society than the nuclear family. Even in the nineteenth century, this arrangement had been at the center of the kinship ideology: the father, the mother, and the children, rather than maiden aunts or mothers-in-law, comprised the central elements in the family circle. Social theorists expressed the concern that the addition of relatives into the hallowed circle would bring dissension and ultimate ruin. Samuel Butler was only one of many anxious English and American analysts. "I believe," he wrote in 1885,

> that more unhappiness comes from this source than from any other—I mean from the attempt to prolong the family connection unduly and to make people hang together artificially who would never naturally do so. The mischief among the lower classes is not so great, but among the middle and upper classes it is killing a large number daily. And the old people do not really like it so much better than the young.[66]

Such pronouncements revealed three central middle-class concerns. First, by the early decades of the twentieth century, scores of social critics were convinced that the enclosed nuclear family was the ideal—and most congenial—arrangement for family members. Abraham Epstein, the pension proponent and expert on aging, asserted that the happiest families were those without extended kin. In 1928, he declared that "we all know among our acquaintances, some people whose young lives have been made pitiably wretched, and in some instances totally ruined, by the constant 'pestering' of an old father-in-law or mother-in-law."[67] Both the elderly and their children, he seemed confident, would be far happier if they could afford to live in separate dwellings.

Second, family experts viewed nuclear households as the proper environment for raising children and ensuring their moral upbringing. Nowhere was this belief expressed with greater vehemence than in the early-twentieth-century attack on the practice of boarding. According to a 1910 report of the U.S. Bureau of Labor, for example, the custom of boarding had little proper place in the American home. The practice, the report explained, was extremely detrimental to family members: "the close quarters often destroy all privacy, and the lodger or boarder becomes practically a member of the family. . . ."[68] The institution, which for so long had been an accepted part of middle-class life and an important source of revenue to the aging, was now seen as a sign of working-class immorality. It was, social analysts declared, an outright attack on the primacy of kinship relations.

Finally, welfare advocates were concerned about the economic impact of extended families. Middle-aged adults, it was feared, were constantly being forced to make irreconcilable economic judgments over the allocation of valued resources. In supporting their elders, they robbed the young; in providing for their children, they dismissed the longstanding obligations they owed to their elders. According to welfare authorities, members of extended families seemed to be faced with an insurmountable predicament: either they provided for their children's growth and education or they saved the old from the shame of the almshouse. Epstein's state pension argument emphasized the economic problems of trying to support the elderly. "It seems cruel," he wrote,

> to force any father or mother in this twentieth century to decide between supporting old parents and contenting themselves with a little less food, less room, less clothing, and the curtailment of their children's education, or sending their parents to the poorhouse or to charitable agencies to accept the stigma of pauperism, and thus assure themselves of more food, more room, more clothing and a better education for their children which would help them become more proficient workers.

In contrast, Epstein asserted, a state pension would "increase filial affection and respect for parents," who were no longer a burden to their middle-aged children.[69]

The concern over the quality of life within the complex family was not limited to "experts." Even the old themselves reported that they would be far happier in separate households. In a 1937 article published in *Saturday Evening Post* and reprinted in *Reader's Digest*, the anonymous author, a seventy-three-year-old woman, wrote, "when declining health and declining finances left me no alternative but to live with my daughter, my first feeling was one of bitterness." The author pledged to make herself as little of a burden as possible through numerous rules: "I must not be around when she was getting her work done, or when she had her friends in. I must ask no questions and give no unasked advice. I resolved to spend the greater part of each day alone in my room."[70]

Given such middle-class views, family experts and welfare advocates came to view complex family settings with increasing hostility. Not surprisingly, perhaps, their criticisms gained credence as the middle class moved away from such households and working-class populations grew affluent enough to adopt them. By the early twentieth century, the extended family no longer seemed a sanctuary of middle-class love and affection. Its value for children, and even for the old, had been seriously challenged. In the experts' views, such family arrangements came to symbolize working-class impoverishment. Only the poor and the immigrant, it was assumed, would live in this manner; all others would choose to reside independently.

The impact of the changing middle-class family, however, should not be exaggerated. Before the development of the welfare state, the family remained the key support for the old and the central agency for their relief should they become dependent. As we shall see in chapter 2, in the working-class family economy, the aged were best served if they could persuade an adult child to remain in the home and contribute wages into the family fund. In the middle class and among the most prosperous of working-class families, older people might amass sufficient assets to retire and maintain independent households, allowing their children to dwell in their own residences. Even for these fortunate aged, however, life was not completely secure; sickness, a sudden loss of assets, or widowhood could undermine even the best of plans.

The Social Security Era

For the families of the middle and working classes alike, the Great Depression had a dramatic and often uncontrollable impact. Severe economic dislocation led to the failure of a fifth of the nation's commercial banks and to the loss of nine million families' life savings.[71] For the elderly, economic collapse spelled disaster as they watched their hard-won assets vanish, and with them their hopes for an independent and secure old age. In city after city, urban dwellers, unable to pay their debts, had to forfeit their homes.[72] In rural areas, the family's inability to meet even its property taxes and ordinary bills led to the repossession and auction of thousands of family farms.

Real estate in farm, village, and city had, of course, served as the elderly's protection for old age. It often represented the only important asset among farmers and in the working class. The collapse in the value of property and widespread forfeiture symbolized only too well the insecurity of old age in the United States in the twentieth century.

The dramatic rise in unemployment also challenged traditional means of care of the old. Widespread unemployment meant that families that had prospered through shared incomes were no longer able to meet the needs of all, and certainly had no hope of generating surpluses. Nuclear families were shattered; by 1940, over 1,500,000 married women lived apart from their husbands.[73] Moreover, families that had been able to establish independent households found the retention of such homes difficult. In many cities, families "doubled up" to cut expenses; they relinquished the ideals of separate households and privacy for simple subsistence.

Nowhere was this more true than in the South. There, as many as one-sixth of all urban dwellers shared apartments. The case of Ruby and Elton Cude of San Antonio, Texas, illustrated well the plight of the suddenly impoverished middle class. From 1932 to 1936, the Cudes and their two young children struggled to live independently in their own home. By 1936, however, the financial burdens had became too great, and they were forced to move to Ruby's parents' residence. The house sheltered not only her parents but also her two younger sisters, an unemployed uncle from Mississippi, another uncle with his wife and two children, and a boarder. Although the Cudes were middle class in upbringing and life-style, their experience during the Depression undermined their ideal family structure and challenged their hopes for the future.[74]

The real or incipient collapse of individual households helps to explain the widespread popularity of Social Security. The Depression hit directly at the traditional means of establishing family security. It stripped individuals of their savings and property; it forced families into complex—and often highly stressful—living arrangements that they had long worked to avoid. It even threatened the most respected with the ultimate disgrace: if all family resources were gone, the elders might be forced to take their place among the paupers in the nation's almshouses.

Social Security directly addressed these fears and met the widespread desire for financial and residential independence. Guaranteed monthly checks removed the anxiety over family failure and assured steady if limited support in old age. In their increasingly generous provisions after 1950, however, Social Security benefits had far greater implications. The family economy, which had so long determined household structure, no longer controlled intergenerational transfers. For the first time, the independent household—first realized in the nineteenth-century village, then increasingly favored by the twentieth century's prosperous middle class—came within the grasp of all but the poorest Americans. Rising real incomes after the Second World War released many from the demands of the family economy, which had required corresidence with children. Even among the working class, higher Social Security benefits permitted retirement, security, and the formation of the autonomous household.

The consequent change in the typical household structure of the elderly was far reaching. In 1900, more than 60 percent of all persons aged sixty-five and older resided with their children. Whether as household head or as a dependent of their offspring, the elderly shared residences with the young, uniting their assets and abilities as well as their conflicts. In the 1950s, however, the recipients of Social Security began to establish a clear pattern of separate residences.[75] The allocation of pensions brought on two new related trends: steep declines in complex family living arrangements and striking increases in independent, autonomous households. By 1962, the proportion of the old who lived with their children had dropped to 25 percent and by 1975 to only 14 percent.[76]

While the trend to independent households has affected men, the most significant transformation occurred in the residence patterns of widowed and single women. In 1940, 58 percent of elderly women who were not living with husbands resided with kin; by 1970, only 29 percent of these individuals shared homes with relatives.[77] In the past, widowhood generally had presented women with difficult residential choices. Upon the death of their husbands, many had been forced to restructure their lives in the homes of their kin. In doing so, they had lost their authority as head of household and become dependent; they had found themselves reliant upon the good will and financial support of their offspring. With Social Security, such radical changes were no longer necessary or expected. By the 1950s, most aged women had the financial resources necessary to continue residing in their own dwellings.

Such stable residence patterns for old women conflict with the interpretation of modern old age presented by some sociologists and historians. Several scholars have focused on the dramatic changes that occur in the life of the present-day elderly, marked by abrupt exits such as retirement and the empty nest. Yet they have generally failed to consider that, in the past, aging women often experienced a dramatic break that required great adaptation. Upon the death of their husbands, they shifted from being the spouse of the head of household to being dependent upon the generosity of their children. Rather than marking the continuity of old age, such alterations in roles and residences represented a radical change. Social Security allowed the majority of older women to maintain an autonomy often lost in previous eras.[78]

The independent residential patterns of the old do not imply a modern neglect of the elderly. Rather, they reflect a longstanding preference of most individuals to live autonomously. Contemporary investigations confirm that when able, the elderly choose to live in their own households. In one study, three-quarters of the elderly African Americans and nine in ten of the white elderly persons opposed residing in a multigenerational household. In the survey, nearly all elderly individuals agreed that "it usually does not work out too well for older people to live with the children and grandchildren."[79]

The desire for an autonomous household is hardly new; it has long been the model of preference for most Americans. The recent popularity of the independent household structure means neither that the elderly have been deserted by their families nor that the young devote far less attention and care to the old than in earlier eras. As we noted earlier, contemporary investigations of the elderly's family life have found intergenerational exchange to be vibrant, instrumental, and essential to the elderly's well-being. Independent residency does not equal abandonment; the number of people within the household is certainly not equivalent to the strength of the family or the importance of intergenerational exchange. Children continue to provide assistance to older people in amounts far greater than any government-sponsored programs, while the secure economic standing of most of the elderly allows many to give aid to their offspring.[80] The circumstances of both old and young permit them to exchange resources and support while maintaining independent households.

In the past, guarantees of such independence were rare. Many older people were forced to rely on the family in more direct and intimate ways. Although only a minority lived in extended households, others formed complex living arrangements. Adult children or nonkin, such as boarders and lodgers, occupied the same houses as the elderly. Within the household itself, goods and services were exchanged to assure individual subsistence. In the preindustrial era, most adults spent their lives as parents of children and adolescents; few survived to witness the maturity and family formation of all their offspring. In the nineteenth century, however, a decline in adult mortality and earlier childbirth meant that a far greater number of aged individuals saw their children establish their own families. Complex household structures, then, were most commonly found in the industrial era, when demographic conditions first made such family arrangements highly likely. Rising life expectancy translated into the survival of more individuals into old age who then shared their homes with relatives.

But complex household arrangements were also influenced by economic conditions. For blacks in the South, extension was dictated by the constraints of sharecropping. Contracts were awarded to those who could provide numerous family members as laborers. For the working class in the industrial era, the family economy relied on keeping older laboring children in the household. Upon the death of their husbands, women were especially likely to become dependents in their children's households, as autonomous economic survival became increasingly tenuous.

As economics shaped the complex and extended household, relative wealth also determined which families were least likely to establish such households. Generally, complex family structures did not occur among the very poor. In most periods, such individuals lacked the resources necessary to respond to family needs and exchange desired necessities. Nor were such arrangements likely to be found among the very wealthy. Their considerable affluence had always allowed them to meet the ideal of the separate household. Autonomous arrangements also became prevalent in the nineteenth-century villages of the United States, where older men and women had fewer offspring upon whom to rely and had amassed the resources necessary to live independently.

By the first decades of the twentieth century, rising levels of wealth extended the opportunity for autonomous households to more and more Americans. But as the Great Depression of the 1930s demonstrated, the permanence of such arrangements remained perilous; ill fortune, bad health, or economic decline could force the newly autonomous middle class into co-residence with their relatives. For working-class families, the Depression had still more severe consequences. Even before the 1930s, they had a pervasive fear of the almshouse and hostility for the condescending private charities of the pre–New Deal era. With the Depression, these anxieties often became reality, forcing families to revert to household arrangements and intrafamilial support that they had assumed were no longer necessary. The Depression's broad impact weakened middle-class objections to public welfare and encouraged the enactment of Social Security. Undoubtedly the most popular of all New Deal measures, it was also the most transforming, for it revolutionized the household and family relationships of the elderly. For the first time, most aged individuals were assured sufficient income to support independent households. Increases in Social Security allocations firmly established the present-day trend of living in isolated, autonomous dwellings.[81]

These changes in household arrangements were supported by cultural assumptions and prescriptions. American ideology has always stressed the centrality of the family and its role in supporting kin. Seventeenth-century ministerial injunctions as well as nineteenth-century middle-class ideology reinforced a belief that the family should give aid and shelter to its members; to rely upon public welfare was a certain sign of moral and economic failure. As a result, when necessary and economically feasible, families pooled income, shared living space, and supported dependent family members. In the twentieth century, however, families more commonly observed another longstanding ideal: separate residences became the basis for enhanced kinship relationships.

The establishment of the autonomous household, however, has not led to the desertion of the old. The continued strength of family relations discovered in recent studies attests to the importance of family networks rather than household arrangements. Although adult children are now less likely than their historical peers to remain in parents' households or to take a needy parent into the home, they are much more likely to have an aging parent depend upon them for some type of assistance. While the pressures upon these adult children are different in nature from those of the industrial era, they are likely to occur with far greater incidence. With the aging of the population and the declining number of children, greater proportions of middle-aged persons must provide some form of assistance to their elderly kin, even as their own families demand their attention. The magnitude of such care has, in fact, raised great concern. Significant and often expensive obligations for the support of elderly family members fall primarily upon middle-aged women, who are already responsible for children, husbands, and, often, their own careers.[82]

In the mid–twentieth century, therefore, the elderly and their families face new challenges. As in the past, demographics and economics determine the range of choices, while the two cultural norms, which balance family responsibility against autonomous living, set the stage for debate. If the family can meet the demands of a larger and older population, it will have realized the goals that history suggests have always guided it: close and instrumental kinship relationships, without members of the extended family being forced to share the same household.

Family, Property, and Security. The Johnson Family, 1895.

Throughout American history, property and assets stood at the center of the search for security in old age. The elderly with land and wealth tended to retain positions of power and exert authority over other family members. In this photograph, Eliza and George Johnson pose in front of their village home with their two daughters, Laura and Alice, Eliza's brother John Ellis (leaning on porch), and family friend William Bronk (seated). Courtesy of the Nanticoke Valley Historical Society.

Family Circle, 1902.
This photograph of a fiftieth wedding anniversary places an affluent couple in a position of prominence in their kinship circle. Far from being deserted or isolated in the industrial era, the elderly retained a strong presence in the family. Courtesy of the Museum of the City of New York, the Byron Collection.

Daughters of the Elderly. Abiantha Watkins and His Daughter, 1891.
Before Social Security, complex households included those in which unmarried
daughters lived with their aging parents and cared for them until death. In 1891,
Abiantha Watkins posed with his unmarried daughter, Carrie, who takes her place
behind him. Courtesy of the New York State Historical Association, Coopers-
town.

"Gibbon Sisters in Their Alley Room, 5 Vandam Street" by Jacob A. Riis.

In *How the Other Half Lives*, Jacob A. Riis vividly portrayed the poverty-stricken inhabitants of New York City. He voiced the popular belief that old age led to impoverishment and institutionalization. In describing the elderly sisters, Riis wrote, "There was before them starvation or the poor-house. And the proud spirits of the sisters, helpless now, quailed at the outlook. These were old, with life behind them. For them nothing was left but to sit in the shadow and wait." The Jacob A. Riis Collection, #284. Courtesy of the Museum of the City of New York.

Coping with the Depression, 1933.
The inability of the family economy to protect the aged was dramatized during the Depression. Here, two members of a San Antonio family carry the last supply of groceries given out by Central Relief before it closed in 1933 for lack of funds. Courtesy of *The San Antonio Light* Collection, University of Texas Institute of Texan Cultures at San Antonio.

Experience and Industry, 1900.
Industrialization did not automatically degrade older workers. This photograph shows the supervisors of Amoskeag Manufacturing Company on the roof of the mill. Their skill and experience had led them to positions of authority in industry. Courtesy of the Manchester Historic Association.

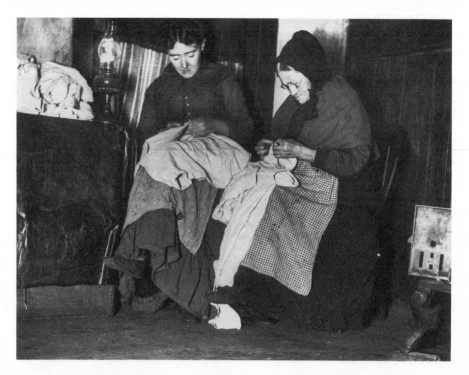

"Two Sewing Women in an Elizabeth Street Attic" by Jacob A. Riis.
Women's skills made vital contributions to the family's well-being, as illustrated
in this 1890 photograph which shows an elderly seamstress sharing home work
responsibilities with a younger family member. The Jacob A. Riis Collection,
#146. Courtesy of the Museum of the City of New York.

"The Smith" by C. H. Gilbert.

In the early twentieth century, the elderly were often depicted as diseased and dependent. Yet such images did not go unchallenged; other attitudes toward age were also evident. In this often reprinted photograph from around 1910, an elderly blacksmith is shown to be skilled and vigorous. The portrait, however, may have relayed an ambiguous message. While the old man is shown as accomplished, the skill he demonstrates harks back to an earlier, preindustrial era. Courtesy of the Library of Congress.

"Old Time Wood Sawyer, New Bern, N.C."
African American men and women worked later in life than any other group, a product of their inability to amass property or assets. At the turn of the twentieth century, a sawyer and his wife display the tools of their trades. Courtesy of the Library of Congress.

HOME
FOR AGED INDIGENT WOMEN.

BY-LAWS FOR THE INMATES.

The inmates will at all times be required to treat the Managers and the Matron with deference and respect; and to pay strict attention to all rules and regulations for the government of the house—they will also endeavor by a quiet, gentle and lady-like deportment to diffuse an air of cheerfulness and good feeling through the house—and by acts of kindness and forbearance to gain the esteem and promote the comfort and happiness of each other.

Every inmate, except in case of sickness, will be expected to attend the devotional exercises of the family.

Those who are able, will be required to make their own beds, and sweep their own rooms every morning; and to assist those who are unable to do the same.

They will also be required to sew, knit and assist in such domestic duties as the Matron may request.

A general table will be provided for the inmates; at which all who are able will be expected to take their meals—if indisposed, a suitable meal will be prepared and sent to their rooms.

No intoxicating drinks or strong stimulant shall be used in the house—except by order of the Physician—and in such cases they must be administered by the Matron.

Washing and ironing shall, if practicable, be done on Monday and Tuesday of each week.

All that is necessary for the comfortable support of the inmates of the home, shall be provided from the fund of the Institution—no individual, therefore, will on any account be permitted to leave the Institution to solicit assistance or procure work, unless by permission of the Visiting Committee.

No person will be allowed to interfere, or find fault with the Matron, but if any one has cause for complaint, application must be made to the Visiting Committee—who will receive any statement, and take such order thereon as they may think proper.

If any inmate wishes to visit her friends, she must obtain permission from the Matron; whom she shall inform of the place where she intends to stay, and the probable length of the visit; in order that no uneasiness may exist on her account, and that in case of sickness or accident, the managers may know where she may be found.

The time of making visits, as well as their frequency, is left to the discretion of the Matron.

Every inmate shall have the privilege of attending what church she pleases on the Sabbath.

There shall be a religious service performed in the house, on some part of every Sabbath day. It shall be the duty of the Visiting Committee to invite the clergymen of the city to officiate in turn.

The Rules for the Poor, c. 1850.

In the nineteenth century, private organizations opened old-age homes as alternatives to the almshouse for individuals of specific ethnic and religious backgrounds. While clearly more pleasant than the poorhouse, the homes often posted stringent regulations for their "inmates" and were not hesitant to expel individuals who failed to follow the rules. Home for Aged Indigent Women (New York), By-Laws. Collection of Carole Haber.

"Passport to the Poorhouse."

In the first decades of the twentieth century, labor and fraternal organizations undertook campaigns to convince the public of the need for old-age pensions. This 1925 illustration depicted an emerging belief about the fate of elderly workers. Dismissed from industry because of his age, this man and his wife have few alternatives but to seek shelter in the almshouse. From *The Eagle Magazine*, January 1925.

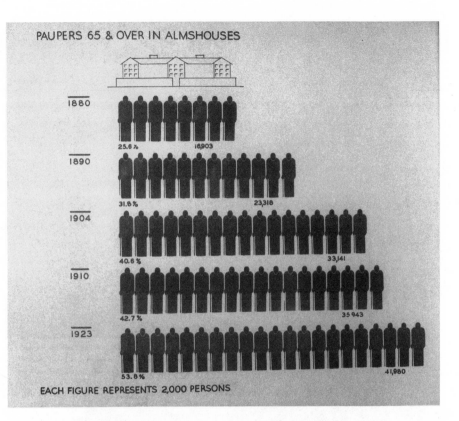

PAUPERS 65 & OVER IN ALMSHOUSES

1880   25.6 %   16,903

1890   31.8 %   23,318

1904   40.6 %   33,141

1910   42.7 %   35,943

1923   53.8 %   41,980

EACH FIGURE REPRESENTS 2,000 PERSONS

The Need for Economic Security in the U.S., 1934.
Studies by social scientists and government agencies often used the growing presence of the elderly in America's almshouses as a proof of the impoverishment and displacement of all the aged. This chart, presented by the Committee on Economic Security, was designed to build support for the Social Security Act. "The predominance of the aged in almshouses," explained the text, "is a sign of their increasing dependency. . . . " Little attention was paid to the fact that the elderly who were institutionalized had remained constant at about 2 percent since the nineteenth century.

THE GRANDFATHER'S ADVICE.

Honor thy Father and thy Mother

Wisdom of the Aged.

    In the preindustrial era, cultural advice stressed the balance that existed between generations and the harmony that grew out of reciprocity. In these two pictures, the artist emphasized the role of the old in sharing knowledge and moral wisdom as a "gift" to future generations. Courtesy of the American Antiquarian Society.

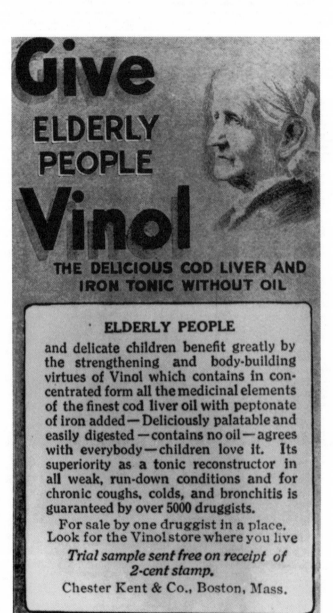

Maintaining Vigor.

The medical model of senescence in the industrial era provided a scientific basis for defining the entire stage of life as one of disease and degeneration. Although scientists generally agreed that there was little hope of returning "senile" tissues to their adult state, patent medicines guaranteed that they could aid "weak, run-down conditions." The Vinol ad equates old people with sickly children and promises to restore their vitality. Advertisement for Vinol, *McClure's Magazine*, November 1913.

There is no loneliness where there is a Radiola

Radiola 20 with five Radiotrons $115.

℔Five reasons for the amazing success of the new Radiolas
tried, tested, and perfected

Fighting Loneliness.

In the early twentieth century, magazine advertisements often portrayed the old as out of touch with the modern youthful world. This 1926 ad for Radiola touches on the theme, although it takes a novel approach. While the departure of the young couple for a night on the town might leave the old woman alone and isolated, the copy assures the reader that "there is no loneliness where there is a Radiola." Advertisement for Radiola, *The Literary Digest*, October 16, 1926.

HOW A MAN OF 40 CAN RETIRE IN 15 YEARS

It makes no difference if your carefully laid plans for saving have been upset during the past few years. It makes no difference if you are worth half as much today as you were then. Now, by following a simple, definite Retirement Income Plan, you can arrange to have a monthly income guaranteed to you for life, beginning fifteen years from now.

Not only that, but if you should die before that time, we would pay your wife a monthly income as long as she lives. Or, if you should be totally disabled for six months or more, you would not be expected to pay any premiums that fell due while you were disabled, and you would receive a disability income besides.

$150 a Month beginning at age 55

Suppose you decide that you want to be able to retire on $150 a month beginning at age 55, and you qualify for the following Plan. Here is what it provides:

1 A check for $150 when you reach 55 and a check for $150 every month thereafter as long as you live.
2 A life income for your wife if you die before retirement age.
3 A monthly disability income for yourself if, before age 55, total disability stops your earning power for six months or more.

Best of all, the Plan is guaranteed by a company with over half a billion dollars of insurance in force. If you want to retire some day, and are willing to lay aside a portion of your income every month, you can have freedom from money worries. You can have all the joys of recreation or travel when the time comes at which every man wants them most.

The Plan is not limited to men of 40.

You may be older or younger. The income is not limited to $150 a month. It can be more or less. And you can retire at any of the following ages: 55, 60, 65, or 70.

What does it cost? When we know your exact age, we shall be glad to tell you. In the long run, the Plan will probably cost nothing, because in most cases, every cent and more comes back to you at retirement age.

Write your date of birth in the coupon below and mail it today. You will receive, without cost or obligation, a copy of the interesting illustrated booklet shown below. It tells all about the Phoenix Mutual Retirement Income Plan. Send for your copy now. The coupon is for your convenience.

Planning for Retirement.

After the enactment of Social Security, retirement became an expected part of the life cycle. Private insurance companies capitalized on the fears of insecurity and offered "retirement income plans" to supplement the government program. A good old age was now tied to leisure and to independent living. Insurance company advertisement, *Newsweek*, 1940.

2

Wealth and Poverty

The Economic Well-Being of the Aged

FOR MUCH OF American history, the economic circumstances of the elderly have been closely linked to the families in which they lived. Until the Social Security era, an economic strategy based in kin relationships seemed natural to most Americans, who depended upon one another in youth, middle age, and old age. The elderly's reliance on the family declined during the industrial period, but Social Security abruptly ended its domain. After the New Deal, intergenerational transfers replaced kinship exchange, and the state, rather than the family circle, mediated the disposition of resources.

Most observers have explained the transition from family to state as a response to the growing impoverishment and isolation of older Americans in the industrial era. Seeking to explain the economic dependency they believed inevitable for older persons, early-twentieth-century reformers indicted industrialization for depriving the elderly of the financial and familial security they had commanded "back on the farm." By the 1920s proponents of state old-age pensions had fully developed the critique: since a modern economy had made the elderly vulnerable, responsible governments had little choice but to institute welfare programs based on age.

The crowning achievement of reformers, the Social Security Act of 1935, was buttressed by the conviction that the elderly could not prosper in an urban, industrial society. In 1937, Justice Benjamin Cardozo wrote for the majority in the Supreme Court which upheld the constitutionality of Social Security legislation. He found "the number of [the aged] unable to take care of themselves is growing at a threatening pace. More and more our population is becoming urban and industrial instead of rural and agricultural." Cardozo relied on Social Security Administration studies that found that "the major part of the industrial population . . . earns scarcely enough to provide for its existence." Unable to save, "industrial workers in [urban] areas . . . reach old age with few resources." [1]

The belief that all the aged "are poor, frail, and . . . in need of collective assistance" remains the dominant paradigm in scholarly and popular discourse about the elderly's past. Even critics who think old people presently receive an inordinate share of national resources assume that "during most of history, to be old was to be poor."[2] No single statement, of course, adequately describes the complex and highly varied economic experience of older men and women throughout American history.[3] Many elders have faced poverty in old age; their abject circumstances shamed Americans, who believed old people deserved good treatment. But most older people fared well by the standards of their time, and their economic circumstances clearly improved during the industrial period. As we shall see, since the colonial era, the elderly have enjoyed relative advantages over the young. Despite its mythical qualities, however, the preindustrial agricultural economy provided relatively low living standards to persons of every age. In sharply raising per capita income, industrialization enhanced the well-being of older persons, rather than undermining it. By the early twentieth century, ordinary working people could expect a degree of prosperity and an accumulation of assets unimaginable in previous eras.

On the eve of the Social Security Act, therefore, the American elderly could not fairly be described as an impoverished population. Nonetheless, an intractable problem of poverty remained, especially among elderly women and aging members of low-income groups, such as African Americans. Even the more fortunate in a laissez-faire society faced risky and difficult calculations as to the resources necessary to secure a comfortable old age. In making estimations, they relied on the principle of a family economy. Although generally successful, this strategy remained uncertain, and the exchange of resources it demanded led to conflict between kin. As the history of the family in chapter 1 suggested, the Great Depression of the 1930s convinced many Americans that the state rather than the family should provide support in old age.

Preindustrial America

In the eighteenth and early nineteenth centuries, the elderly dominated the economic resources of their communities. Distributions of wealth in the colonial era clearly favored older men and their wives. According to data from 1774, displayed in figure 2.1, young men had relatively little wealth, but males tended to accumulate resources as they grew older. Wealth peaked in late middle age, then declined slightly. Even after the age of seventy, elderly men possessed nearly twice the net worth of the average individual. Using probate records from the 1770s, Alice Hanson Jones found that men's assets rose "up to a peak around age 60, or a plateau from about age 60 to 65 or even older. Thereafter, there is some dropping off in average wealth in later years." Studies of a variety of regions in seventeenth- and eigthteenth-century America

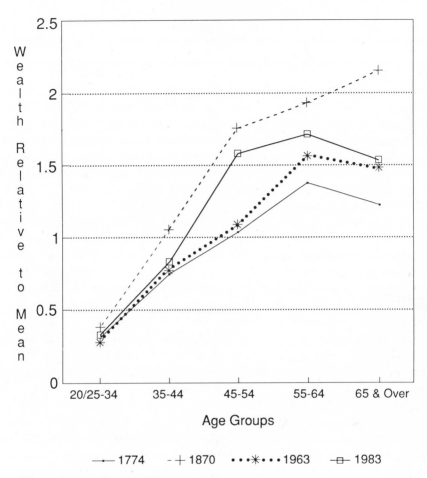

Fig. 2.1. Relative Wealth of Males by Age, 1774, 1870, 1963, 1983

reveal the same rule of reward to age. Assessing both wealth and living standards in colonial Connecticut, Jackson Turner Main found that elderly men fared extremely well; only a small proportion experienced indigence in old age. Most poverty was, in fact, a temporary condition linked to youth. Young Americans could look forward to better conditions as they grew older. Remarkably consistent across time and place, the early evidence on the relationship between age and wealth bears as well a close resemblance to later data, echoing mid-nineteenth- and twentieth-century patterns.[4]

The evidence also corresponds with studies of New England and the Middle Atlantic communities, which reveal the financial power of older generations.[5] As individuals aged, they came to control crucial resources in agricultural societies; relying on a family-based economic system, older men and their wives exerted authority over their children. In colonial America, aging landowners rarely transferred all their property to their heirs before death. By holding on to land, they assured themselves of the presence and productive labor of their offspring. Elderly parents, whose loans, gifts, and bequests molded the prospects of sons and daughters starting out in life, capitalized on the labor of mature children. Cultural prescription as well as the opportunity to inherit encouraged children to honor their parents, to delay marriage, and to contribute labor to the family enterprise. These intrafamilial arrangements underwrote the financial security of older people in the preindustrial era.

While men had legal control over most wealth, this economic life cycle applied to women as well. During married life, women shared in the prosperity (or poverty) of their husbands. In female spheres of activity, women's financial power also increased with age.[6] Once widowed, women rested their fortunes on their ability to retain control over the assets built up during married life. In early America, the chief resource of most widows lay in the estates of deceased husbands. Unless otherwise specified in the will, a woman received the traditional "widow's third," her intestate portion. Designed to keep widows from dependence on children or public charity, the intestate law provided a standard of living tied to the size of the estate. The widows of rich men and widows who received more than the customary proportion could live well. Some adroitly managed their assets and added to the value of their estates.[7]

Although colonial elders had more possessions than younger persons, wealth measures based on means disguise highly skewed distributions. The assets of the very wealthy, usually older men, produced impressive averages. But some persons in their seventies had fallen into debt, and many others had only a small amount of property. Moreover, the data used to estimate wealthholding are biased toward the rich, since these individuals tend to possess taxable property and to leave wills. While age often led to greater prosperity on farms, the process did not necessarily occur in colonial cities. Some historians find considerable poverty in urban areas and argue that age had only moderate influence in increasing wealth among urban workers. Others maintain that inequality became more extreme after the Revolution.[8] Most important, the relative affluence of older persons must be set within the context of general scarcity in preindustrial society; as one historian concludes, "luxury . . . rarely existed regardless of age."[9] Colonial Americans enjoyed a high standard of living by the measure of their time but remained quite poor by modern criteria, even at the height of their wealth.

These conditions were not limited to the colonial period. Census data from the mid–nineteenth century confirm the positive association between age and wealth, its uneven distribution in the population, and the relative poverty of all Americans before the industrial revolution. In an analysis of evidence from the censuses of 1850, 1860, and 1870, Lee Soltow concluded that the "average individual experienced handsome gains in real wealth as he progressed through life." The strong relationship between age and mean wealth among men in 1870, displayed in figure 2.1, mirrored eighteenth- and twentieth-century patterns. The value of estates increased across the life span. In 1850, free males aged seventy to ninety-nine held real estate with a mean value of $2,439, ten times the worth of the estates of aged men twenty to twenty-nine. In 1870, the wealth of men sixty-five and over exceeded that of any other age group. In addition, possession of any amount of real estate or personal assets rose from near 0 percent among twenty-year-old men to 80 percent of men in their fifties, falling slightly after age sixty.[10]

High mean wealth again disguised general poverty. At midcentury, about 30 percent of men sixty-five and over owned less than $100 in assets, and 70 percent less than $800.[11] These levels of wealth meant that most older people avoided dependency only by continuing to work, their assets certainly insufficient to support retirement. Still greater extremes of poverty characterized certain regions and classes. Per capita wealth in the South was less than half that reported in nonsouthern states in 1880, and southern blacks commanded much less than this low proportion. As described in chapter 3, slaves had no opportunity to build up wealth and, in their old age, depended on slavemasters' benevolence. After emancipation, slaveowners no longer had any responsibility for aging former slaves. Freed blacks had not been able to accumulate property during their working lives. If not sold away, their children had worked for the profit of the master rather than the parent. For such individuals, old age was indeed a period of stark indigence. If they could not work and had no family members at hand, they fell dependent upon highly deficient and racist public welfare systems.[12]

But African Americans were not alone in their impoverishment. In the preindustrial era, reliance on public or private charity occurred commonly enough even among the white elderly. The aged appear regularly in poor-relief records: old paupers wandered from town to town or received meager allotments of outdoor relief. Some had lost their health and ability to work; others had arrived at old age with neither income nor assets. This poverty-stricken condition was especially marked among elderly single women and widows. Although some widows retained the wealth of their husbands or even increased the estate, others endured economic hardship in old age. If a husband died propertyless or dictated an unfavorable distribution of resources, a widow had little choice but to become dependent on her children or charity.[13] Some aged women received maintenance provisions in the wills of their deceased husbands; these contracts stipulated that heirs provide support so long as the widowed mother did not remarry. Maintenance provisions were customary in every region of the colonies. They persisted in nineteenth-century agricultural society, and similar contractual arrangements have been discovered in rural areas in the twentieth century. Although designed in part to protect the widow, maintenance provisions at times reduced her traditional intestate portion of the estate. At first judged by historians to be a benign precursor to Social Security, maintenance contracts could be pernicious. In contrast to community property rights of today, patriarchal laws gave men almost complete power over assets, even those women brought into marriages. Husbands composed wills that removed women from positions of authority in the family and limited their share in the estate.[14]

Whatever their intent, maintenance wills and other devices hardly sufficed to protect widows, since the impoverished older woman emerged as a symbol of destitution in early America. Such poverty generally inspired a charitable response; both public and private charities acknowledged the right of the aged poor to receive assistance. This practice also reflected English poor law, which permitted support to a large proportion of the aged population.[15] Needy elders were required first to seek relief from their kin. Indeed, family members reluctant to fulfill their obligations might be prosecuted. But public authorities regularly extended support to elderly unable to obtain family assistance. In following the English practice of classifying the aged among the "worthy poor," town officers furnished elderly persons with cords of wood and monthly rent or sent them "round the town," rotating their place of residence among the homes of neighbors. Welfare officials judged old women to be especially worthy, and the earliest forms of private charity sought to redress their poverty.[16]

In the nineteenth century, critics of traditional welfare practice advocated an austere and punitive "scientific charity." Their successful reform campaign led to severe restrictions on both public and private relief. As we argue in chapter 4, this philanthropy had deleterious consequences for the aged: indigent elderly often faced the choice of moving into the poorhouse or being denied assistance. Yet even such stringent relief programs could not overcome the American belief that impoverished older people had a natural right to assistance. As a result, they appear in every account of early public and private charity. Their presence, however, was less a reflection of the economic vulnerability of old age than a confirmation of the strong principle that the aged poor deserved support. Indeed, this enduring principle gained additional credibility as the military experience of aged men became the basis for granting assistance. Beginning with Revolutionary War pensions, national and state governments provided a variety of resources to veterans of war. These benefits included small monthly allotments to old soldiers disabled in the course of battle as well as land grants to veterans of the War of 1812. Although these federal provisions were sporadic, they provided a type of pension to a large number of elderly Americans and demonstrated the early success of the aged in lobbying for and receiving government aid.[17]

For most elderly men and women in the preindustrial era, therefore, old age brought economic advantages rather than hardship. Except for elderly slaves, the aged tended to control essential assets and income-producing property in an agricultural economy. By retaining possession of land and maintaining authority over the labor of their children, they preserved economic independence in old age. Those who reached senescence with few assets or power could appeal to their communities for charitable support. Public and private welfare officials judged the veteran and the dependent widow to be legitimate recipients of benevolence. But even the fortunate among the aged lived a life bounded by the general poverty of preindustrial society. In 1850, the mean value of real estate held by aged men sixty to sixty-nine amounted to $35,000 in 1990 dollars.[18] Since the very rich strongly influenced this average, the homes and farms of the majority of the elderly had much less value. During the succeeding industrial era, the opportunity to accumulate considerable assets spread to a much larger range of the population. A new economic system provided higher standards of living and greater savings for old age, even as elders continued to rely on the traditional strategy based in the family.

The Industrial Era

According to conventional explanations, industrialization reversed the longstanding privileges of old age. Incapable of competing in modern labor markets, unable to save enough to be independent in old age, and increasingly isolated from their families, the elderly emerged as the primary victims of rapid economic change. By the early twentieth century, intellectuals and reformers in the United States had framed a bitterly critical view of industrialization's effects on older people. (See illustration, 'Gibbon Sisters in Their Alley Room.') Advocates for the elderly began to recommend broad relief policies that would allow the elderly the measure of dignity that sentiment in the United States deemed appropriate for them.

Indeed, a very large number of elderly Americans had already begun to receive assistance through the Civil War pension system. Building on the moral appeal of indigent old age as well as veterans' service to the nation, the system spread from rather modest beginnings to a far-reaching program by 1900. Responding to patriotic appeals to assist poverty-stricken veterans, federal and state politicians liberalized eligibility requirements. Benefits for soldiers wounded in the war soon broadened to include those who had merely served, then to dependents distantly connected to the veteran. While at first applicants had to be injured in battle or needy, by the early twentieth century neither incapacity nor need—but simply age—served as the basis for gaining a pension. According to the policy of the Pension Bureau, merely by virtue of their advanced years, men over seventy were labeled "wholly incapacitated" and deserving of support. While not based on any clear analysis of who needed help, Civil War pensions covered a large percentage of older Americans by 1900, particularly those of Anglo-Saxon or early immigrant background. Perhaps one-third of all men sixty-five and over, and, through them, widows and dependents, received federal or state payments at the beginning of the twentieth century.[19]

The political popularity of Civil War pensions attested to the early appeal of welfare based on age. Veterans' relief, however, held little promise for younger workers or for recent immigrants. Soon to make up the majority of the aged population, the industrial working class depended on finding ways to secure both a reasonable standard of living for family members and an adequate accumulation of resources for old age. Many achieved these goals by relying on the family. Instead of undermining traditional support systems, industrialization encouraged industrial workers to use families to balance life-cycle demands. The factory economy had highly beneficial consequences for many of the aged, and its positive effects were founded upon a family strategy.

Two surveys of the U.S. working class provide the primary evidence for these conclusions. In 1889–90 and again in 1917–19, U.S. government officials took cost-of-living surveys of working-class families, listing income from any source as well as expenditure for all items.[20] More than 6,000 families participated in the nineteenth-century study and 12,000 in the 1917–19 survey. Although more broadly representative of U.S. workers than most evidence, the samples have several deficiences, including failing to include female-headed households. While findings must be tempered by deficiencies in the sampling techniques[21] and a lack of cohort evidence,[22] the data shed a unique light on the life-cycle experience of industrial workers and their families and on change in economic well-being across the heart of the industrial era. Using 1918 dollars for both surveys, figure 2.2 displays the median earnings of male household heads as well as the total income generated by their households. As we discuss more fully in chapter 3, industrial workers' income experience did not follow the positive relationship to age found in wealth measures. The five-year age groups in figure 2.2 show that in each period older males' earnings fell well below those of younger men. Young couples could see clearly that by their middle age, the household head's earnings would be relatively low, at the very moment when growing families required

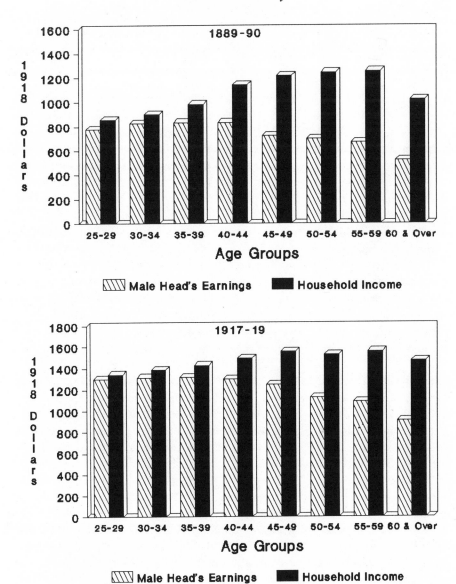

Fig. 2.2. Male Heads' Earnings and Total Household Income (Medians), 1889–90, 1917–19

higher expenditure. To meet the expected shortfall, households relied on a family-based economic strategy, a central feature in U.S. working-class experience.[23]

This financial strategy depended on both the paid and the unpaid labor of family members; wives and children, as well as male heads of households, played essential roles. The success of the family demanded the unpaid work of the wife and mother.[24] Raising dutiful children constituted a wife's most important economic function, since the family eventually relied on children's wages. In one respect, the costs of raising children, in direct expenditure and in wives' labor, became a form of savings. The "useful child" fit the needs of working-class families; children constituted "a natural asset" owing to the relatively low costs of raising them and their early entry into the labor force.[25] John Bodnar's studies of immigrants reveal that parents "eager to increase the income of their household" encouraged children to work; children expressed their fealty to the family by "turning their wages over to their parents in an almost ritualistic manner." When you worked, one immigrant explained, "you used to bring your pay home and give it to your parents. And whatever they feel they want to give you, they decide." Stacia Treski recalled that her parents "wanted fifteen dollars a month from me. . . . They wanted it every month."[26]

In making these demands, aging parents exerted great authority over the lives of their children, as they had in the preindustrial era. They planned careers, seeking to turn children toward objectives that would be advantageous to the family as a whole. As Caroline Ware's study of New York City demonstrated, this familistic emphasis persisted in ethnic communities into the 1930s. Parents still believed that a child ought "to sacrifice his own interest or ambition to promote the welfare of the family."[27]

In most accounts of working-class families, such patterns of behavior have been explained as part of a struggle to survive. Scholars have maintained that parents who coerced their children into the labor market or relied upon their wages simply had little choice. Without such actions, it is assumed, the old would have faced destitution; by putting children to work, they kept the wolf from the door. Bodnar concluded that working-class families in the industrial era were "primarily concerned with survival" and "achieved little in the way of savings." Like Bodnar, Mark Stern also emphasized the close margin of existence in working-class families. While families that included older working children did well, the departure of children and the loss of their wages were devastating. "With all the children gone," wrote Stern, "the old couple would again be impoverished."[28]

Other historians, however, view the family economy quite differently. They reject the convention that survival preoccupied working-class people, arguing that these men and women had ambitions for success and made plans by which to achieve it. According to Eva Morawska, the collective efforts of Eastern European immigrants often led to ownership of property and accumulation of savings. In her surveys of ethnic communities in New York City, Ware found that the addition of children's earnings dramatically improved families' economic conditions.[29]

The cost-of-living studies confirm this more optimistic assessment. They demonstrate vividly the centrality of the family economy in the industrial era, prove the importance of children's wages to the economic welfare of the aged, and reveal a broad opportunity for success in this period. In Figure 2.2, a marked contrast exists between the male household's life-course income and that of his household. While his wages appear to fall across the life cycle, children's wages, rents, and other sources increase; as a result, household income tended to rise well into the late middle age of the household head. In both 1889–90 and 1917–19, median household income reached its peak when the head was in his mid-fifties, two decades after individual male earnings peaked.

Figure 2.3 shows that children's wages constituted the primary source for additional income. Despite falling shares from the chief breadwinner, middle-aged men and women could expect greater income from their children and from assets. In the nineteenth-century survey, for example, nearly 30 percent of households with heads over sixty took in boarders, in contrast to fewer than 10 percent of heads in their thirties.[30] Although the 1917–19 sample excluded larger boarding and lodging households, the sum of rent received and other nonearnings income for households headed by men sixty and over was twice that of younger men. But the key was children's wages. In 1889–90, after household heads reached forty-five years of age, children contributed at least one-quarter of the mean household income. In the oldest households, they provided one-third of total income. Children's earnings became substantially less important for most households in the 1917–19 survey; but for households headed by men sixty and over, children still contributed nearly a third of the total family income. Rising male earnings across this thirty-year period allowed more parents to keep children out of the labor force (the average number of working children fell from 0.6 to 0.3); the oldest households, nonetheless, still required their help. In these households, an average of 1.2 children worked, a figure only slightly lower than the 1.3 characteristic of the 1889–90 elderly.[31]

As shall be seen, the net result of rising total income was to maintain high consumption levels in older households while improving annual savings. In essence, children's wages and other income ensured that standards of living would remain high as the aging male's earnings slipped below the standard for younger men. Moreover, these additional sources guaranteed that surpluses would be available each year to build up the older couple's assets.[32]

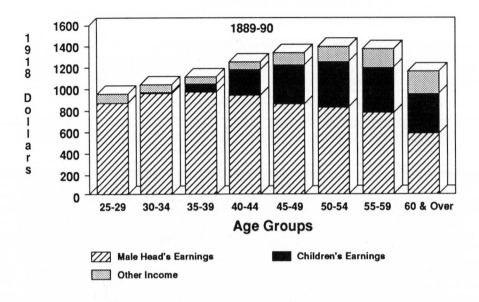

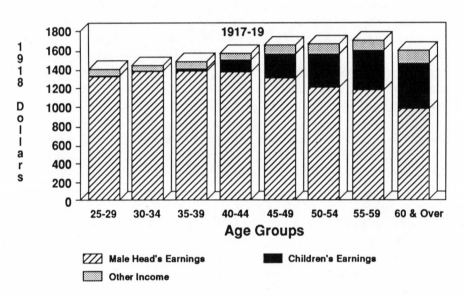

Fig. 2.3. Composition of Household Income (Means), 1889–90, 1917–19

older households do better (handwritten)

Expenditure inevitably rose as families grew and matured. But high consumption costs in older households did not occur simply because there were more mouths to feed. Even as the head entered late middle age and some children departed the household, per capita expenditure remained high. Persons in older households had excellent living standards, above the average for all households. In the nineteenth century, the oldest households reported $231 expenditure per person, in contrast to $224 per capita expenditure for all households; in the twentieth, they spent $319 to $308. Rising real income allowed families to shift consumption away from food toward other items. In the nineteenth century, expenditure on food made up 47 percent of the expenditure in households headed by men sixty and over; in the twentieth, such households spent 39 percent on food. Little evidence exists that this decrease was the result of older people depriving themselves in order to balance budgets. In 1917–19, the oldest households reported higher than average per capita expenditure for amusements, vacations, books, and newspapers.[33] Comparison of the two surveys graphically demonstrates the rapid improvement in standards of living across the industrial era, even in the households of the aged. Said by many to have suffered most bitterly in the move from farm to city, the elderly had household incomes 44 percent greater in 1917–19 than in 1889–90 (from $1,019 to $1,472), and their per capita consumption had risen by 38 percent.

Despite generous expenditure in older households, annual savings tended to be higher in these families as well. Figure 2.4 indicates that median annual surplus rose across the life course, peaking in late middle age in both surveys. Older men had access to larger surpluses than younger, more highly paid wage earners. In 1889–90, households headed by men thirty-five to thirty-nine reported a median surplus of $23; those sixty and over had $53 in annual savings. In the 1917–19 study, older households reported median surplus at $89, in contrast to $65 for men in their late thirties.[34] With the collective effort of family members, including the unpaid labor of the wife and the earnings of children, working-class Americans could do more than survive; they could build up considerable savings.

In all likelihood, parents controlled these surpluses, at least in the short term. Families generally expected boys to turn in the greater part of their wages, and most assumed that girls who worked would hand over all their earnings. Describing a family in New York City, Ware's interviewers reported that a working daughter turned "in all her earnings to the family fund. She has no [additional] privileges because she is working."[35] Given the exact description of expenditure items in the surveys, including distribution of funds to family members for education, amusements, and other discretionary purchases, surpluses constituted for the most part the savings remaining in the hands of the parents. The aging couple certainly captured payments on the

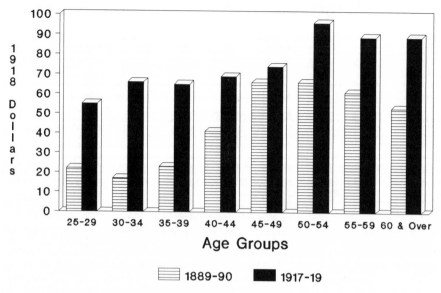

Fig. 2.4. Median Surplus, 1889–90, 1917–19

principal in real estate loans, which amounted to more than 20 percent of the mean surplus for households in 1917–19.

Over a lifetime, even moderate surpluses promised considerable accrual of assets in the last stage of the life course.[36] Ignoring interest, a simple summation of median savings between age twenty-five and sixty-five in 1889–90 yielded assets of $1,745. The same calculation produced $3,015 in 1917–19. Mean surpluses yielded about $5,000 in each survey. The average accumulation probably fell between the median and mean. Since accrual did not depend entirely on the high wages or regular employment of older males, households that did not suffer severe misfortune during the industrial era could expect to save between $2,500 and $5,000 in assets by the time the head of the household reached his mid-sixties.

These estimates correspond remarkably well to the wealth reported for older people in industrial states in the mid-1920s. Two studies in that decade offer a convenient test for the accrual process inferred from cost-of-living data. In 1925, the Massachusetts Commission on Pensions' *Report on Old-Age Pensions* employed "a representative sample of the entire non-dependent population" of the state. Interviewing 17,000 persons sixty-five and over, the commissioners found that 41 percent possessed assets worth $5,000 or more ($4,245 in 1918 dollars). Another 20 percent owned property and other items valued between $1,000 and $4,999. In 1926–27, the National Civic Federation followed similar methods in surveying 15,000 persons sixty-five and over in urban areas of the Northeast. Over 40 percent reported wealth of $5,000 or more, and 19 percent $1,000 to $4,999, almost exactly equal to Massachusetts results. Given that assets tend to be underreported, these figures represent conservative estimates of the level and range of wealthholding in the older population. They suggest that older Americans did grasp the accumulation opportunities suggested by surpluses in the family economy.[37]

These levels of wealthholding also mark a dramatic improvement in the capacity of ordinary workers to build up savings, an improvement for which industrialization appears responsible. In 1870, 70 percent of all males sixty-five and over had less than $1,000 in savings in 1918 dollars. In the industrial working class of 1889–90, half of the men could expect to possess more than $1,700 in savings, and by 1917–19 median saving exceeded $3,000. Such wealth had very positive effects on economic well-being, even when the income received by the household was low. Assets in housing and durables (such as sewing machines) provided services that would otherwise require expenditure. When necessary to sustain customary standards of living, wealth could be converted into income as cash or credit.

Annuitizing total wealth provides one way of measuring the intrinsic value of savings and of assessing the economic well-being of older people. Wealthholders may annuitize their assets such that, for some estimated period of longevity, principal and interest are doled out in equal annual allotments.[38] Using this approach, the elderly's economic progress during the industrial era is striking. In the mid–nineteenth century, the elderly enjoyed a status superior to that of the young, but deficient by later criteria. Mean wealth in 1870 (including the very wealthy aged) implies that perhaps twenty percent of men sixty-five and over could finance a ten-year annuity of $231, an amount equal to the expenditure needs for one person in the older households of the 1889–90 sample.[39] The other 80 percent either had to work or to depend on others to sustain themselves and their families. By the late nineteenth century, industrial workers looked forward to vastly superior prospects in old age. Using $2,500 as a likely accumulation at age sixty-five, half of the working-class population could expect assets that would produce $308 per year for ten years. The $5,000 mean accumulation level—wealth held by 40 percent of the aged, according to the 1920s surveys—provided a ten-year annuity equal to $616, essentially equal to an elderly couple's consumption needs by the higher 1917–19 standards.

Economic growth meant that considerable savings could be achieved not only by the wealthiest Americans but also by members of the industrial working class. These savings, as well as the household income generated in the family economy, provided a much higher standard of living to older people than was likely in the preindustrial era. Accumulation of savings certainly protected against the vicissitudes of industrial life: unemployment, illness and death, or strikes. But assets were not simply conceived of as insurance against these risks. They reflected the goal of a secure and comfortable old age, one in which wealth guaranteed respect, status, and independence. Steeply rising home ownership levels among the old across the industrial period provide evidence for such objectives and for the very positive effects of economic growth on the economic circumstances of the elderly in the United States. Between the mid–nineteenth century and 1930, older people became increasingly likely to live in homes they owned and the most likely among all age groups to own this real estate mortgage free.[40]

The cost-of-living studies, along with the surveys of the elderly population in the 1920s, demonstrate the imposing gains in the economic welfare of older persons during the industrial period. According to the surveys, more than half the aged lived in good economic circumstances. The remainder divided into three approximately equal groups: one having sufficient means, another at the verge of dependency, the last wholly dependent on family or charity. Combining earnings and potential income from wealth, about half the elderly had incomes equal to or exceeding the average earnings of male workers in the 1920s. Another 15 percent had a combined income between $600 and $1,000, which exceeded a subsistence budget for an elderly couple. About 17 percent reported less total income, and a group of equal size reported no income or property.[41]

The last category was patently dominated by single and widowed women. As in preindustrial society, wives' fortunes in the industrial period reflected those of their husbands. Both the Massachusetts and the National Civic Federation reports showed that married women fared best in all distributions of wealth and income. Widows had benefited, however, from legal modifications during the nineteenth century that strengthened their property rights. A husband's death less often threatened a woman with alienation from the property she had brought into the marriage or with disownment from the assets that she and her husband had accumulated by years of work.[42] Some women traded property rights to children for support, a device commonly used by farmers' widows. In cities they could also choose to open their homes to renters and, as keepers of boarding and lodging houses, use their property to provide for themselves.[43]

But older women's circumstances remained unappealing. In the 1920s surveys, the proportion of widows reporting no property reached twice the level of all other women. These women, who faced very poor choices in the labor market, had exhausted their savings or transferred assets to children, and many fell dependent upon kin. As a last resort, they were forced to rely upon public or private charities. Not surprisingly, elderly widows crowded the caseloads of welfare workers, who recognized their plight and their appeal to Americans' charitable impulses. Other groups faced hard times in old age as well. Immigrants had a better-than-average chance of ending up in the almshouse, and the economic status of African Americans often failed to improve with age. Many remained impoverished throughout the life cycle.[44]

Despite imposing economic growth, therefore, segments of the elderly population continued to be highly vulnerable. Nonetheless, poverty had clearly diminished during the industrial era; the majority of the aged had achieved unprecedented levels of well-being. It is ironic that the movement for state welfare gained strength in a period of increasing prosperity for the old. As the Civil War pension system withered away in the early twentieth century and ethnic political organizations gained power, working-class representatives and progressive reformers brought forth a variety of proposals for state relief for the aged. Although cost-of-living studies and other surveys provided strong evidence for relatively comfortable conditions among older persons, pension advocates claimed that most faced poverty.

Until the 1920s, the old-age pension movement achieved few successes. In that decade, the vigorous support of the working class provided the political foundation upon which a number of state pension laws passed.[45] Opposed by business interests and a middle class hostile to public charity and taxation, and severely restricted in scope, such laws nonetheless prefigured the strength of the demand for state relief in the 1930s. The old-age pension movement demonstrated once again the appeal of welfare for the aged, even in the most prosperous of times.

The Social Security Era

Amid the Depression of the 1930s, the coalition opposed to state relief disintegrated; much of the middle class joined in the demand for government old-age programs. The private sector's promises of financial security in old age rang hollow for those who had lost homes, jobs, and businesses, whose savings and investments had been wiped out, or who found their private pension reduced or eliminated.[46] A virtually irresistable popular pressure led to liberal state programs and to the federal Social Security Act of 1935. Continued unabated for decades, the expansion of benefits fundamentally altered the original character of the Social Security program, especially the relationship between the premiums workers paid and the benefits they received. Amendments in 1939 undermined the actuarial principles embedded in the Old Age Insurance provisions of the act; legislation in 1950 virtually abandoned insurance standards in an attempt to stem the growth of noncontributory pensions under the Old Age Assistance title.[47]

As a result, by the 1950s, Social Security had begun to provide largely unearned benefits to recipients, while administrators and politicians maintained the myth that these payments amounted to "insurance" that had been paid for by taxes on workers' earnings.[48] Unquestionably, the system recast the economic history of the aged. Dependence upon the state replaced dependence on the family. As has been shown, familial strategies had been much more complex than the occasional sheltering of an impoverished parent. One of the family's most important functions was to provide income that compensated for relative declines in the earnings of older men. Through reliance on the young, households headed by aging men maintained high consumption while still accumulating surpluses. During the industrial era, this system succeeded in providing a relatively high degree of prosperity to older people. Nonetheless, a family-based strategy had several demonstrable drawbacks; the exchange of valued resources required clear sacrifices by kin. By the 1950s, the family economy had been abandoned by the majority of Americans. The aged as well as the young embraced a state-mediated system that transferred resources between generations rather than between family members.

This momentous shift has not disturbed the historical superiority of the aged in wealth measures. Relative wealth data from 1963 and 1983, shown in figure 2.1, exhibit an arresting similarity to those drawn from the eighteenth and nineteenth centuries. Although the Great Depression eroded the wealth of Americans in every age group, the extent of loss among the elderly cannot be determined.[49] But after the Depression, reward to age can once again be observed. In 1962, consumer units headed by persons fifty-five or older made up 35 percent of the population but owned 56 percent of all personal wealth. In 1983, households headed by persons sixty-five and over held mean assets of $227,464, while those under age sixty-five possessed $133,820. Elderly households controlled more than one-quarter of all household wealth in the United States. Because older households tend to be smaller, elderly individuals possess still greater per capita margins. As a result, even excluding the present value of their pensions (i.e., the wealth necessary for annuities equal to such benefits) as well as certain nonliquid assets, "the elderly were more than twice as rich in terms of individual wealth as the average individual" in the United States in 1983. Although wealth does decline after age seventy-five, households headed by persons fifty-five to seventy-four clearly dominate contemporary wealth distributions, both in home equity and other forms of assets.[50]

As in the past, inequality of distribution characterizes the aged population. In 1983, the top 5 percent of elderly households owned more than half of the wealth in their age cohort. Some evidence exists that economic inequality may be greater in the elderly population than in other age groups, making the use of mean averages particularly suspect. But medians follow a similar pattern. Median wealth in aged households reached $64,000, while the median for all households was about $40,000.[51] Although more modest *age = wealth*

and more representative of average experience, medians still underestimate the wealth of the aged because they do not include the value of the elderly's Social Security and private pension benefits. Given the rapid expansion in such benefits during the last two decades, the aged have undoubtedly achieved higher relative wealthholding than in previous periods.[52] The positive relationship between age and wealth stands out, therefore, as a constant characteristic in American history, despite sweeping changes in the economy and in governmental policy.

Most analyses of the economic well-being of the aged, however, focus on income rather than wealth. Social Security, as well as the spread of seniority provisions, has transformed the income experience of workers across the life cyle. In chapter 3 we describe the improvement in the relative status of older workers since World War II. During the industrial era, workers past age forty had lower earnings than younger men. In contemporary cross-sectional profiles, male earnings do not decline until workers are well into their forties. Studies that follow cohorts across the life course find that most older workers experience no decline in income whatsoever until retirement. These improved conditions reflect the effect of seniority-based compensation. Mass retirement under Social Security has, on the other hand, introduced an unprecedented drop in individuals' earnings at specified retirement ages. In addition, the earnings of other family members no longer compensate for the falling income of older workers. Although comparisons of recent data to evidence in the cost-of-living studies remain inexact, they confirm the decided shift away from family economy strategies. In 1990, household income (from earnings, welfare, or any source) peaked when the household head was forty-five to forty-nine, earlier than in the industrial era. Nearly all of this income was generated by a single earner or by a husband and wife. Household income also declined precipitously at retirement ages. For the sixty-five and over group, median income was about half the median for all households—a pattern quite distinct from the high levels in even the oldest households in 1889–90 and 1917–19. In contrast to previous periods, most older Americans in the present era have retired and no other workers live in their households. Social Security and other pension benefits provide nearly all their income.[53]

Although the total income available to the household now exhibits abrupt declines, Social Security benefits have risen sharply in real terms since 1950. Surveys of Old Age Insurance beneficiaries during the 1940s found that median annual income fell in real terms across that decade as benefits failed to keep pace with inflation.[54] During the first decade of the operation of Social Security, the elderly's economic status may, in fact, have deteriorated. Older people abandoned family strategies—and reliance upon the "family fund"—and attempted to live on small government benefits. Amendments in 1950 restored the buying power of Old Age Insurance benefits, and subsequent improvements, especially amendments in 1972 that tied Social Security benefits to the cost of living, have greatly enhanced the income levels of older Americans. These benefits have had no actuarial relationship to the premiums workers paid; retirees have, as a result, received a very high return on modest contributions. Most important, a regular and guaranteed stream of income frees the aged from pressures to continue working and to maintain the family economy, demands inherent in their last years in the past.

The relatively low income in older households, therefore, inaccurately represents their economic status and disguises marked improvement in well-being since the 1940s. Research using 1951 and 1952 data found that 45 percent of aged couples had receipts insufficient to meet a modest budget, and 30 percent had too little to meet a subsistence budget appropriate to the 1950s.[55] This analysis allowed only a small reduction in budgetary needs for those who owned homes. Later studies corrected biases in income and wealth data and annuitized wealthholding in homes and other property. Research that annuitizes assets and corrects for household size and underestimation of unearned income finds that on average the elderly are substantially better off than the nonelderly.[56]

Even when annuitization is not used, the corrected per capita income of the elderly now equals that of nonelderly adults.[57] Estimates of economic well-being that do not assume that the aged could liquidate their homes and other assets but do adjust for differences in taxation, cost of durables, and household size and composition show that the elderly cannot presently be seen as disadvantaged. For all practical purposes, they have an equal standard of living and much superior assets, particularly in housing.[58]

Certainly, during the last thirty years, the spread of private pensions and the increasing generosity of transfer payments through Social Security have sharply reduced the poverty rate in the elderly population. These rates have fallen below those among the nonelderly, even when wealth is ignored and income is the only criterion. Between 1966 and 1990, official poverty rates for the elderly declined from 29 percent, or twice the national average, to 12 percent, a level below the national mean.[59] Having retained their superiority in wealthholding, the aged have benefited from rising Social Security payments and other programs targeted to older persons (such as Medicare). Without such transfers, more than 45 percent would have incomes below the poverty line.[60]

During the Social Security era the aged have maintained or regained a level of economic well-being that had always been relatively high. Nonetheless, even in the 1980s, when their fortunes appeared to have reached new heights, a significant fraction had few assets and relied almost entirely on Social Security for income. And despite drastic shifts in history, the victims of poverty have remained remarkably consistent: women, African Americans, and Hispanics constitute the core of the impoverished in the elderly population, just as women, African Americans, and immigrants were its majority in previous eras. In 1981, the median annual income of men sixty-five and over was $8,173, while that of older women was merely $4,757. According to a study that estimated poverty among the elderly between 1939 and 1979, female heads of household, nonwhites, and Hispanics were consistently poorer than white males. In 1990, the poverty rate among women sixty-five and over exceeded 15 percent, twice the level for men; it exceeded one-third for the aged black population and for black women reached 38 percent. As a result, women make up more than 70 percent of the impoverished aged; African Americans and Hispanics constitute a disproportionate share of these poor women.[61] Now, as in the nineteenth century, the impoverished tend to be female, widowed, and from groups that had low incomes even in youth and middle age.

Despite the persistence of poverty, the conditions of the most vulnerable have improved under Social Security. Because benefits have been tilted in favor of poorer individuals, Social Security has given women, African Americans, and other low-income workers substantial gains over returns from a private system based on premiums. The 1939 amendments greatly improved the economic welfare of widows who did not work outside the home, protecting them from having to enter the labor force at an advanced age or to rely on children. Social Security benefits for wives and dependent children provide income not based on any labor market activity. Indeed, the real income of older women has improved substantially in recent decades, primarily because of these federal transfer payments. Although often criticized for failing to redress the poverty of elderly women, Social Security has profoundly improved their economic welfare from that common to earlier eras.[62] As chapter 1 revealed, the opportunity for older women to live separately from their children, even if on very low incomes, is largely a consequence of Social Security benefits.

But the richest elderly have also shared in the largess of public welfare and have profited more than other aged persons from tax-subsidized policies for private pensions, real estate, and other retirement mechanisms. All the elderly have secured returns on their Old Age Insurance taxes that no private system could have provided, and through Medicare and other age-based programs, they have enjoyed a series of substantial transfers from younger generations.

As economic conditions worsened in the 1970s, public intergenerational exchanges provoked a debate over whether the elderly received more than a fair share of our nation's resources. Should such policies continue, critics asked, when other age groups, particularly children, faced increasingly hard times? The history of the American elderly provides useful guidelines for this debate. The longstanding tendency to equate old age with poverty stands out as a curious error in our historical consciousness. In the preindustrial era, advancing age usually led to greater command over the productive resources of society; most older men and their wives enjoyed wealth substantially above the average. While many critics have argued that the factory disrupted the privileges of the old, economic growth during the industrial era substantially improved their well-being. Social Security did even more: it protected the persistently vulnerable subgroups—women and low earners—while ensuring prosperity for the majority.

Given industrialization's contribution to a better life for older people, it is perplexing that reformers in this era blamed the factory for the impoverishment of the aged and demanded the allocation of state pensions. To such advocates, however, the grinding poverty of some older people became painfully visible in the new urban setting; like other social problems, it contrasted starkly with rising standards of living and the obvious affluence of the United States. Social commentators did not have to seek far to find desperation in old age. Elderly paupers filled the almshouse wards and old widows dominated charity rolls. In a culture that professed to honor the aged, such impoverishment caused acute embarrassment, a shame dramatically expressed in D. W. Griffith's 1911 film *What Shall We Do with Our Old?* The Massachusetts Commission captured well the paradox of poverty in the midst of plenty: "One striking and exceedingly important fact disclosed," it wrote in 1925, "is that the largest groups are at the extremes; elderly people either have means reasonably sufficient . . . or they are destitute."[63]

This destitute minority, though, could hardly have inspired a system so broadly generous as Social Security. Instead, its origins lie elsewhere, in difficulties and tensions endured by Americans of every age who lived and worked within the family circle. Although the family strategies of the preindustrial and industrial eras succeeded, leading especially in the latter period to high standards of living and considerable savings for older persons, they had severe shortcomings. One problem lay in this device's inherent inefficiency in predicting the future. At the family level, it was difficult to assess with any precision the future needs of the aged: how long they would live; how well their investments would do; how much their children would contribute; and what new costs, such as medical care, might arise. A broadly based social insurance system could assess these risks more accurately, but isolated families faced considerable uncertainty. This insecurity led, as we shall see in the next chapter, to a reluctance on the part of older men to retire.

Uncertainty led as well to another cautious behavior, a continued, intense reliance on family members, a reliance distasteful to both young and old and one that provoked discord and conflict within families. To prepare for an expected decline in earnings and a host of less certain eventualities, older men and women looked to their children's wages. By capturing some of these earnings, they were able to maintain surpluses in the face of faltering personal income. Such use of family members' earnings surely represents a retirement tax. The same penalty, in another form, occurred when adults took aging mothers, fathers, aunts, or friends into their homes. As chapter 1 reveals, both contemporary social gerontology and historical research find that such duties engendered controversy and strife within families, especially when they abruptly ended education for children, compelled co-residence of generations, and restrained the life choices of younger persons.[64] Family members may have consented to the use of children's wages and labor time, the termination of their education, and their entrapment within the parental household, but such obligations created tension. All generations preferred autonomy.

While economic growth during the industrial era reduced intrafamilial tensions, it could not remove them. The Depression of the 1930s was a grim reminder, and not only to the working class, that no level of wealth could guarantee against the threat of becoming dependent on family members. The result was a demand for a public welfare system that arranged exchanges between generations outside the family. As proponents maintained, comprehensive social insurance guaranteed the elderly a steady flow of income, whatever their longevity, and a broad plan assessed risk far more efficiently than family schemes. Social Security replaced intrafamilial strategies with intergenerational ones, spread risk across the entire population, and depersonalized taxation. It did not create affluence among older people and it did not repair damages for which industrialization has been blamed. Social Security did, however, remove the connection between economic well-being and family. It made the aged the children of the state.

3

Work and Retirement

IN THE HISTORY of work, as in the history of economic well-being, Social Security emerges as the decisive catalyst of change. Until this legislation was enacted, most men and women retained occupational roles well into old age. In the Social Security era, however, retirement became the expected and normal state of life for elderly men. For older women, national legislation did not create as sharp a break in experience; continuity or gradual change in occupational tasks still characterized the lives of the majority who did not work outside the home. Nevertheless, the effects of mass retirement extended to these women as well as to the growing numbers who, having returned to the labor force in middle age, then retired in their sixties.

The standard explanation for the shift from work to retirement as the normal experience of old age echoes the impoverishment model evident in the history of welfare: industrialization deprived people over fifty of meaningful work, forced them into unemployment, and mandated a public retirement system.[1] The elderly's loss of occupational status marked them as powerless victims of the modern world. In this chapter we reassess the work and retirement experience of older Americans from the seventeenth century to the present and challenge the conventional account. Economic systems did not fix the fate of the older worker, although they presented new conditions and choices. Preindustrial American society neither guaranteed employment for older workers nor forebade retirement; an industrialized economy did not make older workers obsolete. Moreover, while industrialization presented new obstacles and opportunities to the aged, its effects pale beside the radical impact of Social Security, which made retirement rather than work the expected experience in the last stage of life.

Even in this unprecedented consequence, Social Security could not erase every trace of the past. In the preindustrial, industrial, and Social Security eras, a sharp dichotomy divided the aging population: older workers and retirees appeared either as privileged members of society or ranked among the most disadvantaged. In each period, seniority raised income and improved job security for some workers, paving the way to prestige in the work force and a comfortable retirement. For others, age brought hard times. Hidden in the obscure labor markets of the preindustrial period, unemployed or underemployed older workers emerged as a distinct social problem in urban, industrial America. In the Great Depression of the 1930s, their plight served as a warning to younger men and women that poverty and dependency might be their fate in old age, provoking many Americans to call for public retirement programs. But Social Security—which set retirement at age sixty-five—could not solve all the problems of aging workers. To a large degree, their difficulties had arisen in youth and middle age rather than at the edge of retirement. Although Social Security's adequacy provisions have improved the retirement standards of low-income workers, they remain excessively dependent on its benefits for survival.

Are these contemporary adversities also due to lower productivity among men and women past age forty-five or fifty or sixty? Researchers have not determined in any precise way the relative ability of older workers, but few scholars accept the overwhelmingly negative view common in earlier historical periods. Decline in capacity by age is highly variable by individual and by occupation; on average, people in their sixties experience relatively minor losses in productivity, although steeper declines occur at later ages. Work performance and safety records of the elderly usually remain well above those of workers in their twenties and thirties. Other qualities that come with age, such as conscientiousness and greater loyalty to employers, often compensate for age-related deficiencies.[2] For the most part, the obstacles and difficulties commonly reported by older job seekers arise out of personnel policies that, in fact, favor elderly workers within firms. Age-related declines in ability to work, therefore, have only limited usefulness in explaining the unique circumstances of the elderly. Seniority programs, pension plans, age-hiring restrictions, and, above all, Social Security, have combined to restructure radically the work life of the contemporary elderly.

Preindustrial America

According to historians of the New England colonies, old age in early America was rarely marked by a complete withdrawal from labor.[3] Elderly men headed households well into advanced age; relying on sons for labor, they delayed the transmission of land and assets to children. Seeing themselves as active farmers, men seldom considered themselves "retired." Their aging wives continued to be instrumental working partners in the farm enterprise, and their economic roles extended to a separate, female sphere of market activity. As dairy operators, midwives, and weavers, women directed daughters' work, added to the wealth of the family, and created a basis for their own autonomy.[4]

Although failing physical condition reduced the ability to toil, it did not make aging men and women idle. Older property owners remained closely involved in farming and with the family that provided a labor supply; they continued to be active participants in the preindustrial enterprises that combined land and labor. Richard Barker of Andover, Massachusetts, illustrated the vital power aging fathers could possess. In 1670, Barker permitted his eldest son to marry at age twenty-seven, and granted him a portion of land on which to build a house. Not until his son reached age forty, however, did Barker deed him the property outright. Barker did not grant even this belated independence to his other sons. Only upon his death in 1693 did they inherit land. Until that time, the aging landholder managed the business of the farm, controlling the careers, marriages, and wealth of his heirs.[5] Based in the family farm economy, such authority provided the majority of older men and women with a setting for vigorous economic activity and high social standing. Since the farm was the central productive unit and age led to ownership, older men and their wives possessed impressive resources and often worked or managed a work force until late in life.[6]

Historians have been far more successful in tracing the careers of powerful old men such as Richard Barker than in tracking the lives of the less prominent. The rich elderly sank deep roots in communities: they sat at the front of the meeting houses, assumed positions of political importance, and composed wills ensuring the respect of kin. Not all elderly people in the colonial period, though, had access to prestigious work or a comfortable retirement. These old persons found the last years to be quite different. Landless aged men spent their final days intermittently employed as laborers. Others discovered that their declining strength made work impossible. Wandering from town to town or begging alms from neighbors, they received, at best, charity, and at worst, scorn and neglect.[7]

Similarly, single women and widows faced an uncertain future. In contrast to their married counterparts, they had much poorer prospects in old age. Single women did not enjoy the position of the farm wife, whose work was critical to the family's success. Even women who had been married could not be sure that years of work would protect them in old age. Despite the collective nature of the family farm, the husband retained legal control of the estate. A widow's life depended largely on the terms outlined in his will. If granted control of the estate, women often became proficient farmers and expert businesswomen; under their direction, family estates could prosper. Less affluent widows operated boarding houses, managed stores and taverns, worked as midwives, or hired out their children.[8]

Other husbands provided for wives through maintenance contracts, a form of annual pension discussed in chapter 2. These wills detailed both the widow's rightful assets and the obligations her heirs owed her so long as she remained unmarried. For the most part, they compelled women to retire from active management of the farm, giving over authority to the next generation. Widows with control over assets had a number of options. They could continue to operate farms or businesses; or, if they chose to reduce or quit work, they could sell their property for cash or arrange for annual rents from real estate, land, and stock. In the South, slave-owning women could rent out their chattels. Such arrangements functioned as a retirement system for widows who did not manage farms or enterprises, providing women in both northern and southern colonies with support in old age.[9] Yet not all elderly women had sufficient financial resources for support in old age. Public relief records, the charity dispensed by ministers, and the early private organizations directed toward needy aged women showed that many ended their lives as members of the "deserving poor."

By the late eighteenth century, land scarcity in New England and the ready possibilites for the young on the frontier undermined the patriarchal power upon which the elderly had founded their colonial entitlements.[10] Aging farm couples responded by making *inter vivos* agreements, often with the youngest son. In exchange for land, the aging couple retired from active farm management but received stipulated support from adult children. Although some aging widows operated the farm, most turned it over to children in exchange for support or used its market value to finance retirement. In early-nineteenth-century Vermont, the widow Roxanne Estabrook sold her farm and used the subsequent mortgage payments to provide for herself and her daughters for the next fifteen years. Another widow sold Scott George a portion of her farmland, and he became her "surrogate son," agreeing to care for the elderly woman thereafter.[11] In preindustrial America, therefore, the work and retirement options of rural whites depended largely on the worth of the farm. Elderly men and women often remained active participants in the business of farming. Valuable property allowed them to hire and manage laborers, encouraged the support of children and neighbors, and, if they chose, underwrote partial or full retirement.

In the antebellum South, elderly slaves had no access to property; they could not control an enterprise nor rely on assets to fund retirement.[12] Defenders of slavery pointed to the lives of older slaves as evidence of the superiority of plantation culture. In contrast to the treatment of workers by the cruel capitalists of the North, benevolent masters did not discard slaves as useless; despite declining abilities, they received food, shelter, and support. Critics of slavery, on the other hand, asserted that aged African Americans who could not work were abandoned by owners. Ex-slave and abolitionist Frederick Douglass claimed that his grandmother had been left in the forest by a supposedly caring master when she outlived her usefulness to him.[13]

Historians have found evidence for both arguments; elderly slaves might experience gross mistreatment or considerate care. Both Eugene Genovese and Jacqueline Jones have concluded that the honorific position of older persons in the slave community made it difficult for owners to abuse them.

According to Jones, aged women held especially influential status among slaves, owing to their mastery of the physical and spiritual "healing arts." Like Genovese, Jones traced the superior conditions of the elderly to West African traditions and the values of the slave community.[14]

While the African American culture may have venerated the old, a more potent shield against mistreatment lay in the considerable resistance in both black and white communities to the abandonment of aged slaves. As a result, owners sought returns in labor from elderly blacks. Facing continued maintenance costs for workers they could not fire, masters responded by setting even the oldest chattels to work; few were given the opportunity to retire. According to the daybooks of nineteenth-century plantation owners in South Carolina, slaves past age sixty or classified as "old" continued to labor. Although some toiled in regular field work, elderly bondsmen tended to be divided between those engaged in skilled occupations and those charged with menial tasks. On one plantation, gangs worked the fields while the owner had Old Isaac making Post and Rail Fence," and Old Toney "Laying off Ground." Daniel Webb, a Charleston cotton factor and plantation owner, reported the death in June 1823 of "Old John the Carpenter . . . not less than 70 years old I think," and in December 1841, he noted that "Old Lenny of Chatsworth died in Charleston—he was my Stockminder & Dairy man & is a great loss—though quite old." Like John and Lenny, aging slaves who had gained experience in crafts continued to work as carpenters, boat and wagon builders, river pilots, and dairymen. Older women cooked, practiced medicine, and ran the nurseries; aging house servants were retained for their experience and perhaps because of the personal regard of the slaveowning family.[15]

Although elderly bondsmen and women generally continued to work, age clearly lessened the appraisal of slaves without skills. Slave records starkly described older field workers as a fraction of a "full hand." At a slave auction in Charleston, "Old Chance . . . aged about 60 yrs.," was listed as a "good quarter hand." On the Coffin farm, an early nineteenth-century Carolina plantation, a count of eight full hands amounted to "16 Old & young people." The Dirleton Plantation Book, completed half a century later, recorded older field workers as "3/4," "1/2," and so forth. Aging slaves without skills but not listed among field hands carried out menial tasks, such as watching stock.[16]

Plantation and auction records attest to the long working lives of African Americans. If they possessed skills, their work retained considerable worth; if they did not, they lost value as field hands or were reduced to menial jobs. Few enjoyed retirement. These documents also reveal that senescence did not protect slaves from the threat of sale and forced relocation. Between 1853 and 1863 the Charleston market offered Kate, an "old nurse," at seventy-five years of age; "Guinea Ben . . . 60 . . . cattle-minder"; "Joe (Ship carpenter, Sore leg)," sixty years of age; Stepney, "Driver . . . 70"; "O Fanny (Children's Nurse)"; and Joe Wallis, sixty, "Head Carpenter." Chattels like "Old Tisker—aged & Blind" were offered for sale within their family group. Others, such as "Joe" and "Pomphrey," each sixty-five, were to be sold as solitary individuals.[17]

Although owners might retire slaves of very advanced age, the slave sales demonstrate that this practice depended on the kindness and continued tenure of owners.[18] Whatever the status awarded old age in African-American culture and whatever defenses the slave community mounted against excessive exploitation, senescence continued to be defined by the economic demands of the slave system, in which returns from labor constituted the prime objective of the master. The structure of slavery guaranteed that advanced age would neither release slaves from work nor save them from sale.

The Industrial Era

Farmers in a Market Economy

By the late nineteenth century, circumstances had changed radically for both white and black farmers. Slavery had been abolished; most agriculture in the United States had become commercialized and market oriented. Depending largely on the region in which they lived, the elderly encountered new intergenerational dynamics. In many parts of older agricultural areas such as New England, the older farmer's lot deteriorated. Industrial employment beckoned sons and daughters away from the farm, and they chose employment opportunities in cities. As a result, the pool of farm laborers, renters, and buyers shrank, and farms declined in value. No longer did the possession of property assure aging men and women sufficient financial resources or the unquestioned support of offspring.[19]

In areas such as the Midwest and West, where agriculture remained quite profitable, elderly farm owners held a more enviable position. Control of property still promised a comfortable old age as well as access to a wide range of options for security in the last years. As in the past, some older men and women continued farming, their activity limited only by health and inclination. Other aging farmers elected to reduce their own labor by hiring hands, leasing sections, or giving parts of farms to children in exchange for assistance. Across the nineteenth century, growing numbers of farmers took a further step and used property to finance retirement. In areas where farm land was economically valuable, ending work became a reasonable option for older people. Through rental and leasing agreements, *inter vivos* transmission of land, or the outright liquidation of family farms, aging couples and widows departed from an active work life.[20] Many appeared to have left the farm, moving to villages and small towns, as suggested by the distinctive households of the village elderly portrayed in chapter 1. Such households were unique for the low and steadily falling labor force activity of older men; between 1860 and 1910, the percentage of older men in villages and small towns who reported occupations fell from 74 to 44, a much steeper decline than in farm or urban households.[21]

The variety of choices available to propertied farmers in the late nineteenth century directly contradicts longstanding assumptions about the occupational status of the rural elderly. Clearly, not every old person continued to farm; the agricultural economy did not automatically lead to long working lives for the elderly. In 1890 and 1930, the size of the agricultural sector in a state's economy had only a weak relationship with the level of labor force activity among older men. The level of tenancy or farm rental constituted a more essential variable. Outside the South, tenancy implied a vigorous farm economy in which young men and women rented property as the first step on the "ladder" to ownership. In such areas, older farmers could secure retirement funds by renting, leasing, or selling farmland. Because of the high price set on farms and their usefulness as a retirement device, older men in agricultural states such as Nebraska were actually less likely to be in the labor force than their peers in industrial states.[22]

In the South, farmers faced harder choices. Here tenancy meant poverty. Cash rent predominated outside the South, but in that region, sharecroppers paid rent with a portion of the harvested crop. A postbellum compromise between the interests of labor-hungry landowners and landless freedmen, sharecropping spread to the poor white population as well. By 1930, according to the census, sharecroppers operated 24 percent of all southern farms and 45 percent of "Negro" farms. These tenants labored under unique contractual agreements with landlords. In contrast to other systems of farm rental, land owners did not seek to ensure payment of a fixed rent. Driven by the proportionate harvest arrangement, they wanted tenants to produce as much as possible, preferably in a cash crop such as cotton. This goal led landlords to consider the laboring capacity of the entire tenant family.[23]

This evaluation had important implications for the elderly. Sharecropping contracts muted questions about the efficiency of aged workers (a central issue in the industrial sector), since the family as a whole formed the laboring unit. Heads of households who delivered a worthy set of laborers received contracts; as a result, even very old household heads remained active participants in the labor force. Having no estate to lure their children to stay at home, elderly African Americans reached out to distant and fictive kin to form a pool of workers, as chapter 1 reveals. Echoing its predecessor slavery, sharecropping led elderly blacks to remain at work.

While fitting the standard assumption of long work lives among the rural elderly, this high labor force activity hardly implied a pastoral old age. Hounded by falling cotton prices and lacking a strong industrial alternative, the South could not escape from poverty. Rather than the first rung on a ladder to ownership, southern tenancy became permanent for many African Americans. Unlike prosperous white farm owners, they lacked property that could fund retirement. As late as the 1940s, therefore, elderly men in southern states exhibited extraordinarily high labor-force activity, primarily because aged blacks continued to work as tenants. In 1930, when almost all older blacks lived in the South, 75 percent of aged black men reported occupations (nearly all as farmers), in contrast to fewer than 60 percent of all white men.[24]

Without any asset to trade for support in old age, the widows of black sharecroppers suffered in still another way. Like older white wives, they had been working partners in the operation and management of the family enterprise—indeed, they were much more likely to have worked in the field. Yet unlike their white counterparts, they received no tangible inheritance upon the death of a spouse. As sharecroppers' widows, they possessed little or no property to finance their retirement or to improve chances of remarriage. As a result, older African-American women—many of whom faced lengthy widowhood—migrated to cities in search of employment. Not surprisingly, these women were three times more likely than older white females to be working.[25]

By the turn of the century, the circumstances of the elderly in U.S. agriculture hardly fit the conventional model. The highest levels of labor force activity occurred among black sharecroppers and aged black women, whose lack of ownership compelled them to continue to work late in life. Prosperous white farmers, on the other hand, had the opportunity to contemplate partial withdrawal from work or full retirement. Rather than mandating the continued employment of the old, vibrant farm areas actually *enabled* aging farm couples to retire. In the villages to which they often relocated, they set up a separate and distinct life-style, one which prefigured retirement in the mid–twentieth century. This option depended on an accumulation of wealth sufficient to guarantee regular income in old age. Aging African-Americans and less affluent white farmers had more difficult choices. The emerging industrial sector, however, offered a new array of opportunities. The economic growth it sponsored first made retirement for the masses a possibility.

Factory Work: From Skilled to Semiskilled

Scholars optimistic about the fortunes of the aged in rural societies generally find industrialization a destructive force. According to this view, the factory regimen initiated a steady decline in the appreciation of older workers. In 1922, Abraham Epstein, an advocate of state pensions, described the pernicious effect of industrialization upon the elderly:

> Modern industry finds little use for [older] workers. It replaces and discards these aged wage-earners as it is in the habit of replacing and discarding the worn-out and inefficient machinery. . . . Modern machine industry [has] less need for expertness and experience and greater use for speed and rapid production. As a result, the younger generation, though less experienced, is continuously crowding out the older and less efficient workers.[26]

Epstein's contemporaries accepted this verdict as an axiom. Early-twentieth-century proponents of relief for the aged had little doubt that industrialization had relentlessly debased older workers, leaving them unemployable and impoverished. In their publications, social analysts envisioned a future of degradation and pauperization that would demand state intervention.[27]

Although some scholars still support Epstein's interpretation, current evidence fails to sustain his view of the factory system. The process of economic growth undermined certain traditional supports but created in their place levels of wealth that enabled a broader spectrum of the aged population to reduce work or to retire altogether. The wage employment that replaced family farming jobs had similarly negative and positive results. Although older skilled workers had considerable authority and status and could achieve security in old age, an emerging semiskilled production system threatened these traditional privileges. Semiskilled workers could not control the pace of work nor guarantee their employment. Aging job seekers also faced discrimination in industrial labor markets and endured long periods of unemployment. Nonetheless, other employees received rewards because of their seniority. Certain firms rewarded long service, giving older employees higher wages and more job security than their productivity warranted and offering pensions after retirement. Most important, a much greater number of older men and women came to expect financial security in old age through reliance on a family strategy borrowed from the agricultural era.

In its initial stages, industrial development had little direct effect on the elderly population. Until the twentieth century, most older workers remained in farming occupations. Their daily working lives were tangentially influenced by industrial and urban growth which expanded the market for crops, while beckoning children to leave the farm. Moreover, older workers in urban skilled trades enjoyed distinct advantages. Clear lines of upward mobility by age appeared in craftwork, the precursor to factory production. Trained by senior men, young apprentices became journeymen as they grew older and more experienced, and if fortunate, they could rise to the status of master craftsmen. In nineteenth-century machinery shops, for example, Thomas

Leary found that the "vocational education of young machinists was carried on primarily by senior men via oral tradition, work-place socialization, and hands-on experience." In skilled occupations, age—rather than being a handicap—led to greater mastery, better jobs, and higher income. Older craftsmen owned the tools and resources necessary to the trade, and they bartered knowledge and training for assistance from apprentices, who were often young kin. The craft system allowed skilled workers to avoid menial, physically demanding tasks by exchanging knowledge for labor. James J. Davis, U.S. secretary of labor in the 1920s, recalled that he began his work life "when an aged puddler devised a scheme to enable himself to continue the physically arduous exertion of the trade" by hiring Davis as a boy helper. In an industrial system dependent on skilled workers, elderly craftsmen maintained active and profitable work lives, providing the young a model for successful careers. Workers came to expect the "possibility of advancement" as they grew older; experience in a craft led to higher income and greater security. Elderly craftsmen retained these advantages and expectations well into the twentieth century.[28]

Since the origins of most industries lay in previous forms of craft and the first factories required only moderate capital, older men possessed another edge over the young. Controlling skills, experience, and assets, they might realize the common ambition of rising from "cub" to "some day be the Old Man of some plant." Prosperous older workers invested assets in machine shops, retail stores, and other enterprises.[29] Even as capital requirements increased, these aged craftsmen retained key industrial positions. The subcontractor, "the platypus of Victorian industry," combined labor and management roles and, with the foreman and skilled craftsman, ran day-to-day operations in late-nineteenth-century factories. In 1903, E. A. Bingham reported that the labor contractor for the Baldwin Locomotive Works was "always an elderly man who has spent many years in the shops. . . . The men know him, trust him, and respect him." Even in what became mass-production industries, such as iron and steel, older men initially controlled much of the production process, earning positions of authority and trust as they aged.[30] (See illustration, 'Experience and Industry.')

Union strength in trades such as cigarmaking provided a number of further defenses for older workers who were members. By restricting entrance to the trade and governing apprenticeship and training, unions heightened the value of the older men's skill. Through their rules, unions restrained the capacity of the boss to speed up the pace of work or to fault the output of older workers; through local hall provisions, they insisted that employers who wanted skilled craftsmen had to hire older union members as well. Union regulations also protected aging members by exempting them from certain regulations, such as allowing the old unionist "to work for a wage rate lower than the rate fixed for the younger member" or relieving them of "payment of all contributions except assessment for death benefits."[31]

Finally, the experience, knowledge, and stability of older employees gave them a good reputation among employers. In 1877, Robert Harris, president of the Chicago, Burlington, and Quincy Railroad, assured the chairman of the road, "It will not be disputed that it was the influence of the older men to which we owed the fact that the men at Aurora did not participate in the late troubles." Experienced employees had superior job security during hard times; their years of service represented hard won skill, knowledge, and stability to employers. Poor treatment of long-service workers could also have distressing effects on the morale of younger workers.[32]

Older women also devised ways to achieve authority at work; they had attained skills and knowledge that made them valuable workers. They ran garden farms, dairies, and stores; were nurses and midwives; and superintended cidering, canning, preserving, cooking, and sewing. Like skilled tradesmen, they trained daughters and other girls in crafts.[33] (See illustration, 'Two Sewing Women.') Women's households tasks may not have been recorded as gainful occupations, but they were central to the success of the family economy. Even within these family enterprises, however, women's work could be devalued by authoritarian husbands or inconsiderate children. A husband's illness or death easily disrupted an aging woman's life, as did her own failing health or abandonment by children. For women who never married, who lacked family support or an inheritance, or who became widowed without considerable savings, old age could be perilous indeed.[34]

Men also faced a host of threats to security in old age. Good jobs were lost due to declining strength, industrial accidents, and poor health. Like the young, aging workers faced sudden unemployment because of the periodic depressions endemic to the industrial economy, the failure or reorganization of firms, or seasonal layoffs. But the consequences of unemployment were much more severe for older men, appearing as vivid testimony to the challenges facing aging workers in industrial labor markets. Older job seekers endured much longer periods of unemployment than younger men. They often competed for jobs that placed greater value on younger men's qualities of strength and endurance. And when they found work, they might be forced to accept lowly and low-paid service occupations, such as watchmen and janitors.[35]

Some of these job seekers previously held skilled positions, and the degradation of their status reveals one of the unsettling features in the late-nineteenth-century industrial economy. Technological and managerial innovation ultimately reduced the authority of skilled workers. Employers relentlessly sought to gain control over production by replacing skilled workers with machines and systematic organization.[36] Where continuous process machinery dominated, managers generally succeeded in restructuring production. In steel, automaking, and other major industries, capitalists broke the hold of craftsmen over the production process. They set up labor systems that relied on easily trained and easily replaced semiskilled workers. Jobs that required no more than a few weeks' training had disastrous implications for skilled workers.[37] The spread of semiskilled work diminished the security that experience, knowledge, and the trade union had given elderly craftsmen. (See illustration, 'The Smith.') Managers rather than older workers now controlled production as well as the hiring and training of job entrants.

In the transition to semiskilled production, older workers suffered yet another blow. The division of labor, which lay at the heart of the transition, broke into simple components the complex tasks once understood only by skilled workers. According to the industrial engineer Frederick Taylor, the profit in dividing up the tasks extended beyond savings in time and wages. Separate tasks could be observed and the time necessary to accomplish them accurately measured. Precise measurement enabled employers to gauge optimum production and to evaluate individual performance.[38] Older workers, who had previously controlled the pace of work, found themselves vulnerable to demands that they meet specific quotas. Although the physical effort required in factory work declined as power machinery took its place and the average hours of work fell, the pace of work quickened.[39] Any tendency to fall below optimum speed became readily apparent, and older workers had little protection against judgments based on productivity.

As a result, the elderly fared least well in industries in which rapid technological change occurred. The swift transformations characteristic of the late-nineteenth-century economy disrupted the privileges of the crafts; once-prized skills became outdated overnight. When hiring criteria stressed formal education, the elderly confronted another challenge. Rapid increases in educational standards in the late-nineteenth and twentieth centuries meant that the average schooling of older persons fell below that of the young. Many employers turned to public schools as a source for job training; when hiring criteria stressed formal education, older applicants found themselves at a clear disadvantage. Struggling in job markets where their educational qualifications fell short, the elderly became "old fogies," the relics of a time when skill and knowledge came with age.[40]

Similar obstacles—and stereotypes—hindered the gainful employment of elderly women workers in the late nineteenth and early twentieth centuries. Most women, and more than 90 percent of those aged sixty-five and over, worked in the home, playing that central part in the family economy described in chapter 2. If compelled to work outside the household, they rarely qualified for the new fields of white-collar employment that required skills

learned in high school or technical training institutes. Younger, better educated women qualified to be teachers, clerks, typists, and hospital-trained
nurses. In the mid–nineteenth century, the nurse had been "portrayed as an
'old lady,'" trained by experience and appreciated for her age. By the beginning of the twentieth century, the skill once assumed to have come with age
came with education in new hospital schools. Administrators, doctors, and
patients expected the professional nurse to be young, rarely past the age of
thirty. In 1900, most elderly women who worked outside the home labored
as domestic servants, seamstresses, practical nurses, and boardinghouse keepers. These vocations mirrored older women's traditional household tasks yet
hardly recognized their vital role and managerial authority in the family
economy. In time, youthful occupations experienced a "graying": professions
once dominated by the young eventually had older practitioners. In 1900, for
example, few older women in Boston were employed as trained nurses; by
1950, many older nurses appear in occupational records. The same aging effect
occurred in white-collar occupations (bookkeepers, clerks, stenographers, and
typists), although older women still failed to meet expected proportions as
late as 1950.[41]

Industrialization also robbed women of homemakers' skills. The goods
they had produced in the home and the crafts they had taught the young
were now the province of the machine. Knowledge gained by years of experience was held in disdain by engineers and scientists. By the early twentieth
century, for example, elderly women who attempted to practice medicine or
act as midwives found themselves faced with numerous professional and legal
barriers. Once a leading source of medical advice, they had become primitive
"old wives" whose remedies counted for little in the scientific age.[42]

Advanced industrialization unquestionably had negative consequences for
certain older male and female workers. For the aging craftsman in an obsolete
trade, the skilled worker facing an assembly line, the aging woman displaced
by professional expertise, old age could indeed be a period of "obsolescence."
But these losses, important as they were, obscured fundamental improvements brought about by vigorous economic growth. In the late nineteenth
century, the first generation of workers who had worked their entire lives in
factories reached old age. The overwhelming majority of these industrial
workers had never attained skilled positions; most had been laborers or opera-
tives, relying on physical energy for their livelihood. For them, aging threatened the essential asset—physical strength. They possessed no skill or
experience that might protect them and were unlikely to have a union to
defend them in old age.

For these, the majority of U.S. workers, the economic vitality of industrialization had clearly positive consequences. In focusing on the fallen pres-

tige of the skilled, both initial critics and more recent scholars have ignored the mass of unskilled men and women who in the older production systems had toiled for skilled workers or under the thumb of the foreman. Semiskilled industries derailed the engine of security for skilled workers, yet it promoted the economic well-being of laborers, a far more numerous group. The transition to semiskilled work meant higher annual income and a greater opportunity to set aside resources for old age. In 1916, R. R. Lutz noted that most automobile factory workers were not "artisans reduced to a lower economic level," being instead, "workers to whom specialization has afforded the means of reaching a higher industrial and economic status." Indeed, high wages became the primary means by which employers in the most advanced industries attracted and retained semiskilled workers.[43]

As chapter 2 revealed, three decades of industrial growth sharply increased the economic well-being of households headed by older men. The data displayed in figure 3.1 show that older men averaged much greater earnings in 1917–19 than their peers in 1889–90, those sixty and over reporting an average gain of 75 percent. Despite the impressive improvement, a persistent bias against aging workers appears to exist in these age-earnings profiles, one that undoubtedly influenced popular perceptions of the fate of the older industrial worker. In both 1889–90 and 1917–19, aging household heads saw take-home pay slip below that of younger men. Cross-sectional data do not reveal how much the lower wages reflected life-cycle effects, such as declining productivity or the desire for more leisure in old age, and how much was due to the cohort effect of younger men entering more lucrative occupations. Strong economic growth in the industrial period obviously made cohort effects very powerful; the youngest age group in 1917–19 earned more than the peak group in 1889–90. Indeed, it lifted all boats: men sixty to sixty-four earned more in 1917–19 than their age cohort had in 1889–90, when they were thirty to thirty-four years of age.[44]

Nonetheless, blue-collar workers saw all too clearly that as they aged their earnings would decline relative to those of younger men. The quick peak and protracted decline in wages distinguishes the industrial era's life-cycle patterns from those of the present, in which, even in cross-sectional data, earnings increase until men reach their mid-forties and then remain relatively stable until retirement (see figure 3.2 and discussion below). The early apex in the industrial era undoubtedly led workers and their wives to make careful, conservative estimates about savings, work, and retirement and to place their faith in a family-based economic strategy.[45] Work and retirement decisions were played out in familial settings, rather than based on an individual's earnings, as is usually assumed. We have seen that the family economy often succeeded handsomely in maintaining both high consumption and regular

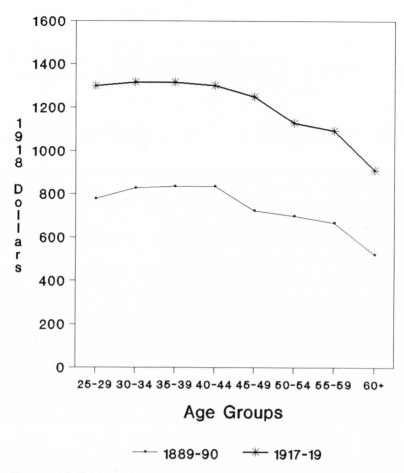

Fig. 3.1. Male Heads' Median Earnings, 1889–90 and 1917–19

(Thousands)

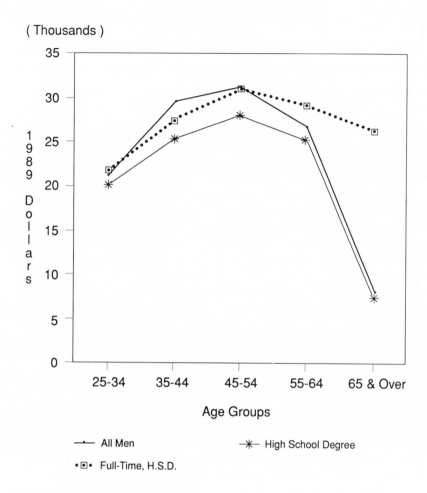

Fig. 3.2. Male Median Earnings, 1989

savings in older households. The accumulation of surpluses reached levels which permitted older industrial workers to consider abandoning work altogether. Given such resources, did workers retire?

Nineteenth-century records prove that more affluent farmers did make this choice, and in the middle class a trend toward retirement can be seen in the late nineteenth century. Unlike those for blue-collar jobs, salaries in middle-class occupations continued to rise through middle age. In addition, more affluent Americans had access to investment information and reliable savings instruments, such an annuities. Engineers, corporate managers, bankers, businessmen, professionals, and politicians enjoyed incomes that made savings for retirement eminently possible. An increasing number of middle-class men worked for firms or agencies that urged aging white-collar workers to quit work and provided pensions to ease the way. Civil service retirement plans, for example, became much more common after 1900.[46] And as we discuss below, a national retirement program—the Civil War pension system—provided a model for leaving the labor force followed by a large proportion of northern white males.

Whether many industrial workers retired, however, remains a contested issue in the history of old age, one difficult to resolve because the terms of the debate remain confused. Relatively good data can be found for gainful employment, the census concept used until 1930, and for its successor, labor force participation. The former measured whether an individual reported having an occupation and the latter whether he or she was actually working or actively looking for work at a specific time. Little reliable evidence exists for retirement itself, that is, whether a worker had made a conscious decision to leave the labor force permanently.[47] Many persons not gainfully occupied or in the labor force are not retired. Among women aged thirty to thirty-nine, very few are in the labor force, and almost none are retired.

The labor force activity of aged men did decline steeply between the preindustrial and industrial periods, although inaccurate measurement of agricultural labor forces and especially of those having the employment dynamics of the family farm, exaggerates the difference. Jon Moen found that the gainful employment rates of men sixty-five and over fell from about 75 percent in 1860 to 60 percent in 1910, remaining at about that level until 1930. Urban rates remained consistently below farm household rates but fell very slowly if at all across this seventy-year period. Part of the decline in overall labor force activity occurred because of a population shift toward less active (and more reliably measured) urban labor markets. The greater share reflected increasingly low levels of gainful activity among older men in a third setting, villages and small towns; these men appear to have abandoned farms and regular occupations.[48]

A number of factors prompted older men to leave the labor force in this period. Advancing age, a proxy for poor health, had strong effects; foreign-born men had lower levels of activity in older age and African Americans higher rates, even in cities. Self-employment opportunities encouraged older men to remain at work, as did a shorter working day. These factors offset each other, since both self-employment and average hours worked per week declined during the first decades of the twentieth century. Greater wealth during this period of strong economic growth undoubtedly increased the proportion of the elderly population that could confidently retire. And eligibility for a Civil War pension induced older men to leave work; in 1910, perhaps one-third of males sixty-five and over received veterans' pensions, although the proportion diminished rapidly thereafter.[49]

But for a much larger number of older workers in the industrial era, retirement remained unlikely. Many simply worked until they died. Others shifted to intermittent labor force activity, a decision that followed the logic of the family economy in which several persons worked. Older men with sufficient wealth and other sources of income for the household could reduce the amount of work they did or leave the labor force for a time, especially if they were sick or less physically able. Aging men might shift toward less demanding occupations, choose to work seasonally, or, if skilled, rely on the high wages they received for short periods of work. The family economy allowed these work choices and sustained the long search for re-employment, characteristic of older job seekers. As late as 1950, older male workers tended to move in and out of the labor force; the abrupt transition from work to retirement that dominates contemporary careers was far less common. Older men in the industrial period exhibited a persistent attachment to occupational roles, only gradually withdrawing from work. On the whole, only the wealthiest, the sickest, or the few guaranteed regular retirement income left work permanently. The very concept of retirement was foreign to many workers. At the turn of the century, even those who had not worked for a full year did not declare themselves to be retired.[50]

The difficulty in calculating what would constitute sufficient resources for old age made workers cautious about retirement. Large savings, investment in a home, business, or other real estate, even the regular contributions of children provided no absolute assurances. Without a guaranteed income stream for an unpredictable longevity, workers could not be confident that savings would hold out, assets would continue to provide sufficient returns, or children would remain dutiful. The unreliability of income in old age before Social Security explains the repeated findings of relatively stable labor-force participation among older men in the early twentieth century. In part, stabilizing rates occurred out of sheer necessity. The Civil War pension system, which had provided support to a large proportion of northern white males after 1890, withered away in the twentieth century. By 1930, certainly fewer than 15 percent of persons sixty-five and over received a regular public or private pension income, often a small monthly payment.[51] Unless provided for by public or private pensions or endowed with substantial savings, older people simply had to work. The alternative was to risk falling dependent upon family members or charity. Even those with seemingly adequate resources faced considerable insecurity if they chose to retire outright. In the free market of the late nineteenth and early twentieth centuries, governments did not ensure against losses if pension plans collapsed or banks failed.[52]

Laissez-faire capitalism also led to discrimination against aging workers. Many analysts have attributed declining labor force activity at the turn of the century to a new "ageism" apparent in employment practices. As one historian concluded, the "elderly's presumed value and apparent status in the labor market was steadily deteriorating."[53] The cult of efficiency and vigor in bourgeois U.S. society inspired businessmen to proclaim the older worker to be incompetent and incapable of competing with youth. Personnel managers established age limits in hiring and made retirement mandatory, ostensibly to guard against ruining their companies with "drones" and "dead weight." These personnel policies harmonized with a growing cultural appreciation of youth.[54] By the early 1930s, openly discriminatory policies encompassed at least one-third of the industrial labor force. In 1929, a conservative business organization reported that 28 percent of its firms had age limits. While only 11 percent of companies in a 1930 California survey admitted they had age restrictions, their employees made up 39 percent of those in the sample. A 1932 survey of 224 firms found 32 percent willing to state they had age limits.[55]

Age-based personnel policies can be rational or irrational, depending on whether the employer makes a judgment based upon productivity. The claim of prejudicial discrimination against the old assumes that employers' actions were economically unwise; sheer prejudice against the aged caused managers to dismiss highly productive and worthwhile employees. Some employers appear to have been guided by this bias. Their proclamations of the inefficiency of older workers rarely had any basis in actual evidence; long lists of the limitations of the aged were more often built from assumptions than facts. Yet ironically, Epstein and other critics of industrial societies often gave credence to a rational discrimination against aging workers by arguing that the elderly were "less efficient" and did not have the capacity to compete in a modern industrial economy. If this assertion were true, the employer who found older workers less productive and had them "turned out like old horses, to search for a living" may have been heartless, but he obeyed rational business principles.[56]

The origins of age discrimination, however, lie less in attitudes toward older workers or in opinions about their productivity than in a crisis in labor management distant from the issue of aging. Capitalists who had replaced skilled workers with the semiskilled found that they had disrupted traditional forms of discipline on the shop floor. Their victory over craftworkers created a new challenge: the incessant turnover and alienation of uncommitted labor. Semiskilled workers had no access to the career lines and hierarchical authority that had fostered self-discipline in skilled trades. Their repetitive work had no intrinsic appeal, their interchangeable jobs bore little investment, and they felt no great loyalty to employers who viewed them as replaceable parts. Because leaving one job and going to another entailed little loss, workers followed an inveterate pattern of quitting and hiring on, as a wage difference or inclination moved them. They engaged in what John R. Commons called "a continuous, unorganized strike."[57] High rates of turnover provoked intense concern among managers in a variety of firms. Rehiring and retraining costs proved expensive, especially since workers often quit at peak production when competing employers offered tempting wage hikes. Beneath the symptom of turnover lay the malignancy of alienation: semiskilled workers had no reason to be conscientious.

In response, early-twentieth-century managers adopted a variety of imaginative personnel policies. These had the paradoxical effect of improving conditions for some older workers while creating disadvantages for others. Most of the new plans sought to increase length of service by rewarding seniority. As early as 1908, Henry Ford addressed the vexing turnover problem by increasing wages in annual bonuses "based on seniority." In 1917, the Studebaker Corporation promised an "annual wage dividend for workers based on years of continuous employment. . . . to minimize the turnover." Such arrangements almost invariably included regulations that the worker be "faithful" and conscientious. Facing turnover rates exceeding 400 percent per year, Ford's more permanent and innovative solution was the wage ladder. By creating a complex set of gradations among largely indistinguishable jobs within the factory, Ford provided semiskilled workers an artificial hierarchy to replicate the traditional advancement of the skilled worker. Rather than being tied to expertise, ranks were based largely on years of loyal service; workers who stayed with the company received higher wages.[58] These "internal labor markets" rewarded seniority as well as productivity, leading firms eventually to provide compensation to older employees greater than their productivity alone warranted.

While a number of nineteenth-century firms linked length of service to higher wages and job security, seniority became a central principle in progressive labor management only after 1900. Personnel managers tied service records to a variety of benefits, from profit sharing to vacations, although job security, wage advancement, and promotion constituted the most important perquisites of senior employees. About one-third of the companies surveyed by state officials in New York in 1907–8 and Iowa in 1913–14 used internal promotion linked to seniority to fill skilled positions. These proportions suggest that one-fourth of all male workers in the period before World War I would achieve twenty years of service with one firm. A National Industrial Conference Board study in 1927 reported that 40 percent of the large firms surveyed used seniority in labor relations policy; a 1932 analysis by the Bureau of Labor Statistics revealed that among automotive and iron and steel firms, about one-third of the labor force worked where seniority provisions were in effect. (These provisions applied largely to male workers; even today, women rarely enjoy returns from seniority.)[59]

Business managers designed seniority systems to meet several goals, including reducing turnover among their most valuable middle-aged employees. Seniority rights may have contributed to the notable stabilization of labor force participation rates in the early twentieth century. Older workers in firms that rewarded service enjoyed higher wages and benefits and greater protection from dismissal than younger employees and had, therefore, good reason to remain at work.[60]

Ironically, the same devices that increased security for some older workers undermined it for others, encouraging the popular and not inaccurate view that employers discriminated against the aged. Prolonged unemployment—probably characteristic of older job applicants in every historical period—became exacerbated by the seniority systems of the industrial era. The enactment of seniority plans, pensions, and other rewards for long service partly explains the protracted periods of job seeking among the elderly. While seniority protected long-service workers in a firm, it penalized older job seekers. Workers who failed to establish a connection to a company or became unemployed in middle age carried several real and assumed deficiencies into the labor market. On average they were less physically able to compete for laboring jobs. Older applicants also tended to have lower educational achievement than young people, and if immigrants, they lacked desired language skills or cultural traits. Middle-aged people had fewer years to repay hiring and training expenses to employers, who also argued that insurance and other costs increased with an older labor force.[61]

For the employment officer in a firm characterized by seniority policies and internal labor markets, older applicants had even less appeal. An aging job seeker did not offer the prospect of long service and high middle-aged productivity for which wage ladders and benefit packages had been created. Management promised steady wage increases to attract capable young workers and encourage them to be hard working and loyal to the company. By hiring steady young workers at a relatively low wage, and offering wage gains by seniority, employers brought order and stability to their labor force. Refusing to hire the aged applicant, while discriminatory under contemporary law, seemed entirely logical in such firms.[62]

In time, however, seniority schemes created an economic dilemma. Compensation based on years of service demanded a cutoff point, since older workers became "inefficient," receiving higher earnings than the young or middle-aged for performing the same work. The solution to the dilemma was mandatory retirement, a rule that a growing number of large U.S. corporations initiated in the early twentieth century.[63] Advocates for the aged often pointed to forced retirement as evidence of virulent age discrimination in this period. The labor policy of the Pennsylvania Railroad demonstrates that the origins of retirement programs lay elsewhere and reveals the intimate connections between seniority, age limits, and mandatory retirement. In an influential labor management policy adopted in 1900, the railroad announced a hiring age limit of thirty-five years, coupled with mandatory retirement at age seventy with a pension to be provided by the company. Although openly discriminatory, the rules had less to do with prejudice against older workers than with problems created by the firm's traditional use of seniority to determine job security and earnings. Long-service railroad workers received very high wages; age limits and mandatory retirement promised to reduce the company's average wage by bringing in young, cheap workers and retiring old, expensive ones.[64]

Industrialization had varied consequences for older workers, but it did not render them obsolescent and cannot explain the mass retirement characteristic of our own time. In the 1920s, perhaps one-third of U.S. employees worked for firms that used age-based labor policies; a still larger proportion of middle-aged industrial employees gravitated toward such companies.[65] Such policies contributed to the bifurcated work experience of older men in the industrial period; many enjoyed well-paid and secure jobs, while a large minority fit the grim picture painted by the advocates of state pensions. Seniority protected older workers (until the mandatory retirement age) but inspired age limits that worked against older job seekers. Although new production and management systems undermined the status of the skilled worker, economic growth improved the conditions of the less skilled. It permitted a much larger number of older people to reduce labor-force activity in old age or to retire from work altogether without being dependent on charity. Industrialization had broadened the range of experience for older workers and increased the probability of retirement; still, as late as 1930 it had not broken the basic connection between old age and work. By 1950, a complete metamorphosis of experience had become apparent: where once

most old men had worked or looked for jobs, the majority now entered retirement. An understanding of this revolutionary change must be sought outside the labor market, in the Social Security Act of 1935.

The Social Security Era

The Depression presented the political opportunity for a redefinition of
the work cycle. While economic development in the industrial era generated
enough wealth for mass retirement, the private market provided few Americans with absolute confidence that they had sufficient resources to quit work.
Older men and women faced serious uncertainties about the income potential
of assets, expenses in retirement, and longevity. As a result, relatively few
severed themselves entirely from work. The 1930s brought the problems of
older Americans into national focus and sharpened the division of experience
among older workers. The chronically unemployed had even less chance to
find work, while company failures and deep cuts in surviving firms' payrolls
threw even long-service workers out of work.[66] Not all older workers suffered
inordinately. Older male employees were initially less likely than the young
to be laid off. In 1930–31, New York manufacturing workers in their fifties
and sixties had greater job security than younger employees. Employers also
favored older workers when rehiring. As a result, until the mid-1930s, unemployment rates for men increased slowly if at all between the ages of twenty-
five and sixty-four, although the duration of joblessness was greater for older
age groups. Unemployment rates actually fell for those sixty-five and over
owing to steady employment for the most secure and withdrawal of the most
discouraged from the labor force.[67]

But unemployment studies in the mid-1930s found joblessness beginning
to rise steeply by age, especially among men, and then remaining very high
even after age sixty-five.[68] Prolonged searches for work extended to members
of the middle class, who had once been the most confident of steady high
incomes in late middle age. This heightened insecurity had an important political consequence. In the 1930s, millions of middle-class Americans shifted
toward support of public pensions precisely because of the stunning failure
of the private schemes that business supported. The best-conceived arrangements for retirement came apart in the stock market crash and subsequent
Depression. Middle-class Americans joined working-class constituencies in
"the overwhelming judgment of the American people" that all men and
women deserved a guaranteed retirement income.[69] With the passage of the
Social Security Act of 1935, the popular goal was achieved. For the first time
in American history, the aged had the assurance of regular income in the
final years, independent of savings and dependable for any degree of longev-

ity. A government annuity, rather than work, assets, or children, would be the basis for retirement.

Social Security thereafter transformed the working lives of the elderly by encouraging them to leave the labor force en masse. Its benefits did support the poor and unemployed elderly (especially women), a group visibly enlarged in the Depression. Its less-appreciated result was to make retirement rather than work the customary state of life for all of the aged. By guaranteeing a secure and regular income regardless of longevity, Social Security induced older workers to retire. The New Dealers, according to William Graebner, intended the act to have exactly this effect.[70] In periods of heavy unemployment, retirement programs could open up jobs for younger persons. New Deal policymakers, joined by a host of politicians and a legion of promoters of radical pension schemes, exploited the popularity of this concept among voters.

Economists, however, generally maintain that Social Security had little impact on the labor market before the 1950s, when Old Age Insurance (OAI) benefits became more generous and more widely distributed.[71] But another Social Security program, Old Age Assistance (OAA), affected the labor-force behavior of older workers at a much earlier date. From 1936 to 1950, OAA provided benefits to more persons than OAI and its average grant was substantially higher than that available in the insurance program. Each state determined the level of aid available and the criteria for eligibility. States with a "pension philosophy" established benefit levels and eligibility rules in a fashion generous to the elderly. These policies fit the temper of the times: in South Carolina, many citizens believed that old people were "entitled as a matter of right" to government assistance; in Boston, the OAA pension paid to "the old Irish lady [was] sacrosanct," and a politician was ill-advised to threaten it. National opinion polls confirmed these local attitudes: the old deserved pensions.[72]

OAA had a sharply negative impact on the labor-force participation of elderly men. As we have seen, before the passage of New Deal legislation, a variety of ethnic and economic specifications predicted differences in the propensity of older men to remain at work. By 1950 a new determinant dominated labor-force decisions. In states where Social Security benefits were high, fewer older men worked. The strongest variable in explaining decline in the elderly's labor force activity between 1930 and 1950 was the ratio of OAA payments to median income. Where assistance payments came closest to replacing income, the labor force activity of older men fell rapidly.[73] These results, based on aggregate data, are confirmed in evidence for individuals. In a sample of older men from the 1950 United States Census, those who lived in states in which OAA benefits compared favorably to potential income had a much lower probability of being in the labor force.[74]

Among men, therefore, the stabilized labor force activity of the first decades of the twentieth century gave way to sharp declines, largely because of public welfare programs.[75] In 1930, 54 percent of men sixty-five and over were in the labor force; by 1950, 42 percent. At present, about 20 percent report labor force activity. During its initial years, Social Security undoubtedly had its greatest impact on the unemployed aged or those holding marginal jobs. Expansion and liberalization of the OAI program after 1950 led to broader inducements to retire. Private pensions have become more common in the same period (covering more than half of all workers), making retirement attractive even to the more secure and privileged employees.[76] Other considerations still influence the labor force decisions of older men, including unemployment rates, technological change, the disruption of traditional industries, and personal and familial characteristics, such as marital status. Although health remains an especially critical factor in the timing of retirement, improvements in health in recent decades imply that new income sources have been the most potent force in reducing elderly males' labor-force activity.[77]

Women's initial reaction to Social Security measures is less certain. OAA constituted an essential resource for women who could not claim OAI through a personal work history or as the widow of an eligible husband. Had it not been for Social Security, women past sixty-five might have participated more fully in the rapid expansion of female labor-force activity after World War II.[78] Women who returned to work in middle age first became a prominent part of the retirement population in the 1960s. In certain respects their decisions about retirement have mirrored those of men. The availability of pension benefits as well as the state of their health strongly influences the timing of retirement for women. (Private pension programs are somewhat less common and substantially less remunerative among women workers.) Their behavior also exhibits features specific to the female life cycle. For older men, marriage and the presence of dependents in the home prompt continued employment; for older women, domestic responsibilities retard labor force activity. A working wife's retirement timing is also influenced by her husband's work decisions, his private pension income, and his Social Security benefits.[79] Among married women, therefore, retirement is not individualistically determined but arranged in conjunction with the circumstances of husbands and families. One striking result is that women, who tend to be younger than their husbands, retire at earlier ages, joining their husbands as they leave the labor force.

Thus the Social Security era has witnessed a decline in the supply of aged workers. Relying on public and private retirement benefits rather than work-related income, healthy older people choose leisure rather than employment. A majority of workers now retire before the "normal" age of sixty-five.[80] The rush to early retirement occurs despite a marked improvement in the status of older workers since the Second World War. Figure 3.2 shows that contemporary males do not reach peaks in earnings until they are past age forty-five, about fifteen years later than in the industrial era. Sharp declines do not appear until age sixty-five and over, when many in the minority who have not fully retired switch to part-time work. Although the crest in income for blue-collar workers still occurs somewhat earlier in life than that of white-collar employees, men with only a high school education achieved their highest earnings between ages forty-five and fifty-four. After a steep climb from their youth, blue-collar workers maintained relatively high wages into their sixties; if they worked full time, they continued to receive high earnings after age sixty-five. These cross-sectional data obscure the still more positive experience of workers during their lifetimes: every recent birth cohort has experienced a steady rise in earnings until retirement.[81]

As a general rule, women's earnings have always been less affected by age than men's. Wright's analysis of southern cotton-mill employees in 1907 showed men fifty and over earned 73 percent of the hourly wage of men thirty-five to thirty-nine; women fifty and over earned 83 percent of the peak. The few working women in the 1917–19 study illustrate the rule: those fifty and over had a weekly wage somewhat higher than the mean for all women and an annual wage that was considerably higher. In the post–World War II era, older women's earnings equaled or exceeded those of younger women.[82]

Although the 1889–90 and 1917–19 cost-of-living studies provide at best an imperfect comparison to modern data, the later peak and the delayed decline in earnings among male workers in recent studies stand out as new phenomena, as does the sharp drop in work-related income at specified retirement ages. Union demands for stricter seniority rules pushed life-cycle profiles to the right, favoring older men. One of the distinguishing characteristics of the rank-and-file union movement in the 1930s was its call for rigid seniority clauses. As one young man declared, "I seen these guys getting laid off—fifty, sixty years old. . . . I said, 'I'm going to be old someday. I want security.' "[83] Management designed seniority systems to be discretionary, but their promises had been deeply internalized by employees. Any violation of seniority rules inspired intense hostility among industrial workers. Although automobile companies tended to retain older workers during the Depression, the industry gained a "notorious" reputation for "discharging older workers who could no longer maintain the pace." As a result, seniority plans became a cardinal principle in the contract demands of autoworkers' unions.[84] According to union negotiators, the plans constituted the fairest and least complicated method of governing employment policies. By using length of service, the order of workers' promotions, layoffs, and rehirings were all readily—and objectively—established, free of management's arbitrary decisions. While management disliked seniority as an absolute rule, it had long had an appeal to personnel officers, and they acquiesced.[85]

Seniority presently governs wage advancement and job security for a very large proportion of the labor force; half of all male workers can expect to achieve life tenure in their jobs. Such programs clearly favor workers aged fifty to sixty-five, who enjoy favorable positions in the U.S. occupational structure, with good wages, security, and superior levels of job satisfaction. But seniority systems continue to present negative repercussions. As in the industrial era, the age limits implicit to internal labor markets make it difficult for older applicants to get jobs. Older workers' adversities arise, as they have in earlier periods, when they lose jobs, especially as a consequence of technological change. After age fifty, job seekers stay unemployed longer and fall into lower job categories if they do find work. These traditional problems have inspired legislation, such as the Age Discrimination in Employment Act of 1967, to correct openly prejudicial policies.[86]

Age-based labor management policies also account for the enthusiastic reception public and private pensions receive among adversarial interest groups. Republicans and Democrats, management and unions, the old as well as the young, have generally applauded the continued expansion of the Social Security system. Workers and management have accepted stipulated retirement ages without much protest. Businessmen accommodated rigid seniority plans because public welfare and private retirement plans siphoned off costly older workers. Throughout the 1950s and 1960s, management improved private retirement provisions and even reluctantly supported the expansion of Social Security. Drawing on models they had implemented for salaried workers, they extended programs in the hope that higher benefits would relieve them of older, relatively inefficient workers. Unions found that the linking of seniority and retirement allowed them to promote the employment and advancement of younger members while meeting the desire of older members for leisure and independence. Despite strict laws against mandatory retirement at stipulated ages, the number of elderly workers has fallen. The average age of retirement is sixty-two; 97 percent of elderly workers choose to retire before the age protected by law. While some complain that they have been subtly forced out, the early age of retirement and the satisfaction reported among retirees suggest that most aged persons voluntarily leave the labor force.[87]

The result is mass retirement. Social Security, more than any other factor in American history, has redefined patterns of work and retirement. Since the preindustrial period, elderly men and women have struggled to find security in their last years. For most of that history, independence could be attained only by controlling children, land, or assets. Most older workers achieved a measure of success in occupational status or in accumulating savings to buffer income declines in old age. Nonetheless, even the industrial era's economic vitality provided only a minority with enough confidence to stop work altogether. Social Security removed the last constraint and brought to an end the expectation that work was the natural condition of life for the elderly. Since its enactment, the history of the older worker has given way to the history of retirement.

4

The Threat of the Almshouse

DESPITE THE RELATIVE prosperity of the elderly, concerns have not vanished over the intractable problem of old-age poverty. Most recently, the rise and fall of the Medicare Catastrophic Coverage Act in the late 1980s revealed the complexity of providing sufficient—and economically sound—long-term assistance for the elderly. The legislation was supported by a widespread and, and as we shall see, long-lived sentiment that the aged did not deserve to end their lives in impoverishment and institutionalization. Its provisions appeared to assure older people and their families that the economic adversities of devastating illness had been met. Individuals would not be required to go on welfare to receive care, nor would spouses or children be forced to oversee the "spending down" of estates before turning to the government for help.[1] Despite its seemingly great promise, however, the law was rescinded by Congress in November 1989. The funding mechanism (which relied on federal subsidies but still required payments by the aged) provoked discontent among affluent older people who had already established private insurance protection.[2]

As a result, the last decades of the twentieth century have witnessed a reprise of a familiar theme in the history of old age: impoverishment and institutionalization still threaten the nation's older population. In actuality, this prospect is less real than conventionally believed. Only about 5 percent of the nation's thirty million persons sixty-five and over live in an institutional setting at any one time, a proportion only moderately greater than in previous decades.[3] Yet the link between old age and institutional care is not based solely on misplaced anxiety. At some period during their advanced years, 40 percent of the elderly will reside in such establishments. Moreover, as the proportion of the aged in the population grows and the longevity of the elderly rises, the likelihood of institutionalization will increase.[4]

The "dread of the poorhouse," however, has never relied on its statistical probability. In the nineteenth and early twentieth centuries, no more than 2 percent of elderly lived in public or private institutions.[5] Yet despite its relatively small population, the poorhouse has played an impressive part in the history of the American aged. As part myth and part reality, institutionalization provided a dominant theme for analysts who wrote about the changing status of the elderly in industrial society. In the nineteenth century, the almshouse assumed a significant role in the care of the dependent old and in the discussion of the assumed needs and capabilities of all the aged. As ever-growing numbers of almshouses began to dot the landscapes of rural counties and the edges of major cities, destitute aged individuals faced the real possibility of ending their lives as wards of the state, housed shamefully in public institutions. For the limited number that met this fate, the almshouse was an undeniable sign of failure and dependency.

Yet even for those who never set foot in the asylum, the threat of poorhouse residency had a potency that could not be ignored; it possessed a symbolic meaning important to the history of old age. Aged laborers and their wives were only too aware that a lifetime of work could be destroyed by unforeseen illness or bad luck; the death of a spouse or desertion of children might leave them alone and impoverished. Reports from almshouse superintendents repeatedly confirmed that even the most provident of elderly persons were not immune from this ignominious fate. Although the *rate* of institutionalization of older people did not show any appreciable change until 1920 and the absolute numbers in the institutions were always modest, the proportion of the aged among almshouse residents rose dramatically. As the function and demographic composition of the U.S. almshouse was transformed during the nineteenth century, the asylum became a highly visible symbol of the frailty and impoverishment of aging Americans. For those convinced that the old faced increasing impoverishment and desertion in the modern United States, the poorhouse became a most useful and visible metaphor for the elderly's ignominious fate.

The effect of the institution, in fact, went beyond symbolizing the extreme and negative characterizations of old age. In the course of the twentieth century, the persistent and widespread fear of asylum residency had a dramatic impact upon welfare policy. The horror of almshouse residency loomed large in the debate over public old-age pensions. The shame of the poorhouse saturated the rhetoric of advocates for state welfare in the early twentieth century and dictated certain provisions of the Social Security Act of 1935. Nor is its legacy forgotten. Widespread aversion to contemporary nursing homes—clearly the descendants of the historic almshouse—continues both to influence congressional legislation and to trouble the national conscience in our own time.

Preindustrial America

During the first decades of colonization, no public institutions existed to shelter the poverty-stricken or debilitated old. Needy—and worthy—elderly individuals received assistance through the auspices of their local communities. In granting support to the old, welfare officials throughout the colonies followed the principles of public charity established by the English Poor Law of 1601. According to its tenets, families were the first source of support for their impoverished kin. By law, parents and grandparents were required to support the young; adult children, in turn, were to assist their destitute elders. As a result, colonial records were replete with cases of officials warning young adults to fulfill their legal obligations to their parents.[6] Aged individuals were, first and foremost, the obligation of their kin.

For those without family, the English Poor Law dictated that responsibility for their support lay with local public officials. Poor taxes provided for regular allocations of food, money, and wood or for the boarding of needy individuals in the home of neighbors. Such assistance was limited by two well-established principles. First, the impoverished had to be legitimate inhabitants of the community. Transients seeking relief were to be "warned out" and sent to their official place of residence; runaway indentured servants and slaves were to be returned to their masters. This regulation applied to all individuals, regardless of age. Even the most senescent found themselves transported beyond the city limits if they failed to prove themselves true citizens of the community. In 1707, for example, the city fathers of Boston repeatedly warned Nicholas Warner to vacate the city. Despite the fact that Warner was over eighty and ailing, the selectmen held firmly to their decision. They did not want any vagabonds, whatever their years, journeying to their town expecting public charity.[7]

The second restriction on granting assistance was that individuals had to be "worthy" of relief. The lazy or indolent would be given little support; such persons were required to labor for their subsistence. The old, however, were traditionally categorized as valid recipients of aid. Given their declining physical condition and assumed inability to be self-sufficient, they appeared ideal candidates for Christian charity and community assistance.[8]

Indeed, throughout much of colonial history, the old who applied for public welfare were usually granted some form of relief. Many, such as Widow Baldwin of Hadley, Massachusetts, or William Baker of Portsmouth, Massachusetts, were assigned to reside with their neighbors; others remained in their own homes, receiving monetary support or essential provisions.[9] At the end of the seventeenth century, however, overseers of the poor in the colonies' largest cities turned to a new way of providing for the poor. In 1664, the city fathers of Boston founded the colonies' first almshouse; by 1713, New York, Charleston, and Philadelphia had established poorhouses as well.[10] In these early institutions, the poor and sick of every age and background were provided with food and shelter.

The asylums for the impoverished initially housed relatively few persons.

Most individuals continued to obtain assistance in their own homes or in the households of their neighbors. City magistrates often assigned boarders to live with and assist elderly women. Extremely decrepit and notably "ancient females" were placed by the local officials in the homes of others and supported by the local poor tax. For most native-born citizens, relief came in the form of "outdoor" assistance: a cord of wood, an allotment of food, or a small monthly payment. Authorities targeted aged women as especially deserving of such outdoor relief. Believing them unable to provide adequately for themselves through employment, authorities supplemented their income with goods and currency. In antebellum Charleston, women beyond the age of sixty comprised an extremely high proportion of those on outdoor relief. According to the city relief roster, they accounted for 20 to 38 percent of all female paupers awarded outdoor assistance. As a group, their numbers filled the list of recipients; only in rare instances were they forced to end their days confined to a public establishment.[11]

In early America, the presence of aged paupers in communities evoked considerable sympathy among overseers and town officials. Few questioned that the elderly had a legitimate claim on public assistance. Towns had an undeniable duty to provide for the old in their own homes or in the households of their neighbors; in the most extreme cases, they were obliged to provide adequate care in the community almshouse. According to the principles of public charity, elderly people deserved assistance even if they had led less than completely pure past lives. Their dire condition could easily be attributed to the natural frailties of age; their impoverished state could be the result of an accident or ill chance.[12]

By the 1760s, the growth of seaboard cities and an influx of immigrants led urban elites to question the efficacy of the traditional welfare system. In Boston and Philadelphia, city leaders voiced concern about pauperism, drunkenness, and vice, especially among transients and newcomers in rapidly growing populations. Confronted by rising and expensive demands for assistance, overseers began to threaten applicants for aid with the "house." They often denied the most impoverished individuals relief unless they entered the institution. Behind such actions lay a strong belief among authorities that welfare had become too expensive. In the late eighteenth and early nineteenth centuries, rising tax rates as well as the elimination of the "warning out" policy led municipal leaders to consider the financial benefits of the almshouse. Although residency in the asylum was often more costly per person than outdoor relief, welfare authorities believed that rigorous work schedules, meager provisions, and poorly heated wards would limit sharply the number applying for assistance. With an interest in restricting public expenditures, officials wanted few able-bodied vagrants seeking comfortable rooms or good meals at the taxpayers' expense.[13]

The authorities' new hope for the almshouse had a clear effect upon the poverty-stricken old. For the first time, large numbers of old men, aged couples, and, at times, even destitute women were required to enter the asylum in order to receive assistance. In 1769, for example, Barnet and Sarah Campbell of Great Barrington, Massachusetts, applied to the overseers of the poor for outdoor assistance. Due to their great age and ailing condition, they expected to receive public charity in their own home. The city's welfare authorities, however, declared that if the couple wished assistance, they had to become inmates of the almshouse.[14]

In the eighteenth century, such attempts to reform the welfare system were often sporadic and inconsistent; by the early nineteenth century, they had become far more systematic and effective. Welfare authorities broadly adopted the theory that alms "pauperized" the poor by making them lazy and dependent. As a result, they violently opposed all forms of outdoor relief and encouraged civic leaders to build forbidding almshouses and workhouses. Punitive institutions, they argued, would discourage the indolent and vicious from seeking charity and might "reform" those incarcerated through strict codes of conduct. Through their enforced discipline, they would warn the idle poor that hard work and a harsh regimen awaited all alms-seeking applicants.[15] As immigration brought millions of poor and socially disconnected foreign laborers into U.S. cities, these principles of relief took on both a new urgency and a highly nativist tone.[16] Overseers of the poor, ministers, and charity experts focused their attention on finding correct solutions to the rapidly rising costs of relief as well as a way of preventing foreign degradation of the American social order. By restricting outdoor relief and creating a rigorous system of work and discipline in the public institutions, they hoped both to dissuade impoverished immigrants from requesting public charity and to discipline all who sought such assistance.[17]

In their transformation of the welfare system, authorities did not alter their beliefs in the worthiness of the old. In forming social policy, they continued to express the conviction that the elderly had a right to receive public assistance. Josiah Quincy, a pioneer in the sweeping reform of U.S. welfare systems, maintained that "of all classes of the poor, that of virtuous old age has the most unexceptionable claims upon society."[18] Yet with the radical restructuring of public charity, the treatment of the worthy old was generally not separated from that of other impoverished groups. In the formation of stringent welfare policies, the elderly became victim to the authorities' antagonism against the idle young, foreign poor, and "vicious." Like far less "deserving" individuals, they too were prohibited from receiving support in their own homes. With the establishment of the almshouse, welfare administrators gave them a choice: they could forgo applying for relief or agree to enter the purposefully punitive and noxious almshouse.

This transformation of the public charity system left a lasting imprint upon the consciousness of U.S. citizens. In its punitive restrictions, it created a broadly based fear of almshouse residency that would last for more than a century. For those in need of relief or struggling to remain self-sufficient, the establishment of the poorhouse as the centerpiece of the welfare system had clear ramifications. The impoverished now faced not only the horrors of poverty but also the very real threat of long-term incarceration. Especially for the old, the new welfare policy translated into a fear of spending their last days in institutions filled with societies' most despised and rejected.

Among the elderly who struggled to remain self-sufficient, such concern was not without some basis. In small towns and rural counties that could only afford one public institution, the impoverished old deserted by children or incapacitated by illness were incarcerated alongside the communities' most depraved and diseased. Housed in the same institution and often in the same ward, they found themselves surrounded by the unemployed, the alcoholic, the vagrant, the orphan, the mentally and physically ill. In large cities, authorities often sought to classify their inmates, restricting the able-bodied and unworthy to workhouses and placing the worthy poor in almshouses. Such attempts, however, invariably collapsed under the weight of financial and demographic pressures.[19] Even in large urban areas, the unfortunate elderly were placed with society's most despised outcasts in numbers that far outweighed their demographic proportion. Between 1830 and 1850, 18 percent of the inmates in the almshouses of Baltimore and Philadelphia were above the age of fifty, even though the individuals of this advanced age comprised only 4 percent of the cities' populations as a whole.[20]

Managing institutions that had been designed primarily for other groups of impoverished and needy individuals, asylum directors did not welcome such large numbers of elderly residents. Few welfare administrators agreed with an English authority's declaration that the incarceration of the aged pauper was necessary to maintain "that essential prop to industry, the terror of starving in old age."[21] Most concurred that in contrast to that of the young, the elderly's institutionalization was primarily due to ill health, desertion, or unemployment. For the old, unlike the lazy, the drunkard, or the corrupt, the almshouse served neither as a deterrent nor a punishment but simply as a residence of last resort.

Because of this philosophy, asylum managers did not structure the institution to reform the elderly or influence their daily behavior. Although the old were expected to fill their days usefully, they were not assigned strict work schedules or allotted harsh punishments. In large urban asylums, authorities even attempted to provide the elderly with particular privileges based on their advanced age, declining physical abilities, and status as "the most deserving" of paupers. In 1835, the Philadelphia Board of Guardians suggested creating three special wards for aged and helpless women: one for those in bad health, a second for those who could sew and knit, and a third for those who were especially good seamstresses. The municipal officials also placed elderly couples in a special "married" ward and granted them favored allotments of food and beverages. In contrast to the young, the old were even allowed at times to leave and reenter the institution. One Philadelphia couple, Mr. and Mrs. George Lighthouse, often departed from the public asylum in the summer to visit their children, then returned for shelter during the harsh winter.[22] Even the more rigorous reformers in the United States believed that the worthy status of the old justified their special care—as long as it was confined within the walls of the pervasive institution.[23]

Yet even with such privileges, almshouse residency was hardly pleasant. While the young and middle-aged tended to use the asylum as a temporary shelter, the old who entered generally remained until death.[24] The institutionalized elderly typically lived out their life's end surrounded by a constantly changing assortment of alcoholics, beggars, unwed mothers, orphans, and the mentally and physically disabled. Nor were elderly inmates guaranteed the most basic amenities. Beset by financial problems and feeling little obligation to many of the foreign residents, welfare authorities operated institutions on strict budgets: food, clothing, and living conditions often went from bad to worse.[25]

The Industrial Era

By the second half of the nineteenth century, the connection between dependent old age and almshouse residency had become ingrained in the nation's social consciousness. As industrialization spread, welfare principles first apparent in antebellum commercial centers became more and more prevalent and powerful. Generations grew up with "a reverence for God, the hope of heaven, and the fear of the poorhouse."[26] This relationship seemed to be verified by well-publicized almshouse records. Increasingly, asylum managers reported, the nation's public asylums were filled with growing proportions of inmates above age sixty; the elderly came to be viewed as the "natural" inhabitants of the public institution.[27] Although, as we shall see, social experts took the growing presence of the old to be a sign of their inevitable dependence, the ever-increasing percentages of elderly residents in the asylum had a more immediate source. The actions of welfare authorities and reformers—rather than the increasing incapacity or impoverishment of the old—led directly to the transformation of the almshouse into a residence for aged persons. By removing other groups of indigent and needy individuals and placing them in separate institutions, officials left the old to become the predominant inmates of the nations' almshouses.

The demographic evolution of the poorhouse first began in the mid–nineteenth century. Previously, the almshouse had mixed individuals of all ages and backgrounds. In the earliest asylums, the orphan had slept alongside the hardened criminal; the able-bodied immigrant had lodged beside the debilitated elder. In the industrial United States, however, welfare authorities deplored the lack of "strict" classification. Without proper separation of the needy, they argued, the vagrant would never be reformed into an industrious worker; nor would the child be shaped into a self-sufficient adult. Indeed, the "indiscriminate" institution was a school for vice rather than a place for eliminating such wickedness.[28]

Given such beliefs, charity experts and municipal leaders hoped to categorize dependents and provide each classification with an environment appropriate to its needs and capabilities. This classification went beyond the separation of inmates that occurred in large urban asylums of the early nineteenth century. Not only did reformers attempt to separate the worthy from the indolent; they also erected special institutions based on the perceived disabilities and handicaps of the inmates. Beginning cautiously with homes for the deaf, dumb, and blind, authorities established a variety of institutions that removed large numbers of the dependent, although assumed reformable, individuals from the almshouse. Children were placed in orphanages or dispatched to the countryside, "juvenile delinquents" were assigned to reformatories, the acutely ill were transferred to hospitals, and "lunatics" were confined to asylums for the insane. In some cities, even able-bodied paupers were removed from the poorhouse and placed in workhouses designed to punish and reform. Here, city officials believed, they would find no more warm winters or free meals. Young and middle-aged adults would either learn to work or would suffer for their indolence.[29]

The creation of the new institutions had a dramatic affect on the demographic composition of the almshouse. Without large numbers of children or young adults, the number of inmates in the asylum declined while the proportion of elderly inmates rose significantly. Immediately after the Civil War, for example, children made up 29 percent of inmates at the Charleston, South Carolina, almshouse. In 1867, the great majority were removed to newly created orphanages. With the able-bodied already confined to a "bettering house" and the insane placed in the state insane asylum, the poorhouse became filled primarily by the dependent old.[30] Similarly, in late-nineteenth-century San Francisco, the average age of the poorhouse residents rose from thirty-seven in 1870 to fifty-nine in 1894.[31] Nationally, the percentage of almshouse inmates above the age of sixty grew from 33 percent in 1880 to 53 percent in 1904 and 67 percent in 1923.[32]

In the early twentieth century, United States census administrators acknowledged this transformation; their reports charted the increasing proportion of elderly paupers within public asylums. "Almshouses," census officials declared in 1910, "are becoming to an increasing extent institutions for the aged."[33] By 1925, the origins of almshouses as deterrents to the assumed laziness of the foreign-born and vicious had long been forgotten. The public institutions, a leading social analyst declared, were beginning to "fulfill the real purpose of an almshouse—that of providing [for] the old and infirm."[34]

National census officials were not the only group to acknowledge the transformation in the composition of almshouse residents. By the early twentieth century, local welfare authorities had come to recognize that their public institutions no longer housed diverse groups of inmates. In 1903, the Charity Board of New York City renamed its public almshouse the Home for the Aged and Infirm. In 1913, Charleston officials transformed their asylum into the "Charleston Home."[35] In the tradition of similar but failed attempts to provide the aged separate and better quarters in earlier periods, administrators and charity experts consciously attempted to eradicate the image of their shelters as punitive places that dispensed only the barest necessities along with the harshest discipline. In their annual reports, New York administrators boasted that they provided "a warm room and clean comfortable beds to sleep in—good wholesome and varied food to eat, a church to go to, plenty of papers, magazines, and books to read." According to the asylums' superintendents, the old could ask for nothing more; after years of struggle, they could now call the almshouse "home."[36]

But the effect of the aged almshouse population was not limited to changes in the names of the institutions. In Charleston, city leaders acknowledged that the large number of elderly inmates had a permanent influence on the operation of their asylum. In contrast to the past, they explained, the inmates were now expected to do little real labor as most were "old and infirm, utterly destitute, and unable to take care of themselves."[37] Above the Mason-Dixon Line, the visiting medical staff of the Long Island Almshouse and Hospital of Massachusetts agreed. "The institution as a whole," they wrote in 1904, "because of the infirm character of its inmates, is gradually and inevitably assuming the general character of a hospital."[38] In such institutions, the growing proportion of resident elderly paupers could no longer be ignored. By the early twentieth century, care of the poverty-stricken old had come to be seen as the true function of the nation's poorhouses.

The predominance of the old was further enhanced by financial decisions made by welfare authorities. Not only were other groups likely to be removed to specialized institutions, but, for budgetary reasons, the old lodged elsewhere were generally transferred to the almshouse. Welfare officials looked to send their aged charges to the least costly institution. In 1883, California allocated one hundred dollars annually for each pauper over sixty. Local officials immediately transferred the poverty-stricken elderly to county almshouses in which the yearly cost of sustenance fell well under the appropriated sum. It was hardly surprising, then, that California almshouses, such as the one in San Francisco, rapidly filled with the old. The confinement of the dependent elderly actually served to increase the coffers of the state's municipalities.[39]

Moreover, such budgetary considerations tended to keep elderly paupers out of alternative asylums and organizations. In the mid–nineteenth century, several private charity associations declined to assist the elderly. Recurring depressions had convinced their leaders that urban poverty was far more extensive than they had imagined. In the face of such need, they began to allocate their limited resources by identifying the most appropriate recipients. In 1853, for example, the New York Association to Improve the Condition of the Poor resolved "to give no aid to persons who, from infirmity, imbecility, old age, or any other cause, are likely to continue unable to earn their own support, and consequently to be permanently dependent." Looking to more hopeful and remediable cases of indigence, leaders of the association argued that the needy elderly could find appropriate support by applying to the guardians of the almshouse.[40]

A similar philosophy guided the policies of antebellum insane asylum superintendents. In the mid–nineteenth century, doctors specializing in the new field of psychiatry optimistically believed that institutionalization was a cure for insanity. Although superintendents rarely specified the proper age for their patients, the demographic structure of their asylums revealed their strong preference for the young. According to a survey of the mentally ill in Massachusetts in 1854, the old had the highest rate of insanity of any age group. In contrast to individuals twenty to twenty-nine who had a reported rate of 189 per 100,000, among individuals sixty to sixty-nine the insanity rate was 735 per 100,000; for those above seventy it was 664 per 100,000.[41] Despite the high incidence of reported insanity, the old were strongly underrepresented in the state's insane asylums. A study of the state hospitals at Worcester and Tauton, the private hospitals at McLean, Pepperell, and Dorchester, and the municipal hospital of Boston reported that fewer than 10 percent of the inmates were above sixty, although 19 percent of the state's reported insane were of advanced age.[42]

The relative absence of the old can be attributed to an age-based pattern of institutionalization. In 1854, 80 percent of all incarcerated insane persons age twenty to fifty-nine were placed in a public or private insane asylum; the remaining were confined to other types of institutions. Among the old, however, placement in an insane asylum was quite rare; only 7 percent of the incarcerated aged insane were residents of such establishments.[43] While young patients were admonished to seek help quickly in one of the new curative institutions, little hope was extended to the old. Beyond age seventy, the insane elderly were generally classified as incurably senile. Asylum superintendents agreed that it was pointless to spend countless hours or great expense on patients who had little chance for recovery or a productive life. "We never intentionally send an insane patient to [the Long Island Almshouse]," explained Dr. Charles T. Gaynor, "except in the case of an old person who is pretty senile and can be treated as well at Long Island as at any other hospital."[44] For such aged and insane patients, the almshouse seemed the appropriate—if far less hopeful—place of residence.

Again, financial considerations determined this institutional pattern. In many states, it was far less expensive to support the aged pauper in the almshouse than in the state insane asylum. Thus until the late nineteenth century, while families that had the financial resources generally either cared for their elderly relatives at home or had them placed in insane asylums, states and local communities had the insane old confined to less costly almshouse cells.[45] Owing to their advanced age, incurable "senility," and impoverished state, the best that could be hoped for was that they would end their lives assured of adequate food and shelter.

This pessimistic view of the dependent elderly had a significant impact on the composition of hospitals as well. Traditionally, hospitals had housed large numbers of poverty-stricken aged patients; their wards served as old-age homes for those without financial resources or available family members. In 1866, the superintendent of Chicago's St. Luke's Hospital noted the presence of "a few very aged men, who are there simply because no where else could they have the decencies and comforts to which none who knew them would deny they are entitled."[46] By the late nineteenth century, however, hospital administrators resisted admitting old, chronic invalids to their institutions. In an attempt to convince the public that the modern hospital had evolved into a scientific center for acutely ill, curable, and paying patients, they advised the elderly to seek other shelter. In the 1890s, the managers of Carney Hospital of Boston radically altered their longstanding admissions policy. Although they had once reserved an entire floor of the institution for elderly persons, they now rejected all "permanently chronic patients." The new hospital, they declared, was no longer the proper place for such impoverished and hopeless individuals.[47]

Far more appropriate for the dependent and senile were the wards attached to the almshouse. By both expelling the old from the institutions for the acutely ill and refusing admission to all such future applicants, hospital managers further contributed to the changing demographic composition of the almshouse. According to Dr. Gaynor of the Boston almshouse, many of his inmates had been rejected by other hospitals simply because they were both chronically ill and elderly. As a result, the Boston poorhouse had become increasingly dominated by aged individuals who were not simply poor but were "in need of care and treatment—hospital patients in every sense of the term."[48]

Other welfare officials agreed. Homer Folks, commissioner of New York City's charities, attempted to convince the public that the almshouse had assumed a new function in society. In the past it had served to punish the criminal and discipline the indolent; now its primary role was to provide medical care for the aged and impoverished. The fact, he declared, "that the inmates of our almshouses, as well as of our hospitals, are definitely removed by physical disability from the possibility of self-support . . . seems to me to be extremely important." Was it not time, he asked, "when the inmates of our almshouse should be considered as more nearly related to hospital patients than paupers?"[49]

In reporting the high percentage of almshouse residents who were elderly and in emphasizing the ailments of most aged poorhouse residents, welfare experts informed the public that age itself was the source of the elderly's numerous infirmities. With increasing years, they argued, individuals could not be expected to perform normally or competently; their senescent state made them unproductive and dependent. Even within the almshouse, aged inmates could no longer be expected to work or contribute to their own maintenance. "It is not possible," explained a trustee of the Long Island Almshouse, "to discriminate between 'old and infirm' and 'old and sick.' These terms at Long Island are interchangeable; the people are sometimes known as inmates of the institution and sometimes as patients in the hospital. . . . "[50] Their advanced age, dependency, and chronic physical state all seemed to be intrinsically and inevitably connected.

This perception was clearly in line with late-nineteenth-century beliefs about aging that emphasized the elderly's inability to remain vital or independent in modern society. Sociological studies, such as the groundbreaking surveys of the Englishman Charles Booth and the subsequent work in the United States by Lee Welling Squier, Abraham Epstein, and other reformers, seemed to demonstrate that old age and pauperism were inherently related. According to Booth, at least a third of all almshouse admissions were due not to individual failures or misfortunes but simply to the vicissitudes of aging. Moreover, both Booth and Epstein stressed that a startlingly high percentage of the noninstitutionalized old lived in or near poverty. "Old age and dependency," Epstein concluded, "are indeed inter-related and too closely associated."[51] The source of this relationship, all agreed (although wrongly, as we have seen), was industrialization. It denied the older worker an opportunity to make a decent living, provided the young with a wage insufficient to support old age, and tore apart the old systems of family support that had sustained older people for centuries. It was hardly surprising, then, that elderly individuals found themselves both abandoned and impoverished in their old age.

Contemporary medical research supported the assertion of inevitable dependency and seemed to offer a scientific explanation for this widespread condition. Since the mid–nineteenth century, elite physicians had defined the aging process as an incurable disease that eventually robbed individuals of their strength and senses. Based on findings of French and German scientists, doctors began to categorize physiological changes in the tissues of the elderly as pathological states for which no cure could be offered. Arguing that the old who attempted to compete with the young were defying their own anatomy and physiology, physicians came to characterize the entire stage of life as one in which weakness and decay became the normal, expected conditions.[52]

For both sociological and medical experts, the large number of impoverished and incapacitated elderly persons confined to public institutions simply confirmed their expectations. Indeed, they believed, it reflected an insidious debilitation and impoverishment of the elderly in the community at large. According to their understanding of aging, all old people were potential candidates for institutionalization. The growing proportion of elderly residents simply supported the contention that most aged men and women were doomed to dependency. "For the great mass of wage-earners," Epstein explained, "inability to maintain their regular employment makes dependency in old age inescapable and inevitable."[53] Many of the aged would share the inevitable fate of tottering "over the hill" to the poorhouse.

By the end of the nineteenth century, such assumptions were not peculiar to sociologists or proto-gerontologists; clearly, the horror of institutionalization had a persistent hold on many Americans. On June 17, 1871, Will M. Carleton's "Over the Hill to the Poorhouse" was published on the cover of *Harper's Weekly*. The poem told the story of an honorable widow of seventy who was passed from child to child until she was relegated to the poorhouse. In the final verse she bemoaned her plight:

Over the hill to the poor-house—my childr'n dear,
    goodbye!
Many a night I've watched you when only God was nigh:
And God'll judge between us; but I will al'ays pray
That you shall never suffer the half I do to-day.[54]

Three years later, David Braham and George L. Catlin wrote a companion piece as a popular song. In their version of "Over the Hill to the Poor House," it was an elderly man rather than a woman who suddenly found himself forsaken by his children. Completely deprived of their support, his destiny seemed clear; he had few alternatives but to enter a poorhouse. In the refrain of the song, the old man lamented:

> For I'm old and I'm helpless and feeble,
> The days of my youth have gone by,
> Then over the hill to the poor house,
> I wander alone there to die.[55]

The authors of both versions were not alone in portraying the almshouse as the inevitable fate of large numbers of upstanding and industrious Americans. In *What Should We Do with Our Old?* D. W. Griffith depicted a hardworking elderly man who was displaced at his job by a younger worker and immediately became impoverished at home. As his poverty-stricken condition led to the death of his wife, he faced the certainty of institutionalization.[56]

The fear of the almshouse played an important role in the consciousness of Americans; it also led to the development of an institutional alternative, the private old-age home. One of the great ironies in the history of old age in the United States is that the same reforms that placed the noxious almshouse at the forefront of public welfare also inspired the creation of far more benevolent asylums. In relegating elderly immigrants to the almshouse, welfare experts worried that some aged individuals—especially the native-born and female—were too worthy and upstanding to be consigned to such a terrible fate. Their past lives had not been filled with depravity or wickedness; they did not deserve to end their lives in the squalor of immigrant-filled almshouses. The solution, many reformers and church groups agreed, was to select the most worthy of the old and house them in newly established, privately funded old-age homes.

The development of these private institutions was, then, intricately linked to the erection of the forbidding public almshouse. In Boston, the same elites who espoused harsh principles of public relief and built punitive institutions led the societies that established private old-age homes. Their actions were hardly paradoxical. In their endeavors, they demonstrated the persistent belief that the old were deserving of compassionate assistance—although such superior care was limited to individuals of appropriate caste and nativity. For them, the problem of worthy, though impoverished, elderly individuals could be remedied not by a reform of the welfare system or even a redesign of the almshouse, but simply by placing certain individuals into more pleasant institutional surroundings.[57]

Continuously in the nineteenth century, the development of old-age homes was motivated by the pervasive fear that worthy individuals—generally of the correct ethnic or religious background—would end their days confined to an almshouse. In 1817, the organizers of one of the nation's first old-age homes, Philadelphia's Indigent Widows' and Single Women's Society, explained the need for charitable institutions through what was to become an archetypal story. Upon visiting the almshouse, its members discovered two respectable aged women forced by poverty to end their days confined to undifferentiated poorhouse wards. The horror of it was overwhelming; here was tangible proof that individuals of their own class could be reduced to shame and impoverishment. For the society, the discovery of such humiliated females became a clear call to action. "We feel grateful," the members explained, "that through the indulgence of Divine Providence, our efforts have, in some degree, been successful, and have preserved many who once lived respectfully from becoming residents in the Alms House."[58]

A similar sentiment motivated the founders of Boston's first old-age home in 1849. As with the Philadelphia institution, the goal of the Association for the Relief of Indigent Females was to rescue worthy elderly women who had "a natural repugnance . . . to be herded with paupers of every character, condition, and clime."[59] Throughout the nineteenth century, founders of old-age homes described their institutions as the only true means of saving from the almshouse "those whose previous lives have been upright and respectable, and for whom almshouse association is cruelty."[60]

The often-evoked description of private old-age home residents as too respectable to reside in the public almshouse implied, however, that these new asylums were not intended for every impoverished individual. The organizers of the institutions obviously did not want women who, as the Indigent Widows' and Single Women's Society stated, had been "inured to the struggles of penury." Their asylum was intended for the unfortunate who had once been middle class—or at least respectable working class—and had fallen into poverty through no fault of their own.[61]

Most important, candidates for private asylums had to come from the proper ethnic background; in contrast to the almshouse, old-age homes were intended to have a homogeneous, native-born inmate population. According to Henry B. Rogers, president of Boston's Home for Aged Women, the mass influx of immigrants into the city had radically changed the character of the poorhouse. Foreigners, he declared, "have taken possession of the public charities . . . as they have of the houses where our less privileged classes formerly resided." Abandoning the almshouse to the immigrant poor, Rogers dedicated the Boston asylum as a haven for those who were "bone of our bone, and flesh of our flesh."[62]

Given the importance of the inmates' caste and ethnicity, the founders of the homes did not leave these elements strictly to chance. Costly entrance fees (often subsidized by charities or individuals), recommendations from visiting committees, and assurances from select church officials or distinguished citizens all guaranteed that the inhabitants of these institutions would be of the proper class and background. Although asylums for other ethnic and religious groups were later established (partly in response to nativist discrimination), the earliest and dominant shelters catered to Protestant, native-born whites.[63]

A slightly different, although equally significant, pattern occurred in the South. In the nineteenth century, few private old-age homes were established in southern cities; to a great degree, the almshouse continued to be the primary shelter for the impoverished old. The explanation for the absence of homes may rest on the varying role ethnicity played in different regions of the country. In the North, the immigrant origins of the almshouse inmates was a source of distress to the organizers of private homes. Above all, they wished to rescue their native-born paupers from living alongside foreigners. In 1827, for example, before the establishment of private homes, the Boston almshouse administrators set up a separate area for "Irish females." In the South, however, the ethnicity of the paupers rarely evoked great concern. Even though immigrants entered their institutions as well, southern superintendents made little attempt to distinguish among their charges or separate native-born paupers from the foreign-born.[64]

For southern authorities, a far more pressing issue than ethnicity was the possibility that African Americans might reside in the institution. In antebellum Charleston, the public almshouse had been officially closed to needy blacks. As slaves, most were the responsibility of their masters; even free blacks were turned away from receiving public assistance. Only in extremely rare cases did African Americans gain entrance to the poorhouse, either at a cost to their owners or at an expense to the city. After the Civil War, though, the institution rapidly filled with ex-slaves. In 1866, 47 percent of the inmates were black.[65] In response, city officials established two separate—and totally segregated—almshouses. By 1878, not a single black pauper was found in the public (and now entirely white) almshouse. Instead, a new institution, the Ashley River Asylum, later called the Old Folks Home, housed the impoverished black elderly.[66]

These dual systems of poorhouses, along with some Confederate and religious old-age homes, may have alleviated the need for an extensive system of private asylums. In many ways, the black almshouse was the equivalent of the northern public institution, especially after the development of private old-age homes in the cities of the Northeast. With its high death rates, limited budget, and meager provisions, it was intended to shelter Charleston's most despised and impoverished citizens—and to warn away others who were considering applying for such assistance. In contrast, the white almshouse was portrayed as a suitable residence for upstanding, although penniless, white residents. The managers of the all-white but public "Charleston Home" proudly described how their ample budget allowed them to provide good food, beautiful rooms, entertainment, and varied reading material to their charges. In their annual reports, their institution was depicted as far more than an almshouse; it had become a haven that any elderly white person could call "home."[67]

By the early twentieth century, even northern welfare administrators such as Homer Folks sought to improve conditions for the elderly charges. To a large extent, these changes were more cosmetic than real. The addition of flowering plants, the distribution of newspapers, even the modification of the asylum's name did little to alter the fact that elderly inmates ended their lives in the most demeaning of institutions. But the attempts of the authorities, as well as the establishment of private, benevolent alternatives, clearly reflected a growing dissatisfaction with the treatment of the nation's impoverished elderly. The traditional conviction that aged individuals deserved compassionate treatment led to numerous outcries against institution-based relief. Inquiries into almshouse conditions found that the elderly had been unjustly crowded into institutions originally designed to be both repugnant and punitive. Despite the best intentions of its superintendents and the efforts of charitable organizations, social reformers asserted that almshouses were nothing more than "concentration camps for the aged."[68]

Early-twentieth-century investigations of the almshouses, however, did not end with simple remonstrances against the institutions. In their critical examinations, progressive social reformers posed a more far-reaching question: given the harsh conditions of the almshouse and the worthy status of the old, why were the aged incarcerated at all? In the search for answers, social analysts repeatedly made two critical and erroneous assumptions. First, seeing that the aged had become a majority of the almshouse population, they assumed that poverty and dependency among the aged had also increased rapidly. In their charts and surveys of individuals *within* the institution, they emphasized the difficulties that awaited even the most providential aged worker. In contrast to past experts who had linked poverty to drink or laziness, they pronounced old age itself to be a cause of dependency. The social reformers concluded—without much in-depth study of the self-sufficient old—that even those who struggled outside the asylum were, in time, likely to be institutionalized.[69]

The first assumption of progressive analysts, however, appears to have had little real merit. The large number of elderly individuals in almshouses was hardly proof that a sudden rise in poverty among the aged had occurred. Nor did almshouse figures reveal that most elderly individuals would eventually come to depend on some form of public relief. Although the poorhouse population was increasingly composed of aged individuals, the proportion of the aged who were incarcerated in them remained virtually unchanged between 1880 and 1920 at about 2 percent. As we have seen, the shift in the demographic composition of poorhouses was the result of specific bureaucratic and financial decisions made by politicians and welfare administrators rather than of rising dependency among the nation's aged population.

The first error, however, led to a second, equally erroneous supposition. Contemplating the assumed rising dependency among the old and observing the coincident ascendancy of an industrial economy, progressive analysts charged that industrialization and urbanization were the sources of the elderly's new vulnerability. Edward T. Devine, Abraham Epstein, Isaac Rubinow, Lee Welling Squier, Arthur J. Todd, and Amos Warner, joined by a legion of other critics, asserted that as long as the United States had been a rural and agricultural land, the old had been greatly respected.[70] The elderly's memory of the past was indispensable; their knowledge and skills had great value. In the modern world, however, the aged were left with few significant roles. The socioeconomic problem of the old man or woman, wrote Isaac Rubinow, "is specifically a problem of modern society, a result of the rapid industrialization within the last century." Relegated to "the industrial scrap heap," the old, not surprisingly, were forced to end their lives confined to the nation's almshouses.[71] In reality, however, this assumption was as inaccurate as the belief in the elderly's ever-growing dependency. As our previous chapters demonstrate, the economic transformation of the nation assisted most aged persons; it did not uniformly harm the elderly or deprive them of all resources.

Yet these errors did not limit the effectiveness of the reformers' arguments or the dominant role their assumptions played in calls for social reform. While patently mistaken, these ideas had striking effects on both the political and social history of old age in the United States. By the early twentieth century, reformers' generalizations about the causes of old-age dependency extended far beyond the limited number of inmates who were confined to asylum wards. Analysts argued that their investigations into almshouse conditions had important ramifications: long lists of individuals waiting to be placed in private institutions, worthy persons still forced to reside in almshouses, and thousands of aged individuals who existed on the edge of poverty all proved the increasing dependency of the elderly in the industrial world.

Confusing growing absolute numbers with increases in rates of incarceration, analysts even argued that almshouse residency had become a threat to hard-working members of the middle class. In 1925, in her influential study *Aged Clients of Boston's Social Agencies*, Lucille Eaves asserted that "the risks of being left without means of meeting [the needs] of old age are not confined to the workers with low earning capacity but are shared by persons in all ranks of society."[72] Though the great majority of aged persons continued to lead self-sufficient lives and despite increasing wealth among older persons as a whole, the lesson from those within the public asylum seemed clear:

poverty in old age was not limited to the traditionally poor; it had become the dominant threat and prevailing fear among the nation's older population.

During the early twentieth century, public welfare advocates, fraternal groups, and state labor federations all exploited this fear in their campaign for new welfare programs. They repeatedly addressed the widespread anxiety that without the intervention of broad social programs, ill chance or bad health could force even the most industrious individuals "over the hill" to the poorhouse. As a pervasive image, the almshouse needed little explanation. "The poorhouse," wrote Epstein, "stands as a threatening symbol of the deepest humiliation and degradation before all wage-earners after the prime of life."[73]

The metaphor of institutionalization as the old folks' inevitable destiny was employed by welfare advocates in three distinctive, although clearly related, appeals. First, as part of an emotional plea for legislation, it symbolized the callous treatment awarded the elderly in industrial society. The poorhouse openly violated the longstanding belief that the elderly deserved respectful treatment. Even in the late nineteenth century, in their successful agitation for a more generous Civil War pension system, veterans' advocates had consistently drawn on the indignity of compelling good U.S. citizens to enter the almshouse.[74] By the twentieth century, according to one social analyst, *almshouse* had become "a word of hate and loathing, for it includes the composite horrors of poverty, disgrace, loneliness, humiliation, abandonment and degradation."[75] An early-twentieth-century illustration in the magazine of a fraternal group, the Eagles, depicted what was to become a commonly accepted image. In the sketch, an aged couple received notification that the man's services were "no longer required," as today "young men only need apply." The announcement was emblazoned with the words: "Passport to the Poorhouse." Notwithstanding their respectable, middle-class surroundings (complete with a needlepoint reading "Bless Our Home"), little question remained as to the fate that awaited them.[76] (See illustration, 'Passport to the Poorhouse.')

Even almshouse administrators began to argue that the almshouse represented an undeserved and heartless fate for its aged residents. In 1897, Ernest C. Marshall, in his *Annual Report of the Institutions Commissioners to the City of Boston*, strongly opposed placing elderly individuals in the city's institutions. Few of the elderly, he argued, had led unworthy lives or demonstrated vices deserving of such treatment. Although their only crime was to have experienced the loss of their children or the depletion of their savings, the city's laws mandated their incarceration. Arguing that "the placing of these unfortunate poor in the almshouse is not the kind, humane or even just way of treating them," he called on his superiors to ensure that "it be no longer said that Massachusetts brings shame to old age, the blush to wrinkled faces, by classing them under the shameful name of paupers."[77]

The almshouse also served a second symbolic function in the campaign for old-age pensions: touted as economically inefficient, it was proof of an antiquated welfare system. Such institutions, analysts contended, were fiscally irresponsible since they required inordinate public expenditure. According to a 1923 Department of Labor study of 2,183 almshouses, each institutionalized person required $440 annually in public expenditure. More than half of these institutions, the study noted, were patently inefficient. Housing fewer than twenty-five inmates, they incurred high fixed costs simply for upkeep and maintenance. With such a large portion of the budget given to building expenses, the inmates had little hope of receiving adequate daily care.[78] Such economic arguments were not novel. Two decades before, a 1903 investigation of Boston's Long Island Almshouse had found that the large budgetary requirements did not result in happy conditions for the aged inmates. Sufficient clothing, comfortable quarters, and ample food were often neglected.[79]

But the fiscal irresponsibility of the institutions went beyond their high budgets and meager provisions. Critics had long charged that the elderly could be more efficiently supported in their own homes. By the 1920s, private social workers maintained that $500 per year would support an elderly couple living in the community. Commissions considering public support of the aged set a pension of one dollar per day per recipient, or $365 per year, as the maximum allotment to be distributed. Both these sums were far less than the cost of supporting individuals in the almshouse.[80]

This economic perspective served to buttress traditional uneasiness about incarcerating elderly people and justified replacing the traditional system with old-age pensions. "It is well known," wrote the Illinois State Federation of Labor in 1923, "that the cost of maintaining an aged person in a public institution is far in excess of the amount it is proposed to pay such person in the form of a pension."[81] In the 1920s, the economic benefits of old-age pensions became a central theme in the movement for state annuities. The Fraternal Order of Eagles, instrumental in the campaign's success, asserted that the almshouse represented not only moral weakness on the part of society but economic failure as well. Incarceration of the old in an almshouse, they argued, actually cost the taxpayer more than an economically sound old-age pension system.[82]

Finally, the almshouse served a third symbolic purpose in the call for the establishment of pensions: its existence, critics charged, not only affected the old but also had grave implications for younger persons as well. For families whose relatives resided in it, the almshouse brought shame and debasement. The dread of almshouse residency was so great, social advocates declared, that individuals and families would take any step to avoid incarceration. According to Reverend George B. O'Conor, director of Catholic charities in the Archdiocese of Boston, the good parishioners of his city's working districts "would rather starve to death" than enter the poorhouse.[83] As a result, relatives made great sacrifices to save their elders from this ignominious fate as well as to prevent the entire family from sharing in the individual's shame. Reformers asserted that faced with a choice of allowing old relatives to enter the poorhouse or keeping necessary funds for themselves, adult children generally relinquished their own economic security and well-being.[84] Such individuals even sacrificed the next generation by placing their own children in the labor market at the expense of their education and future. Consider the dilemma, wrote Mabel Nassau in her 1915 study, *Old Age Poverty in Greenwich Village*, "of the middle generation trying to decide whether to support the aged parents and thus have less to eat for themselves and for their children . . . or to put the old people in an institution!"[85]

Social advocates for the aged were not alone in the utilization of the almshouse as a metaphor for strained generational relations. Leading progressive economists presented similar briefs. "Because of the necessity of supporting the aged," wrote the editors of *The Worker in Industrial Society* in 1923, "the children are frequently doomed to under-nourishment; and to a life in the midst of crowded and unsanitary quarters; to leave school early in life and in their turn to join the ranks of the unskilled."[86] Politicians argued that the threat of the almshouse ensured that resources needed by the young would be spent on the support of increasingly dependent and unproductive aged individuals. "Many married sons and daughters," wrote Massachusetts Senator David I. Walsh in 1927, "in order to spare their aged parents the disgrace of bitterness and pauperism, assume burdens which cannot be borne except at the cost of depriving their children of the rights of childhood and the opportunities of success, and of dooming themselves in turn to an old age of helpless dependence."[87]

In the 1920s, politicians such as Walsh were quick to grasp the importance of the public's fear of dependency in old age and their aversion to the almshouse. As a candidate and as governor of New York, Franklin Delano Roosevelt intensified a theme of his predecessor Alfred E. Smith and focused on the seemingly inevitable impoverishment of the aged worker. In his speeches and legislative messages, Roosevelt described old age in terms well known to welfare advocates. The destitution of the elderly, he declared, was an inevitable "by-product of modern industrial life." With urban and industrial growth, the old could do little to escape institutionalization. Age discrimination against older men, Roosevelt stated, meant that the "aged, worn-out worker . . . after a life of ceaseless effort and useful productivity must look forward for his declining years to a poorhouse."[88]

As governor, Roosevelt echoed the charge of charity reformers: the existence of the almshouse clearly illustrated the overwhelming need for a broad program of state pensions. The incarceration of the impoverished old, he asserted, was both economically and morally wrong. It represented a "wasteful system" that deprived individuals of their hope and dignity. In his acceptance speech and subsequent legislative initiatives, Roosevelt used the existence of the almshouse to justify state action. "We can no longer be satisfied," he declared in 1929, "with the old method of putting [the elderly] away in dismal institutions with the loss of self-respect, personality, and interest in life." With the adoption of an old-age pension, Roosevelt argued, the old institutional poor law might be abandoned altogether and the elderly allowed to retain their self-esteem.[89]

By the late 1920s, Roosevelt, the New York Democratic party, and a growing number of politicians in other states had become convinced that broadly based popular support existed for old-age pensions. Roosevelt warned recalcitrant Republican legislators that the fear of dependency in old age reached many of the constituents. "Judging by the number of letters I am receiving, there is a more widespread popular interest . . . than most of us people in public life had realized."[90] Failure to sense the depth of concern was not only emotionally insensitive and economically wasteful, but could result in political suicide. Nor was Roosevelt alone in his political use of the almshouse as a salient moral and economic issue. In the 1930 New York Assembly elections, Democratic candidates seized on the reluctance of Republicans to agree to pension legislation, arguing that "the poorhouse does not belong in this age of progress," since it "costs the State, or rather the taxpayer of each County, more than a proper system of pensions. So it is not only right but economical to wipe the poorhouse out of existence."[91]

In the critical debate over the Social Security Act in the 1930s, the poorhouse as a symbol reached its broadest audience. The Committee on Economic Security, commissioned by President Roosevelt to examine the conditions of the aged and to recommend legislation, used almshouse statistics to advance the case for a social insurance program. In their 1934 publication *The Need for Economic Security in the United States*, the committee displayed silhouette figures of older men with canes to represent the rising proportion of elderly in public institutions. "The predominance of the aged in almshouses," they concluded, "is a sign of their increasing dependency." According to the commission, significant measures needed to be adopted to rectify what appeared to be an inevitable, widespread trend.[92] (See illustration, 'The Need for Economic Security.')

Although political discussions about the almshouse clearly reflected widespread popular fears about institutionalization, these fears were especially profound in ethnic communities. Such anxiety was not ill-founded; it had roots deep in the historical development of U.S. public welfare. In the nineteenth century, the reforms of the poorhouse reflected elite fears of the "lazy" and "vicious" immigrant. In large part, the punitive almshouse was an attempt to deter such individuals from seeking assistance and to control those who applied for aid. Similarly, the establishment of private old-age homes was based on the desire of the elite to rescue the native-born from the immigrant-filled almshouse. As a result, alternatives were created for the native-born old while the almshouses became dominated by foreigners and their descendants. Surveys revealed that their numbers in the institutions far exceeded their representation in the community. By the twentieth century, the public institutions were cited as proof of the inherent inferiority of foreign groups. The dominant presence of such groups, however, was hardly accidental. To some degree, the high proportion of publicly supported foreign-born resulted from conscious attempts by welfare administrators to place "the better type" of pauper—individuals who shared their own ethnic background—in private charities, leaving almshouses to immigrants and their children.[93]

In the first years of their arrival in the United States, these immigrant groups had little control over such welfare programs. They could neither defy the almshouse system nor establish their own programs. As these groups gained political and economic power, however, they attacked the ethnocentric prejudices reflected in institutional policies. In 1923, James M. Curley, the Irish mayor of Boston, lambasted the Protestant-dominated welfare structure in the state and city and excoriated the "pauperizing" of old people in city institutions, the separation of elderly married couples, and their seclusion in "drab and desolate" buildings far from their neighborhoods and friends. His solution, as well as that of other ethnic politicians and the Catholic Church, was the distribution of state pensions that allowed older people to remain in their own homes and neighborhoods rather than resorting to public incarceration.[94] Roosevelt was also fully aware of such ethnic concerns. In his 1928 platform and campaign, he carefully attempted to attract labor and ethnic groups who had long sought the enactment of old-age pensions.[95]

By the 1930s, the attack on the almshouse had gained great momentum. Critics expressed bewilderment as to how the institution could have come into existence. It seemed to play no ethical role; its costs far outweighed any possible benefits. In their arguments for state pensions, however, both welfare advocates and politicians displayed little historic memory. Their characterization of the fiscal irresponsibility of the institution, the immoral treatment of its inmates, and its effect on future generations bore faint similarity to earlier expectations or assumptions. Nineteenth-century proponents of the public asylum had always known of the great expense of incarceration. They had been well aware that on an individual basis, outdoor assistance was less costly. In their opinion, however, the almshouse would reduce the cost of welfare by limiting the numbers on public relief. By erecting a harsh, forbidding institution, charity officials believed they would discourage individuals from seeking relief and supply assistance to only the most debilitated and desperate.

By the twentieth century, the criticisms of welfare reformers revealed that the perception of the institution and its inmate population had dramatically changed. According to surveys of charity officials, aged almshouse residents had little hope of avoiding institutionalization. The great majority of individuals within the asylums were there, according to Roosevelt, not as "a result of lack of thrift or energy" but "as a mere by-product of modern industrial life."[96] The evolving nature of industrial society and the unavoidable physical degeneration of older people doomed them in ever-growing numbers to the shame of incarceration. In the call for national pensions to replace the institutions, therefore, welfare advocates no longer believed that the almshouse served as a deterrent to indolent members of the lower class. Rather, in the opinion of a broad spectrum of Americans, it had become the inevitable—and the extremely unjust—final "home" for large numbers of elderly individuals who deserved far better treatment.[97]

The Social Security Era

In the movement for a Social Security system, the almshouse assumed a powerful role. As an emotional symbol it represented the horror of modern old age; its very existence seemed to prove that pensions had to be provided to all aged men and women. By the 1930s, business, state, and federal old-age pension programs directly addressed the seemingly widespread threat of incarceration. In part, these plans were designed to save the hard-working and industrious (although now unemployed) elderly from the ignominious fate of poorhouse residency. Pension advocates often took direct aim at the almshouse, declaring that monthly payments to the old would finally cause the demise of the long-hated institution.[98] Even the Supreme Court employed the symbol of the ominous almshouse when asserting the constitutionality of the Social Security Act. Writing for the majority in 1937, Justice Cardozo proclaimed that "the hope behind this statute is to save men and women from the rigors of the poorhouse as well as from the haunting fear that such a lot awaits them when journey's end is near."[99]

Justice Cardozo's characterization of the reformers' intention was apt indeed. The provisions of the Social Security Act of 1935 clearly reflected the New Dealers' attempt to destroy the longstanding institution. "We were," recalled Pennsylvania's deputy secretary of public assistance, "rather enthusiastic to empty the poorhouses."[100] Moreover, New Dealers had little desire for the public to equate state pensioners with poorhouse paupers. Thus in the federal legislation, residents of public institutions were categorized as totally ineligible for any form of old-age assistance; all others, whether residing in privately funded institutions, alone, or with families, could receive state and federal assistance.

Not surprisingly, the legislation did have a significant impact on the composition of the almshouse. States and counties chose to support the elderly in the most cost-efficient manner. The old-age assistance title in the Social Security Act carried a sizable federal subsidy for assistance in the recipients' homes or private quarters but prohibited such aid in public institutions. It was obviously far more economical for state and local officials to provide federally supported old-age assistance than to pay the full cost in a public institution. In Kansas, officials rapidly transferred county homes to "private" control, although the supervisors usually remained the same.[101] In Charleston, S.C., New Deal legislation ensured that most impoverished elderly individuals in the city and county would receive support through pensions rather than institutional shelter; by 1938, 1,360 persons were granted old-age assistance.[102] Sharing in a national trend, Charleston's almshouse population declined. In 1949, the city ruled that the public almshouses fulfilled little function. Most of the twenty-seven inmates, municipal officials declared, could be better treated by receiving relief in their own households.[103]

Not all the destitute, however, could be returned to their own homes. Charleston's authorities conceded that some aged individuals were in need of extensive medical care; they would be placed in local sanitariums. Similar actions were taken by city and county officials throughout the country. As public almshouses closed their doors for lack of federal assistance, the infirm elderly were placed in private boarding houses and asylums. Many of these establishments had already existed as informal nursing homes. Among the "most dramatic changes" induced by the Social Security Act was the encouragement it gave to a formal nursing home industry. With federal support, proprietors transformed what once had been boarding and rooming houses into more formal "homes for the aged."[104]

Despite pension advocates' assertions that state annuities would eliminate all such homes, the continued need for institutional care for a small proportion of the elderly had not been completely unforeseen. In the early 1930s, welfare authorities such as Homer Folks argued that the government needed to recognize the dual function of the almshouse. The great majority of elderly residents, he stressed, were placed in public institutions not only because they were poor but also because they required extensive medical care. According to Folks, only about 15 percent of the institutionalized old were able to live independently on a pension. "The others," he declared, "are physically infirm and sick, and have various kinds of ailments and conditions that require personal attention of the kind that you could not get in an individual home; [they] require nursing or medical attention . . . in some sort of institution." Testifying before the New York Commission on Old Age Security, Folks argued that the government should consider not only the allocation of pensions but also the creation of an institutional provision for the support of the sick and ailing.[105]

Neither the federal nor the state government took action on Folks's recommendation. In the course of the nation's welfare history, the almshouse had become a symbol of failure and shameful treatment of the aged, far too pernicious to be granted broad federal support. Despite its relatively small inmate population, it stood as a symbol of an outdated and ruthless welfare system. Not surprisingly, then, New Dealers excluded almshouse residents from Social Security and limited the ability of public institutions to provide for the debilitated elderly. As a result, the infirm elderly turned to newly created and largely unregulated private facilities.[106] Displaced from the poorhouse and unable to receive support in any public medical institution, the debilitated old became the prime subjects of the burgeoning private nursing home industry of the late 1930s and 1940s.[107]

By 1950, it had become clear that the attack on the almshouse had served its purpose. Fulfilling neither a charitable nor a medical function, the 200-year-old institution had finally lost its central role in the welfare system and could be treated more generously. This assessment, as well as the lobbying of public hospital associations, convinced Congress to amend Social Security to allow federal support to individuals in both public and private medical institutions. The 1950 legislation, along with the Medical Facilities Survey and Construction Act of 1954, cemented the role Folks had foreseen for public nursing homes. While the old almshouse had become obsolete, federal support of public and private institutions made the nursing home the new shelter for society's most dependent and debilitated old.[108]

The greatest incentive to the private industry, however, came with the passage of Medicare in 1965. According to the legislation, aged individuals were eligible for support for up to 100 days of nursing home residency, following a three-day hospital stay. As a consequence, the nursing home industry, which had grown steadily in the years following enactment of Social Security, grew rapidly. Between 1960 and 1976, the number of homes increased by 140 percent, the number of nursing beds by 302 percent, and, most significantly, the revenues received by the industry by 2,000 percent.[109]

For over 300 years, American beliefs about the worthiness of the impoverished elderly have remained virtually unchanged. Since preindustrial times, authorities have judged the aged pauper to be deserving of community relief. In dispensing charity, they generally linked the impoverishment of the old to their declining abilities rather than to controllable vices or indolence. Yet despite this persistent belief, the aged poor have been dramatically affected by changes in welfare systems directed at other groups of indigent persons. In the nineteenth century, hoping to limit relief and control the poor, welfare reformers forced recipients of public assistance into noxious poorhouses. Grouped along with the alcoholic, the orphan, and the vagrant, elderly persons in need of assistance were threatened with institutionalization. By the late nineteenth and early twentieth centuries, their incarceration assumed an additional significance. The isolation and predominance of the aged in almshouses and private old-age homes became a broadly accepted symbol of the declining status of the old. Rather than simply being the result of bureaucratic decisions, their dominant presence in the asylums seemed visible proof of inevitable debilitation and dependency. In a modern industrial society, most aged people, it was assumed, would ultimately require some form of public care.

Although almshouses no longer exist, such institutional anxiety still concerns the nation. The elderly's longstanding fear that their days would end in the almshouse has a clear parallel in the contemporary belief that the nursing home might be their fate.[110] This widely shared fear aptly demonstrates a significant fallacy in the arguments of early pension advocates. In their desire to eliminate the almshouse, reformers overestimated the effects of Social Security. Misreading the almshouse evidence, they predicted that the distribution of monthly annuities would eliminate the need for long-term institutions. As recent history reveals, however, a considerable minority of older people continued to require such care regardless of government stipends. By the 1970s, in fact, the outcry against nursing homes rivaled the early twentieth-century attack on the almshouse. According to consumer groups, it appeared little had changed. While some institutions offered high-quality care, many simply warehoused the old and provided waiting rooms for death.[111] As the recent debate over catastrophic illness revealed, the institution continues to influence the experience of growing old in the United States.

Yet the impact of the pension advocates cannot be dismissed. The movement for old-age pensions served to alter radically the condition and concerns of the nation's elderly. Social Security helped the most impoverished of the poor, especially of immigrant origins, avoid the horrors of the poorhouse. For millions of others, it alleviated the desperate—if somewhat unfounded—fear that they might be thrust into a demeaning institutional environment. And for still more Americans, the children and grandchildren of the elderly, the New Deal measure created the assurance that they would not be forced to choose between providing for their own needs and rescuing their elders from the threat of almshouse residency. In shutting the poorhouse door, Social Security removed the dread of an institution that had cast its shadow over the elderly for more than 200 years.

5

Advice to the Old

FOR THOSE IN almshouses and old-age homes, old age had a distinct meaning. While they received little veneration, they were often treated with
compassion and sympathy. In the eyes of welfare authorities and charitable
executives, the advanced years of the dependent old justified their need for
special treatment. For the noninstitutionalized elderly, age also had special
connotations. Although until the mid–twentieth century the old never comprised more than a small fraction of the population, they were hardly invisible or ignored. In contrast to other portions of the life cycle, their stage of
life never needed to be "discovered" as a distinctive segment of existence.[1]
From the sermons of seventeenth-century ministers to the writings of early
twentieth-century pension advocates and the publications of professional gerontologists in our own time, the last stage of life has received wide social
attention. Across nearly four centuries, the American elderly have been advised, criticized, romanticized, even dissected. They have been the subject of
thousands of sermons, hundreds of medical publications, and scores of stories, poems, and advice books.

Over the centuries, depictions of old age have dramatically changed. The
counsel of colonial ministers, who admired the wisdom of age or castigated
their congregations for improper conduct to the old, differed greatly from
the guidance of mid-twentieth-century financial experts, who advised the old
on their investments and retirement strategy. Strikingly different approaches
to old age reflect the values of different historical periods as well as the con-
trasting backgrounds, training, and professional interests of the authors. Yet
the importance of these admonitions has displayed a certain constancy. By
cautioning the elderly on their behavior or by counseling others in society
how to act toward the old, they reveal widely shared beliefs about the proper
characteristics, needs, and roles of the aged in American society.

In this chapter, we explore advice given to the elderly from the preindustrial period to the twentieth century. Even broadly considered, such advisory pronouncements must be greeted with great caution. The course of
American history never provided an era in which all elderly persons were
spoken of with great reverence; nor was there ever a period of total gerontophobia, in which every old person was treated with disdain and dishonor.[2]
At no time in the past, therefore, were all assertions about old age consistent

or unvaried. For every author who spoke about the worth of the old, another in the same period decried their frailties or belittled their weaknesses. For some, gray hair could be a sign of great wisdom; for others, it was simply a mark of obsolescence.

Yet despite such inconsistencies, advice literature to and about the old has reflected broad perceptions of old age that have changed across time and make up a significant part of the history of old age. Through admonition and interpretation, writers, physicians, ministers, and social experts have attempted to make sense of growing old and understand the numerous changes that came with the aging process. Although their expressed views of senescence did not always reflect the reality of the elderly's experience (and, at times, conflicted greatly with that reality), they offered an important source through which to trace the evolving meaning of growing old in the United States.

In the pages that follow, we focus on three general paradigms of old age. In the preindustrial era, authorities generally advised the old to fulfill—and enjoy—their reciprocal roles and obligations. They saw old age as a distinctive and well-defined segment in the stages of life, which corresponded with other life divisions and marked a divine balance among the stages. In the industrial era, experts depicted ideal old age in remarkably different terms. Rather than providing links to the past for later generations while depending harmoniously on their descendants' love and assistance, the elderly came to be depicted as suffering from an inescapable disease that affected every aspect of their existence. By the early twentieth century, this evolving medical and professional model of aging had become the dominant theory for explaining old age and defining the elderly's place in the universe. Old age was a period of life to avoid or delay; individuals were to search and plan for ways to live like middle-aged adults and thwart the advances of age. In the mid–twentieth century, a third paradigm appeared. Experts tended to discount both the medical model of aging and the importance of generational balance and harmony. Elderly individuals were advised to strive for their own independence and self-sufficiency. A good old age became synomous with autonomy.

Preindustrial America

"If any man is favored with a long life," wrote the esteemed—and elderly—minister Increase Mather, "it is God that has lengthened his days."[3] In his last years, Mather pondered the implications of his longevity. Like many of his fellow ministers, he believed that the attainment of old age was rarely an accident. God, he maintained, had determined exactly which persons were to live beyond the prescribed "threescore and ten." Without God's explicit intervention, their lives would have ended far earlier. Advanced age, Mather concluded, was an unmistakable sign that the individual had lived a favored and righteous existence.

Increase's son Cotton Mather, an eminent minister and respected scientist, agreed. In *The Angel of Bethesda*, the first medical treatise written in the British colonies, the younger Mather advised the elderly to thank God directly for their extended life spans. Every day, he instructed, the elderly must implore why they are "not *feeble* and *Sore broken* and roaring by reason of Disquietness of . . . Heart and under those Terrible Distempers which Defy the *Physicians* and which Torture the *Patients* and under which *all the Days* of the Afflicted are *Evil Days*." A healthy long life, Mather concluded, had little to do with doctors or medicine; it was nothing less than a God-given miracle.[4]

This religious perspective informed much of colonial writing on old age. Ministers, it was assumed, were the logical authorities on growing old. Physicians, as Cotton Mather's medical treatise proclaimed, had little to offer the old; the long lives of the elderly were sure signs that they had escaped the intrusions of disease and the often fatal interventions of doctors. In colonial society, therefore, a formal definition of old age and the explanation for its existence were left largely to clerical interpretation. From their pulpits, ministers attempted both to explain the purpose of growing old and to define the qualities best suited to the elderly.

For the New England clergy, there seemed little question that old age symbolized an important stage in the life cycle. In a society in which death was a constant companion and few people reached "threescore and ten," senescence was endowed with great religious significance. For many ministers, the attainment of advanced age was undeniable proof of God's plan for an ordered universe. Without old age, it was assumed, the world would lack harmony and balance; with senescence, the order of the universe was easily defined and apparent. "There is," explained Reverend Samuel Willard, "that Relation and Order that arises from the Condition of Many, whom God's Providence disposeth to dwell in such Societies. . . . There are in all Places, some that are *Aged*, and others that are *Younger*, and both of these in Plenty are promised to a People whom God has blessed."[5]

According to leading seventeenth-century philosophers and ministers, such balance was essential in the definition of social structure. The rights and duties of individuals were delineated not by themselves but as they related to others in the community. Individuals became parents only upon the birth of their children; men assumed the role of husband only upon marriage to their wives. Without the complementary object, their status became meaningless. A minister could not hope to preach without his congregation, nor a ruler expect to command devoid of subjects. Instead, society was composed of reciprocal relationships that defined the distinctive status of individuals and placed them in their proper standing in the universe.[6]

For those who gave advice to the old, the importance of such mutual relationships was clear. Above all else, ministers warned, individuals should be aware that the life stages were distinct and balanced. Each phase had been endowed with immutable and complementary roles and obligations. According to divine plan, the old clearly could not survive without the assistance of the young, nor the young progress without their elders' wisdom. (See illustration, 'Wisdom of the Aged.') Rather, communities functioned harmoniously when individuals fulfilled the qualities best suited to their age and avoided all other, seemingly inappropriate, behavior.

Most ministers advised the old to recognize that old age necessitated numerous adjustments. The elderly had to acknowledge the benefits—and the limitations—that came with great age. Leading clerics such as Samuel Willard and Cotton Mather agreed that the old possessed virtues of great importance. According to their sermons, the old were to maintain constant sobriety, gravity, orthodoxy, temperance, charity, patience, and soundness in judgment. And, ministers advised, if the elderly persisted in these noble qualities, they would find their high status in society guaranteed. The young, in search of guidance and knowledge, would naturally turn to the advice of their graying elders.[7]

Yet as old age had its advantages, it also had its liabilities. The same ministers who vividly portrayed the glories of aging did not hesitate to list its accompanying horrors. In his *Addresses to Old Men and Young Men and Little Children*, Cotton Mather enumerated the disadvantages in detail:

> The sun, the light, the moon and the stars begin to be darkened with you; that is, your parts are under decay; your fancy, your judgement are failing you. . . . Your hands now shake and shrink, and must lean upon a staff. . . . Your thighs and legs now buckle under. . . . Your teeth grow weak and few, and are almost all rotted out. . . . Your eyes become dim, and clouds disturb the visible powers in them. . . . You become deaf and thick of hearing. . . . You can't without some difficulty go up a pair of stairs, and are in danger of stumbling at every stone in the street. . . . Your backs are so feeble that instead of carrying anything else, they can scarce bear themselves.[8]

Such bodily alterations were the physical signs of the dramatic changes that came with age. Their advance marked the end of customary roles and the establishment of new obligations. Where once the elderly had strength, they now had wisdom; where once they enjoyed unlimited energy, they now had gained long years of experience. In old age, ministers counseled, declining physical ability was exchanged for moral authority. Most important, the old were to understand that they set the standard of proper behavior for the rest of the community. In so doing, Reverend Samuel Willard stated, their "good example [would] be acknowledged and imitated."[9] Those of extreme age were never to be content with purposeless leisure or lapses in conduct. Rather, they were cautioned to spend their remaining years doing an "Abundance of Good," acting always as paragons of virtue.[10] In every action, they were to show that their long lives had resulted from consistently following the path of righteousness.

Yet in following this advice, the old were also expected to know their place. Wisdom acquired through a long life did not necessarily mean that the elderly made the best political leaders; accumulated experience did not suggest that they were to ply their trades unceasingly.[11] Repeatedly, ministers cautioned the old to put aside the tasks of their middle age. With the wisdom of age, ministers declared, the elderly were to admit that their growing weaknesses required them to retire from the obligations of middle age. "Old folks," cautioned Cotton Mather, "often can't endure to be judged less able than ever they were for *public appearances*, or to be put out of offices. But good, sir, be so wise as to *disappear* of your own accord, as soon and as far as you lawfully may. Be glad of a *dismissal* from any *post*, that would have called for your activities."[12] Not surprisingly, then, ministers congratulated those individuals who acknowledged their own limitations and passed control to the next generation.[13]

As the old were cautioned to relinquish public matters to the young, so too were they advised to be ready to cede the private role of head of household to the next generation. Upon seeking shelter in the homes of their offspring, they were cautioned to be aware that they no longer possessed the authority of their younger days. Such advice seemed especially pertinent to the adult children of aging widowed women. "Your mother, or your husband's mother may live with you," John Wesley declared, "and you will do well to shew her all possible respect. But let her on no account have the least share in the management of your children. She will undo all that you have done; she will give them their own will in all things. She would humour them to the destruction of their souls if not their bodies to [*sic*]."[14]

The clergy's counsel to the old was clear: to attempt to continue in public or private life as they had in the past would be to go against the sacred order; to accept their new functions in life would be to understand the divine plan.[15] Not surprisingly, ministers were quick to condemn the elderly when they acted in ways judged unbecoming. "For them that stagger with age," declared Cotton Mather, "at the same time to stagger with drink; to see an old man reeling, spewing, stinking with the excess of the taverns, 'tis too loathsome a thing to be mentioned without very zealous detestation."[16] While such behavior might be pardoned in the young, it was unforgivable in the elderly. "The frequent sight of gray hairs," wrote Reverend Nicholas Noyes, "is a lecture to men against levity, vanity, and youthful vagaries and lusts."[17] According to the admonitions of the clergy, the old were selected by God for extraordinary life spans. As chosen individuals, they must give little hint that their days had ever been—or still were—filled with transgressions and sin.

Nor were the old to concentrate on their infirmities and diminishing abilities. In *A Word to the Aged*, Reverend William Bridge harshly berated the old for their weaknesses. Elderly people, he declared, are

> too drowsy and remiss in the things of God . . . too covetous and tenacious for the things of the world . . . too timorous and fearful . . . too touchy, peevish, angry, and forward . . . very unteachable . . . they think they know more than others . . . hard to be pleased, and as hard to please others . . . full of complaints of the present times, . . . [and] full of suspicions, and very apt to surmise, suspect, and fear the worst.[18]

Ministers cautioned the old against complaining about the losses and limitations and advised instead that they accept their new position with "Christian resignation."[19]

This new role for the old clearly had an implication for the actions of the young. According to the ministers' depiction of universal order, God had purposefully created reciprocal roles and functions. In sermons, therefore, the clergy not only advised the old about their changing obligations but also admonished the young as to their evolving duties to their parents. Most clearly, once the old began to decline in power or activities, their children became responsible for their daily necessities. "It is," declared Reverend Willard, "part of the duty of Children to take care of their Parents in their age and need." Such filial care once again revealed God's harmony and order. Adult children, Willard explained, would now return to their parents "the love and care expressed to us in our infancy and Childhood."[20]

Not all young adults, however, followed the dictates of biblical order. Ministers often castigated their congregations for failing to respect the old or pay them the honor they deserved. In *Solemn Advice to Young Men*, Increase Mather reprimanded the young for their most inappropriate behavior. "To deride aged persons because of those natural infirmities which age has brought upon them," he wrote, "is a great sin."[21] "Yet," Mather conceded in another sermon, "how common is it to call this or that old person 'old such an one' in a way of contempt on account of their age."[22] Moreover, not only did the young sometimes ridicule the old, but they even failed to support them in their senescence. From the pulpit, ministers strongly berated such ungrateful offspring for the sins they committed. "Children," thundered Reverend Samuel Willard, "that have been the charge of their Parents, to bring them up to be capable of doing something, should not presently, in hope of doing better for themselves, desert their helpless Parents, as think it now time to look to themselves, and let them shift as they can."[23]

Ministers, however, saved their harshest criticisms for children who failed to care for their widowed mothers. Widowhood, according to Cotton Mather was "a state of Affliction." A world of women without husbands clearly lacked the balance that defined the ministers' view of the universe. Mather characterized the life of the widow as especially difficult: "if the widow is bereaved of the Main Support that after the Death of her Husband Sorrows Embittered by New Anxieties and Encumbrances coming upon her; Debts to be Paid and Mouths to be fed."[24] The clergy did not hesitate to intervene in family matters; they readily exercised their authority to persuade adult children to support their elderly relatives.[25]

But it was not only the clergy who stressed the importance of reciprocal roles and obligations. In colonial America, such relationships also served as a foundation for legal statute and intervention. According to colonial law, parents were responsible for the well-being of their children; in turn, middle-aged adults were accountable for the welfare of their aging kin. Authorities automatically turned to the families of the old when aging individuals became unable to support themselves. By so doing, they maintained the equilibrium of social relations: where once the aging adults had provided for them, they now assumed the care of their elders. For families who failed to fulfill their obligations, however, authorities were quick to intercede and restore social harmony. Individuals who neglected to support the family were promptly chastised as well as penalized through the assessment of sizable fines. With little hesitation, magistrates advised, then enforced, the fulfillment of reciprocal obligations.[26]

The importance of mutual responsibilities—both to the elderly and to their children—extended well beyond the Sunday sermon or the legal statute. In colonial society, proper conduct on the part of all family members was essential for the maintenance of intergenerational peace. From birth, children had been taught to "honor thy father and mother"; to show disrespect to the old was to reject biblical injunction.[27] Thus, few social mechanisms existed that allowed the young to challenge the decisions or usurp the power of the old. Harmony within the family depended primarily on the elderly coming to terms with their evolving position and voluntarily passing control to the next generation, while the young accepted their new responsibilities and graciously paid their elders the respect they deserved.

In giving advice to the community, however, neither ministers nor magistrates appeared especially anxious about the state of the family or the nature of relationships among generations. Despite specific cases of neglect and indifference, they assumed that most individuals would fulfill their obligations and understand the symmetrical nature of the universe. Above all else, they argued, social interests and expectations linked one generation to the next. As individuals grew old, they simply assumed the appropriate characteristics and responsibilities of the next life stage. Like their elders before them, young men and women would eventually—with God's grace—grow old. In time, they too would become either the recipients of respect or the targets of contempt and disdain. Thus their advice to the young was simple: the old were to be addressed as they themselves would choose to be treated in their final years.[28]

In colonial society, therefore, advice to and about the elderly rarely depicted old age as a serious social problem. Some persons clearly failed to respect the old; their conduct then received the condemnation of ministers and, often, the intervention of political authorities.[29] Yet the place of the aged in their communities was never really questioned. Old age, like every other segment in the life cycle, simply had its own distinctive characteristics and obligations. As long as aged individuals fulfilled their prescribed roles and responsibilities—and accepted their limitations—the lives of the young and the old seemed intricately related.

At the end of the eighteenth century, advice to the old continued to echo the sentiments of these colonial origins. Ministers still argued that a long life was directly due to the intervention of God. The old, they were sure, had a distinctive place in the universe; respect for them continued to be praised as a virtue.[30] In the early nineteenth century, however, recommendations that the elderly realize their limitations and pass control to the next generation became more strident. Numerous northern Protestant evangelical ministers cautioned that the old should be aware of their diminished powers; they should hardly attempt to continue in the ways of the young.[31] Elderly individuals who refused to recognize and accept their transformed status, in fact, were characterized as having a pernicious effect on both their congregations and their communities. According to evangelist Charles Finney, "the traditions of the old" hardly inspired correct behavior in the young. Rather, they stood as "the grand sources of most of the fatal errors of the present day."[32] Denouncing "old fogies" who controlled access to congregations, young ministers demanded that the elderly resign themselves to a lesser role both in the church and in the world. Through their persistent attempt to retain power and authority, the old disturbed both heavenly command and earthly order.[33]

Such sentiments were expressed not only by young clerics but by their elder counterparts as well. In the first half of the nineteenth century, elderly preachers stressed the need for the old to understand that their time had long passed. The old should peacefully accept their departure from positions of wealth and influence. "It is," declared the seventy-year-old Presbyterian minister Albert Barnes, "an advantage to the world that men should die; that having accomplished the great purpose of life, they should give place to others; and that what they have gained in any respect should go into the common stock for the good of the world at large, and for the benefit of the coming generations, rather than that it should be retained by themselves under the form of vast monopolies."[34]

In giving such advice, ministers continued to stress the natural balance of generations and the order of the universe. No longer, however, did they focus upon the elderly's role as repositories of wisdom or keepers of sacred traditions. Indeed, nineteenth-century experts often challenged the assumption that the old possessed valued skills and experiences. In a rapidly changing society, the old only gave voice to a universe that had long passed; they knew nothing of the demands of the modern world. Ministers cautioned the elderly, therefore, to recognize their changed status. Old men had little hope of regaining their financial, intellectual, and physical powers; elderly women were no longer seen as the molders of social mores or standards. Aged women, for example, were chided by ministers for clinging to the vanities of the past. "Now she is an old woman of fashion," Theodore Parker exclaimed.

> wearing still the garments of her earlier prime, which, short and scanty as they were, are yet a world too wide for shrunken age to fill. . . . Poor creature! In youth a worm; in womanhood a butterfly; in old age, your wings all tattered, your plumage rent, a 'fingered moth'—old, shriveled, sick, perching on nothing, perishing into dust; the laughter of the witty; the scorn of the thoughtless; only the pity of the wise and good.[35]

Such admonitions reflected the ministers' rather ambiguous attitude toward the elderly. From their pulpits, these ministers depicted old age as a period of decline; the old, they advised, had to give way to the young. Yet the "old fogies" whom the ministers portrayed were far from impotent. According to their characterizations, the old were hardly victims of market forces or servants of the young. While clerics beseeched the old to withdraw from active life, they recognized that the elderly had the ability to control the young and dictate the course of their lives. In their portrayal, the old were often cast as domineering and authoritative individuals who unwisely refused to cede their "vast monopolies" on power. In contrast, aged men and women fulfilled their divinely ordained posture when they ceded responsibility and control to the next generation and passively planned for the heavenly reward.

For such nineteenth-century evangelical ministers, the old had three possible functions in modern society. First, they were to demonstrate to the young the proper posture for the last years. Above all else, the elderly were to demonstrate the benefits of living a righteous life and the vile consequences that awaited those who lived in immorality. Many preachers argued that a decrepit old age was a clear sign that the individual had not adhered closely to the natural laws of God: if aged individuals had lived with evil, they would die in sin. In giving such advice, ministers expressed little faith in the intercession of physicians or their medical treatments. Righteousness alone ensured that an adult would experience a "ripe" and serene old age. "There is nothing more beautiful," declared Lyman Beecher, "than a serene, virtuous, and happy old age; and such an old age belongs to every individual's life, if he only knows how to build it."[36]

Second, as the elderly could demonstrate correct Christian resignation, they could also teach the young how to meet death with dignity and serenity. In formulating such advice to aging Christians, ministers emphasized the inherent and inescapable connection between old age and mortality. Previously, the clergy had routinely cautioned all individuals of the need to prepare themselves for their possible demise. As a belief in the ability to control mortality among the young and middle-aged became more widespread, the old became the only sure candidates for imminent extinction. "If old age be the utmost boundary of life," declared Corlandt Van Rensselaer in 1841, "how forcibly are we reminded by it of the certainty of death."[37]

Finally, the elderly of the early nineteenth century served a third function: if beset by poverty, they could receive the community's benevolence and charity. As we have seen, the aged had always qualified as members of the worthy poor; their presence in society allowed the more fortunate to express their compassion. According to historian C. D. Hemphill, etiquette books of the period advised the young to visit the old or to entertain them in their own homes. But such behavior did not reflect a desire to benefit from their experience. Rather, the elderly were portrayed as being in need of kindness; the attention of the young was born out of the individual's proper upbringing and Christian compassion.[38]

In the early republic, ministers were not the only group to discuss the natural passing of the generations or the importance of meeting death with dignity. Nor were they alone in putting little faith in the ability of doctors to change the nature of the elderly's final days. At the end of their lives, for instance, Thomas Jefferson and John Adams expressed little confidence in the knowledge or skill of physicians. At eighty-six, after suffering a serious leg wound, Adams described his experience with the nation's leading doctors. Following their advice, he experienced two months of pain and discomfort. "I verily believe," he wrote to Jefferson, "that if nothing had been done to it but washing it in warm water it would have been well in three days."[39] Jefferson too had negative experiences with established medical procedures. In 1818, he sought relief from rheumatism by taking the therapeutic waters of hot springs. As a result, he complained to Adams, he suffered "imposthume, general eruption, fever, colliquative sweats, and extreme debility." The result of such intervention, he argued, was little more than to make a healthy old man sick.[40]

Not surprisingly, then, neither man relied heavily on the counsel of doctors, although both suffered from increasing disability in their final years. Throughout discussions concerning the nature and meaning of old age, they hardly considered the need to extend their lives through extraordinary medical measures. They merely congratulated themselves that increasing bodily weaknesses were not accompanied, or preceded, by a loss of intellect. As they approached extreme age, they awaited death with the hope that it would occur before they lost mental acuity. They agreed, in fact, that death had its place; if given the choice, neither would elect to live eternally as aged individuals. "When all our faculties have left," Jefferson asked rhetorically, "or are leaving us, one by one, sight, hearing, memory, every avenue of pleasing sensation is closed, and athumy, debility, and mal-aise left in their places, when the friends of our youth are all gone, and a generation is risen around us whom we know not, is death an evil?" The answer, the men concurred, was no. "There is," Jefferson declared, "a ripeness of time for death, regarding others as well as ourselves, when it is reasonable we should drop off, and make room for another growth. When we have lived our generation out, we should not wish to encroach on another."[41]

Such perceptions were not limited to the nation's elite. In their advice to children and grandchildren, elderly middle-class women in the new republic also spoke of the irremediable decline that accompanied great age and accepted the natural replacement of generations. For them, as for Adams and Jefferson as well as the evangelical ministers, old age and death were natural parts of the life cycle. As a result, they generally expressed concern over the prospects of their heavenly reward, rather than the indefinite continuation of life.[42] In 1825, New England matron Elizabeth Prescott wrote her friend Nancy Shaw that little could be done to assuage her age-related illness. It was, she explained, God's way of "reminding us that this is not our home and teaches us our duty to prepare for another and better world."[43] As such degeneration was part of the divine plan, doctors were assumed to have little expertise. "When a weakly person comes to be near three score and ten," Elizabeth Drinker advised, few remedies existed. "If they can keep from a large share of what is caller bodily pain," she wrote, " 'tis all that some of us ought to look for."[44]

Rather than relying on the care of physicians, such elderly women usually turned to the support of their kinship network. As they had once nursed their children and grandchildren in their adulthood, they hoped—and generally expected—that their family would provide for them in their final years. After being reassured by her son and daughter-in-law that she would always be cared for, Elizabeth Denny Ward wrote that their attentiveness comforted her and "takes away anxious care that might otherwise arise and distress the mind." Like numerous others, she hardly expected or invited expert recommendations or intervention; in her advice to others, she stressed only the importance of family and friends.[45]

To physicians in the new republic, such attitudes were hardly unexpected. They had their leeches and tonics, but they possessed no elixirs that guaranteed the extension of life. While they advised the young on ways to preserve vital energy and treated most diseases with little regard to the age of their patients, they had few recommendations specifically devised for the old. Even the renowned—and extremely interventionist—Revolutionary-era physician Benjamin Rush did not consider elderly patients to be ideal subjects for heroic medical measures. In his study entitled *Medical Inquiries and Observations*, Rush devoted a chapter to exploring the reasons for longevity among a group of healthy octogenarians. He concluded that the key to their long lives lay not in the actions of physicians but in the deeds of the individuals themselves. They had been temperate in food, drink, and activity, while moderate in politics, religion, and work. Moreover, each had been blessed with ancestors who achieved great age. For Rush, these elderly individuals served primarily as examples to others of the means of attaining long lives. The secret to their advanced years lay in reasonable habits and rational beliefs.[46] As with the ministers, old age served as a lesson on how to live correctly.

Yet despite Rush's failure to prescribe extreme medical intervention, his counsel on aging differed somewhat from the advice given a century earlier. He expressed little interest in the notion of divine mediation. "I do not believe," he wrote in 1797, "that [the] faculties of the mind are preserved by any supernatural power, but wholly by the constant and increasing exercise of them in the evening of life."[47] According to his Enlightenment-era philosophy, specific decisions made by the elderly themselves rather than the intercession of God or the actions of physicians determined both the quality of their days and the prolongation of lifespans.

While Rush applauded the long lives of the old and their ability to teach the young about longevity, his view of old age was sentimental at best; in its romanticization, the ideal old age lost power and importance.[48] As characterized by Rush and early-nineteenth-century ministers and writers, the correct old age was primarily a time of reflection and passivity. Although they possessed no visible infirmities, old men and women would simply come to accept their fate and focus serenely on the passing of life. By giving such advice, commentators emasculated men in old age, endowing the entire last stage of life with passive characteristics and behaviors. Their view of ideal male senescence contrasted sharply with mid-nineteenth-century stereotypes of proper middle-aged male conduct. Rather than being authoritative or domineering, models of senescence were compliant and acquiescent. Exchanging business ventures and monetary pursuits for piety and domestic serenity, they were to approach their inevitable demise with submissiveness and resignation.[49] When the Old Man's Home of Philadelphia opened its doors in 1865, its founders stressed this transition. While young men were assumed to be intelligent, independent, and vigorous, old men no longer possessed these traits. In the second annual report, the managers of the home wrote:

> The very name of manhood gives the idea of strength and ability to labor. Hence our first duty was to convince others of that which our own experience has taught us, namely that there is no class of humanity so sadly powerless to aid themselves, so useless in any of the ordinary duties of the household and so unwelcome among strangers as destitute men.[50]

Women, too, were to pass their roles of importance to the young and take up their positions as dependents of their offspring. No longer assumed to be wise counselors to the young or retainers of skill, they served few useful functions in society. With old age, they had become the ideal recipients for sympathy and benevolence.[51]

In the mid-nineteenth century, a new model of old age slowly began to emerge that increasingly emphasized the apparent dependency of old age while ignoring its previously recognized assets and values. In Europe, elite pathologists and physicians gradually formulated a view of old age that also challenged the notion of generational reciprocity, divine harmony, or even the elderly's symbolic value. Their pathological studies seemed to support the increasingly strident tone of the ministers and writers. Scientific research, they argued, definitively proved that the elderly had little to contribute to society and were obliged to cede former roles and responsibilities to a younger generation.

Midcentury French and German physicians espoused a medical model of growing old that stressed the inescapable physical and mental deterioration of all aging individuals. According to elite clinical pathologists, even normal old age was accompanied by critical deterioration. In advancing years, they cautioned, the body underwent highly destructive changes in the cells, bones, and tissues. In autopsies performed on the old, European physicians routinely discovered evidence of calcification, ossification, and general degeneration. Such alterations, they concluded, were so common to the old as to be considered basic to the aging process itself. Merely by growing old, individuals developed the exterior symptoms and internal lesions that were evidence of specific, extremely serious illnesses. Old age, rather than being a normal state in the life cycle, became characterized as a pathological process that transformed healthy and active individuals into complete invalids.[52]

By the mid–nineteenth century, the emerging medical model began to have an impact upon thought in the United States. In 1838, Dr. Isaac Ray began to use the new medical understanding of old age as a means of identifying the particular needs of the elderly. His depiction differed sharply from Benjamin Rush's optimistic characterization. He spoke little of the assets or moral lessons that came with advanced age; he neither guaranteed that a virtuous youth would lead to a healthy old age nor assumed that most of the old would retain their mental astuteness until their ultimate demise. Rather, in his influential *Treatise on the Medical Jurisprudence of Insanity*, he depicted the last years of life as ones often beset by both physical and mental incapacity. With their increasing years, he argued, large numbers of individuals suffered the obvious decline of old age. Memories weakened, intellects grew dim, even skin, cheeks, and eyes reflected ever-declining capabilities.[53]

For Ray, this unceasing degeneration had important ramifications. The eminent doctor cautioned his professional readers that both medical and legal authorities had for too long ignored the needs and limitations of aged patients. When dealing with aged property holders, he counseled, the legal system generally failed to recognize the distinctive characteristics of advanced age. Time and again, the courts rejected petitions to award guardianship over the elderly, stating that their degree of incapacity did not meet the standard definition of complete insanity. For Ray, however, the courts' tendency to equate old age with other stages of life was both inappropriate and dangerous. According to his medical conception of advanced age, large numbers of old persons required professional attention and care. Their loss of reason, he stated, arose "simply from that impairment of the mind so common in old age"; they were, without doubt, "more or less" insane.[54]

Inherent in Ray's use of the medical model was a belief that rather than providing a balance of generations, aging often disrupted the family and led to dissension. The question of guardianship, he predicted, would always be "disagreeable." In place of family harmony or kinship balance, he substituted the certainty of intergenerational strife. Selfish relatives would press for guardianship; increasingly demented elderly individuals would be unable to realize their limits and would not voluntarily cede power to the young and healthy. While Ray rejected the argument that guardians would have to be appointed for all elderly persons, he warned that large numbers of such cases existed and would require medical and legal intervention. In disputes in which such individuals possessed considerable wealth, he counseled, "there always comes a period sooner or later when interdiction is required."[55]

In such circumstances, Ray advised, the family should rely on the intervention of a wise and impartial medical counselor. Only an experienced authority had the ability to separate physical disability or longstanding habits from increasing mental incapacity.[56] Although Ray stressed that even the most highly trained expert had to act with great caution, he believed that little actual harm was done if the incompetency of the old was declared a bit quickly. "Although we take from him the control of his property," he wrote, "even while his faculties are sound enough to make him capable of performing the duty himself, yet we are only prematurely taking a measure which a few weeks or months will generally render absolutely necessary."[57] According to the European medical model of aging, most aged individuals would eventually be beset by serious and disabling illnesses that required the intervention of experts.

By the mid–nineteenth century, Ray's conception of old age and his opinion about legal interdiction had had considerable impact. As legal historian Margaret K. Krasik has demonstrated, the medical model of aging dramatically altered legal attitudes toward elderly petitioners.[58] Before then, courts generally devoted little attention to the question of guardianship of the elderly. In judging petitions for assuming legal responsibility, jurists generally found old men and women able to handle their own affairs. According to numerous legal precedents, only lunatics, idiots, and those totally without sense were judged to be completely of unsound mind and unable to control property. Even as late as 1836, the Supreme Court of Pennsylvania rejected a petition for guardianship of John Beaumont, an elderly property owner. Although they found Beaumont to be far less capable than he had been in his middle age, they pronounced him far from "entirely destitute of understanding." Relying on the standard definition of *non compos mentis*, the court denied the authority of the lunacy commission over elderly individuals who retained at least part of their reason. The court assumed that such persons could still manage their affairs and play a vital role in their families.[59]

In 1843, however, state courts legally recognized Ray's argument about declining ability in old age and adopted a new definition of old age that emphasized its inabilities and weakened state. According to Judge Patton in the precedent-setting M'Elroy case, an aged individual who disrupted his family and behaved in socially unacceptable ways could be classified as incompetent. In place of the powerful patriarch who played a vital role in the balance of nature or had valued lessons to teach the young, the court substituted the image of a senile old man whose increasing debility and improper conduct—while not evidence of the complete loss of sanity—required "the shield of law be thrown round him, his family, his friends, and his estate."[60]

Most significantly, both Judge Patton and Appellate Judge Huston of the Pennsylvania Supreme Court based their decisions on a new conception of aging that differed dramatically from traditional theories of divine balance or reciprocal roles. The court's ruling was tied directly to the newly emerging medical model of growing old. Rejecting the notion of guardianship only in the case of total loss of reason, Judge Patton cited the importance of medical theory as explained "in the books." Complete insanity was not necessary for guardianship; some faculties of the mind could be deranged while others remained unimpaired.[61] On appeal, Judge Huston supported Patton's decision, declaring issues of insanity "a matter more of medical than judicial cognizance." In place of the traditional understanding of *non compos mentis*, the judges affirmed the importance of relying on current scientific evidence.[62] The medical expert rather than the minister or even traditional legal precedent was deemed the best authority on the aging process.

The Industrial Era

By the second half of the century, the medical model of aging dominated beliefs about old age. In northern advice books to and about the old, the portrait of the powerful, authoritative, and somewhat threatening elder had completely faded, replaced by a depiction of senescence that emphasized its inescapable weaknesses and infirmities.[63] All aging individuals—even the once seemingly strong patriarch—were now characterized as experiencing significant decline with the passage of years. No longer seen as repositories of wisdom or even examples of Christian resignation, they were portrayed as longtime sufferers, weighed down by the inevitable and inescapable infirmities of old age.

This depiction of the elderly reflected a significant evolution in both the nature of advice given to the old and the source of the recommendations. In the industrial United States, new professional groups staked out their claim as authorities over the entire aging process. While ministers continued to discuss the relationship between death and aging, lawyers, doctors, social workers, sociologists, and pension advocates all assumed increasing authority over the interpretation of the needs of the elderly and the meaning of their last days. In contrast to the preindustrial period, the writings of experts on old age spoke little of God's harmony or order. Endorsing and advancing the nascent studies of the earlier pathologists, these new professionals declared that the elderly retained few productive or even functional roles in the modern world. Basing their characterization on the ever-growing—and seemingly unchallenged—number of scientific theories and statistical studies, these authorities emphasized the weaknesses and infirmities of all elderly persons and often assumed that an adversarial relationship existed among family members. In their view, the old could neither provide the young with intellectual lessons nor guide them in proper morality and righteousness. And in contrast to preindustrial advice, even the close relationship to death had lost its sanctity; the approaching demise of the old seemed only to demonstrate their complete obsolescence. According to the admonitions of the new authorities, old age was nothing more than a thoroughly debilitated, dependent, and unworthy stage of existence.

Central to this new conception of aging was the growing influence of the medical profession, as its definition of old age became the basis for wide-ranging advice literature to and about old age. By the end of the nineteenth century, in fact, the warnings about the negative effects of old age had become increasingly extreme. While Ray had concluded that not all elderly people would suffer dementia, late-nineteenth- and early-twentieth-century U.S. physicians often asserted that in old age there was little hope of avoiding "senile" physical and mental deterioration. With increasing age, they argued, both the body and the mind underwent severe alteration. Blood vessels and cells became less efficient; the body had little hope of retaining vitality or recovering from illness. Anatomically, physiologically, and psychologically, the aging body could not be arrested from progressive and inevitable degeneration.[64]

To a great degree, the pessimism of the medical model of aging actually reflected the physician's inability to define the cause of aging or to separate normal aging from pathological decline. Increasingly, scientific studies argued that the line between the physiology of old age and its pathology was difficult, if not impossible, to delineate. I. L. Nascher, the leading early-twentieth-century authority on aging, emphasized the difficulty of deciding what characterized health and what qualified as disease in individuals of advanced years. "It is impossible," he wrote in 1910,

> to draw a sharp line between health and disease in old age. With every organ and tissue undergoing a degenerative change which affects the physiological functions, it is a matter for personal opinion to determine at what point the changes in the anatomic features and physiological functions depart from the normal changes of senility and to what degree.[65]

Not surprisingly, then, late-nineteenth- and early-twentieth-century doctors rarely expected even the most modern therapeutics to effect great change in the old. No treatment could ever hope to restore permanently "senile" cells and tissues to their healthy, middle-aged state; no drug could stop pathological deterioration from taking place. In old age, doctors assumed, the normative progression for the old was from health through disease and ultimately to extinction. "In maturity," wrote Nascher, "nature cures; in senility, nature kills. In maturity the physician tries to aid nature; in senility, he tries to thwart nature and retard the natural senile process which ends in death."[66]

This pessimistic characterization of old age did not deter physicians from creating age-specific diagnoses of elderly persons' ills or tailoring advice distinctly to the last stage of life. The evolving conception of senescence tended to place all aspects of the elderly's existence under the physicians' authority, as they valiantly strove to impede the patient's ultimate fate. Since the entire aging process was equivalent to a severe pathological state, even seemingly healthy old people needed to confer regularly with a physician to monitor their inevitable decline, preserve their dissipating energy, and retard their irreversible degeneration.

Doctors not only felt confident in discussing the care (although certainly not the cure) of senile diseases but also assumed authority over all aspects of the elderly's behavior. According to the evolving perception of old age, to be "senile" was no longer merely to be old; it was to be in need of constant medical intervention. Nascher believed that

> the old man does not know what is best for him; he cannot realize that his organism cannot stand or withstand the strains which were formerly put upon it; he cannot accommodate himself to new conditions brought about by the progress of civilization. If he has been accustomed to a certain routine, he will want to continue in that routine and he will depart therefrom only when the weakened system makes him incapable of continuing therein.[67]

Physicians' admonitions to the old addressed a wide variety of activities and endeavors. According to the predominant view of senescence, no organ could escape experiencing the ravages of time. As ossification and calcification destroyed the tissues of the heart, they also eroded the powers of the mind. In advice literature to the old as well as in medical texts for the colleagues, they dictated a regimen for the aged that emphasized the weaknesses and limitations of all elderly persons. The elderly could no longer hope to retain the physical or mental endeavors of the past. Once they entered advanced age, they had to restructure their lives to conform to the doctors' recommendations.

Most important, the old—especially elderly men—were to retire from the labors of their youth. The industrial pace of work, doctors agreed, tended to dissipate the abilities of the worker. "After sixty," wrote Dr. Alfred Loomis in 1888, "failure to recognize the changed condition and a continuance in the business habits of earlier life . . . are often no better than suicide."[68] Excessive interest in work would lead to a stroke; inordinate labor would tax an already weakened heart. "The patient," declared Dr. Gutherie Rankin in 1904, "must lead an absolutely quiet and uneventful life [and] curtail his business responsibilities. . . ."[69] Doctors advised the old to withdraw from the "hurly-burly" of society and to concentrate on preparing for the afterlife.[70]

Along with their cautions about business and labor, physicians also stressed the importance of the elderly's diet. Indulgences in food or drink were clearly habits of the past. Meals had to be sharply limited in light of the aged individuals' naturally weakened condition. Most physicians advised the old to regulate the amount and types of foods they ate. Like children, they were cautioned to consume only the most bland and easily assimilated meals. Red meats, spices, coffee, and heavy drink no longer suited the senile digestion. If an elderly man "continues to eat as in middle age," wrote Dr. William Gilman Thompson in 1906, "he will become very fat or have gout or rheumatism, and shorten his life." Instead, the old were cautioned to recognize the debilitated state of their intestines and cells and adopt a strictly age-based—and physician-approved—plan of nourishment.[71]

Similarly, doctors advised the old to alter their style and forms of exercise. Certain activities, wrote Dr. Fernand Lagrange in 1891, were "absolutely forbidden." Aged individuals who continued to fence or use gymnastic apparatus were simply signing their own death certificates. Quiet walking, gardening, and gentle horseback riding were far more suited to the aged constitution.[72]

Time and again, physicians argued that they knew more about the elderly than the aged knew about themselves; their advice was not based on simple intuition or sentiment but on indisputable findings of medical research. In language that stressed the authority of the physician and the subservience of the elderly patient, doctors declared the legitimacy of their role as expert. "The physiologic reason for urging care and persistence in retaining elasticity of tissues," declared Dr. J. Madison Taylor, "is to be found in the fact that sclerotic changes, and faulty attitudes, combine to interfere with peripheral vascular competence as well as peripheral innervation."[73] Lay persons could hardly argue with such pseudo-scientific counsel. They could only place their entire way of life in the hands of medical experts.

In giving such advice, however, doctors remained extremely cautious. Unlike longevity experts of the past, they did not believe that such recommendations would lead to revolutionary changes in the old. They could not promise additional years of activity or a revitalization of lost energy.[74] Diet and general routine, wrote Dr. Rankin, could only affect the "time and speed of decay." Ultimately, doctors agreed, the old would experience progressive degeneration, and the patient would eventually suffer "a breakdown at the weakest spot."[75] The aged, therefore, had little choice but to admit their weaknesses and radically alter their lives.

In making such recommendations, the advice of doctors differed sharply from that given by authorities in the past. In numerous articles and monographs, most physicians rarely acknowledged that advanced age could be accompanied by socially valuable characteristics. Their elderly patients neither spoke with great wisdom nor possessed useful experiences.[76] "When an old man utters great thoughts," wrote Dr. George Beard in 1876, "it is not age but youth that speaks through the lips of age."[77] According to the medical model of aging, the elderly demonstrated only increasing physical and mental degeneration. In advice to retire and to redefine life, physicians held out little hope that the old would continue to play a worthwhile role in the community. Above all else, they cautioned, the old had to acknowledge that they were debilitated patients in need of complete care. On the brink of their own demise, they had to alter their lives to ensure survival.

In 1905, this perception of enfeebled old age stimulated national attention and debate as the result of a speech given by Dr. William Osler. Upon his departure from Johns Hopkins, Osler pondered the relative contributions of aging individuals to society. Little question existed, he stated, of "the comparative uselessness of men above the age of forty. . . . The effective, moving, vitalizing work of the world is done between the ages of twenty-five and forty—these fifteen golden years of plenty, the anabolic or constructive period, in which there is always a balance in the mental bank and the credit is still good." For those over sixty, Osler advised complete withdrawal from active life, not only for themselves but for their employers as well. Declaring the "uselessness of men above sixty years of age," he urged his audience to consider "the incalculable benefit it would be in commercial, political and in professional life, if as a matter of course, men stopped work at this age. . . . " Osler added, in a less than serious remark, that the English novelist Anthony Trollope had found a solution to the problem of old age. In *The Fixed Period*, Trollope had college professors retire at age sixty, complete a year of contemplation, then meet their end through the inhalation of chloroform.[78]

Popular newspapers reported widely and sensationally on Osler's speech. While a few took the reference to chloroform seriously, most focused on Osler's view of the value of the old and middle-aged. Arguing that individuals such as Abraham Lincoln and Benjamin Franklin contributed a great deal to the nation after age forty, they attempted to disprove Osler's view of senescent uselessness.[79] But Osler's opinion reflected his own personal experience as well as the implications of medical research. His scheme was indisputable, he declared, "to any one who, like myself, is nearing the limit, and who has made a careful study of the calamities which may befall men during the seventh and eighth decades."[80]

Osler did not expect any great outcry over this address. Medical science, he assumed, had already substantiated the great physical and mental decline that accompanied old age.[81] Moreover, his view of aging was not limited to a few research physicians. The medical model of growing old had spread well beyond the medical community.[82] In 1876, in the midst of a national depression, economist Francis A. Walker had called for the passage of "factory acts prohibiting the labor of all classes beyond the term which physiological science accepts as consistent with soundness and vigor."[83] By the turn of the century, industrial efficiency experts also embraced the idea of the limitations of the elderly worker. Even advocates for the aged adopted the medical model and used it to explain the apparently ever-rising impoverishment of the old. Few challenged the idea that the old were unproductive; experts concurred that old age led most individuals to decline and impoverishment.[84]

By the early twentieth century, the new model had also begun to influence business and government policy. In establishing mandatory retirement programs and age limits for hiring, businessmen justified their actions by asserting the incapacity of the "superannuated man" to compete with younger, more productive workers.[85] As we discussed in chapter 3, the real reasons for mandatory retirement and age limits were far more complicated than simple productivity estimates. Employers, however, used the new medical model as an explanation for age-based labor management policies.

In 1907, the United States government officially recognized the medical implications of growing old. A revision of the rules for the allocation of Civil War pensions linked decreasing physical ability directly to advancing age. According to the new directive, upon attaining age sixty-two, a veteran would be considered "disabled one-half in ability; at sixty-five, he was labeled as two-thirds disabled, and reached complete disability after his seventieth birthday." Such advice to government bureaucrats recognized neither individual ability nor family condition. It simply linked the person's years to declining capabilities.[86]

Even popular culture recognized the notion of declining abilities as the prevailing model for growing old. According to the lyrics of numerous popular songs of the day, the old had little to give the young: their energies had passed away, their decline was inevitable. In tunes such as "Denied a Home" (1895), "Don't Leave Your Mother When Her Hair Turns Grey" (1900), and "There's a Mother Old and Gray Who Needs Me Now" (1911), elderly individuals were portrayed as physically weak and unable to provide for themselves. Their very survival depended on the benevolence of their children. "Don't leave your old home now," advised Chas. Osborne and Ernest J. Symons in "Stick to Your Mother, Mary" (1913). "She's old and gray and wants you to stay. So don't take a year of her life away."[87] According to the lyricists, the old no longer represented a balance of nature or even the preservers of necessary skills. Power had passed completely to the young; the most the old could expect was support and kindness.

Inherent in the words of the songs, as in the prescriptions of physicians, was the notion that aging was a time of loss and decline. Stripped of its role of providing balance to the community, old age seemed little more than a state to be widely feared and strongly despised. Not surprisingly, then, in the early twentieth century, a new type of advice literature addressed the old. In scores of magazines and journals, popular writers admonished the reader on ways to avoid old age entirely. Although they gave passing mention to food or drink, they concentrated on the psychology of "staying young." In articles such as "The Quest for Prolonged Youth," "The Art of Not Growing Old," "On Keeping Young," and "Let's Stay Young Together," experts offered similar advice: deny the process of aging; think and behave as if you were still a young adult. To the readers of the *Forum*, Della T. Lutes cautioned that "a youthful spirit can dominate gray hair or wrinkled hands, if it is not cramped and cumbered by the mental limitations of 'years.'" Above all else, she cautioned her elderly readers, "remember always, *don't act your age.* . . ."[88]

Such counsel differed sharply from the colonial admonitions to recognize one's age and act accordingly. While eighteenth-century experts had argued that aging brought with it wisdom and understanding, early-twentieth-century writers could find little physical or psychological advantage to being old. The aging mind no longer possessed great knowledge; old hands retained little valuable skill. Old age, according to the twentieth-century writers, represented nothing more than "decay, disillusion, weariness."[89] It stood not as a symbol of divine order or a lesson to the young, or as the final point of symmetry in the life cycle, but as the most distressing of obstacles to be denied and, ultimately, overcome.

Given the dire predictions of experts, popular advice responded appropriately: avoid old age entirely. In the early twentieth century, scientific magazines even informed their readers that such a lofty goal was not inconceivable. Reporting on experiments to return youthful vigor to "senile" animals through glandular transplants and grafting, magazines such as *Scientific American* proclaimed that the fountain of youth was at hand. The magazine's editors sharply criticized all individuals who scoffed at the novel experiments. The doubters' lack of belief, they declared, was simply proof of their scientific ignorance. In an extended interview with Dr. Serge Voronoff, who had performed glandular grafting and transplants, a writer described the scientist's experiments with unrestrained praise. Through pictures and descriptions of "senile" animals that had been returned to their youthful state, the reporter held out the hope for the eventual eradication of old age.[90]

In formulating such advice and predictions, popular writers addressed fears of growing old that went far beyond the dependent and impoverished elderly. In the 1920s, fashions and habits emphasized the vitality and distinctiveness of youth. As models of generational rebellion, F. Scott and Zelda Fitzgerald won admiration and widespread imitation for their renunciation of their elders' manners and mores.[91] Such vilification of the "ways of the old" was not limited to an attack on the elderly; in the popular emphasis on the adolescent beauty and spirit, even the middle-aged became targets for denigration. Writers agreed that men and women beyond age forty were hopelessly outdated.[92]

In popular advice literature, therefore, writers often directed suggestions to middle-aged, middle-class men and women who dreaded the passage of years. They as well as the elderly were cautioned to redress any obvious signs of old age. In comparison to the vitality of youth, their sagging bodies, gray hair and wrinkles were visible—although, if possible, concealable—marks of growing uselessness. Writers cautioned their readers that they should never admit to "thinning hair, false teeth, arch supporters, hardening arteries, sagging muscles, [and] failing eyes."[93] In order not to look "out of date," old-fashioned, or unemployable, the public was advised to avoid any hint of oncoming senescence.

The Social Security Era

Throughout the 1920s and early 1930s, such "staying young" articles continued to advise the old on how to avoid looking and acting their age. In giving counsel to avert being categorized as old, the publications spoke directly to the fears of a public beset by social and economic uncertainty. In the maturing industrial economy, the long-standing difficulties of job seeking became more obvious. The extended job searches of the unemployed often exhausted savings and forced them to rely on family or friends. In the Great Depression, as banks failed, mortgages were defaulted, and pension and insurance plans were wiped out, aging men and women lost their planned security for old age and families were once again forced to deal with the issue of old-age support. Among the truly desperate, few alternatives existed; they had little choice but to resort to charity or—for the most impoverished—to submit to the forbidding almshouse. The Depression greatly exacerbated the challenges facing middle-aged workers thrown out of work and, perhaps more important, raised the anxieties of those who remained employed. Despite guidance on looking and feeling young, their advanced years could hardly be denied—or even hidden by hair dye.

The establishment of Social Security clearly addressed the widespread fear of being seen as old and obsolete. It did so, however, by removing work from the life of the aged and replacing it with a new stage: retirement. At first, benefits supported those aging job seekers whose chances of securing new employment were slim. By the 1950s, however, higher benefit levels, rising real incomes during middle age, and private pensions had encouraged active workers to leave the work force permanently. Social Security reduced the worry that gray hair or wrinkles would lead directly to humiliating joblessness, family impoverishment, or complete dependency. Although advice in popular magazines on impeding the onset of old age did not disappear altogether, the allocation of pensions and the resulting growth in retirement created new concerns and interests. With the institutionalization of a period of leisure, a guaranteed fixed income, and an increasing maze of government regulation and bureaucracy, new issues faced the elderly. Advisers soon appeared to counsel the old on how to plan their retirement, finance their economic security, and organize their leisure activities. (See illustration, 'Planning for Retirement.')

Much of this advice reflected new academic interest in the process of growing old. In the late nineteenth and early twentieth centuries, physicians such as Nascher had called for the creation of a specialty in the diseases of old age. Coining the term *geriatrics*, Nascher argued that doctors needed to treat the old by standards and norms that corresponded to their advanced age rather than by comparing their health and abilities to individuals of far younger ages. Without such a specialty, Nascher contended, the line between treatable diseases and normal physiological changes in the elderly would never be discerned. The old would always be perceived as hopeless invalids who, in comparison to the healthy middle-aged, were in a rapid and inevitable state of decline.[94] In the early twentieth century, however, few physicians answered Nascher's call. The limited number of elderly patients, the negative stereotypes of these individuals, and the ambiguous definition of normal and abnormal development in the old all deterred the establishment of the specialty. Devoting themselves to more lucrative and specific fields, physicians failed to award geriatrics the status of a significant medical endeavor.[95]

Beginning in the 1940s, however, such attitudes slowly began to change. With the establishment of the American Geriatrics Society in 1942 and the Gerontological Society of America in 1945, old age became recognized as an interdisciplinary field worthy of research and interpretation.[96] A number of scientists searched for a definition of normal aging different from the pathological model of their predecessors. As with Nascher, the researchers were still troubled by the difficulty of distinguishing normal old age from its pathological changes. "Even pathologists," conceded Edward Stieglitz in 1943 in his groundbreaking collection of articles, *Geriatric Medicine*, "are by no means unanimous in their opinion of what constitutes changes of normal senescence and what alterations are evidences of diseases." Yet Stieglitz and the contributors to *Geriatric Medicine* were far more optimistic than earlier physicians. The field was still in its infancy; he was sure that his call for "base line data of normality in relation to age" would soon be developed.[97] Moreover, the early geriatricians were no longer as pessimistic about relieving the ills of old age. By defining normal old age, they could identify and then alleviate numerous pathological conditions that often accompanied aging.[98] In contrast to past experts, they argued that old age was *not* a disease but a normal and ultimately healthy part of the life cycle.

In the 1940s and 1950s, the research of Stieglitz and his colleagues reflected their medical training. Working largely from a medical model of aging, scientists focused on the physiological and anatomical process of growing old.[99] By the 1960s and 1970s, however, academic gerontology had begun to expand beyond its initial medical focus. Scholars in the new field were strongly influenced by the growing proportion of the elderly in the population, the greater affluence of the old, and the political stature of the Social Security Administration. Incorporating the work of humanists and social scientists, experts explored the social, economic, and philosophical meaning of growing old. These researchers continued to search for definable "norms" in old age.[100] Yet their studies also revealed the dramatic diversity of old age among individuals and cultures. Attacking the stereotypes widely shared by society, they portrayed a far more diverse and complex old age than had been projected by earlier professionals. As the life expectancy of the elderly increased and the proportion of the population over sixty-five rose, writers acknowledged that the old could not be classified as a uniformly dependent and needy group. According to their findings, growing old in the United States was shaped by a vast array of biological, sociological, economic, and individual factors.[101]

No work was more influential in attacking prevailing stereotypes of aging than Robert N. Butler's *Why Survive? Being Old in America.*[102] Awarded the Pulitzer Prize, the 1975 book brought widespread attention to the existence of "ageism"—a word first coined by Butler in 1969—and to the pernicious effects such sentiments had upon the old in the United States.[103] Listing numerous myths about aging that had little basis in reality, Butler attacked popular beliefs that classified the old as unproductive, inflexible, and senile. He called for a new understanding of aging among both professionals and the public at large, one that awarded dignity to the old.

The success of Butler's book led to the publication of scores of advice books for the elderly and their families. In the late 1970s and 1980s, this literature uniformly repudiated the idea that the old were passive victims of their age whose best hope was to take all steps to hide their advancing years. But such contemporary writers, while rejecting the disease and dependence model of the industrial period, did not hark back to the preindustrial model of old age as providing a harmonious balance with youth and middle age. In contrast to the past, these popular writers did not consider—and at times even denied—the importance of divine plan, the balance of nature, or the need to modify the lives of the old according to their inescapable disabilities. Adopting the perspective of the growing body of academic research, writers instead advised the old to understand, then to control, the significant factors that structured their last years. The best old age, they stressed, was based neither on the lessons they could teach the young nor on the denial of their years but on ensuring health, wealth, and, above all else, independence in the final years.[104]

Many advice books first began by attacking prevailing stereotypes about old age. The authors concurred that despite popular beliefs, the old in the

United States were neither lonely, dependent, nor senseless.[105] The great majority of elderly people, they argued, lived autonomous and active—if nonemployed—lives. Unlike past authorities on old age, mid-twentieth-century experts no longer encouraged the aged to seek rest and reflection. Rather, advocating continued activity and involvement, they detailed the best exercise, diet, and habits for maintaining health and well-being—and for actually enjoying old age.[106]

These writers recognized that dramatic changes often occurred to individuals once they withdrew from the labor market. In the late nineteenth century, experts had often promoted the benefits to society of mass retirement of the old. They had portrayed elderly workers as inefficient and enfeebled. The continued employment of the old, they had argued, was a detriment both to the aging individuals and to the nation's overall productivity.[107] Fifty years later, such arguments were neither applicable nor necessary. With the establishment of Social Security, retirement had become the expected and established norm for the elderly. Indeed, to the surprise of many academics who thought work essential to self-worth, older workers began to look forward to retirement. As a result, experts on aging focused on how the old should best spend their socially mandated leisure hours. Retirement, they concurred, did not disqualify the old from continuing to live productively and independently. Detailing the numerous possibilities offered by school, hobbies, volunteer work, and new occupations, they portrayed the "golden years" not as a time of inactivity but as an occasion for new experiences and opportunities.[108]

Stressing the advantages of retirement, experts warned their readers of the need to be financially secure. "Most elderly," wrote David A. Tombs, "want to be independent. They do not want to rely on their children for housing, care, or money."[109] In contrast to the past, mid-twentieth-century advice books did not portray the elderly as helpless individuals who needed to place their lives in the hands of others. Rather, they concurred that if the old were informed about their legal, economic, and social rights, they could control their own fate.[110]

These experts attempted to provide elderly readers with the means of guaranteeing autonomy. Their books, as one author explained, were intended "to offer the knowledge and tools necessary for elderly people to get what they want—in their medical treatment, their finances, and their right to maintain control over their lives."[111] Exploring such issues as Medicare, Medicaid, life insurance, pensions, and Social Security, the authors agreed that in matters of health, housing, or resources, elderly persons who could chart and command their daily lives experienced satisfaction and contentment.[112]

This key sense of independence also shaped experts' counsel on intergenerational relations. In the past, authorities on aging had assumed that the widowed old would eventually reside with their kin; numerous stories and articles listed ways to reduce or eliminate the resulting household tension.[113] The allocation of Social Security, however, had a decided impact on such advice and expectations. Recognizing a principle long upheld by both the elderly and their children (although not always financially achievable), experts now agreed that it was best for the old not to have to reside with relations. By the 1970s, only 14 percent of the old lived with their children; most chose to reside elsewhere. The ideal, writers agreed, was to establish strategies that allowed elderly individuals to dwell in their own households or enter alternate living arrangements that guaranteed continued control and independence.[114]

Yet while experts advised the old to maintain independent residences, they did not ignore the issue of family relations and responsibilities. For authorities on aging, the obligations of the adult children toward the elderly parents were of prime importance.[115] With the increasing longevity and decreasing fertility of the U.S. population, most elderly individuals experienced numerous years of life after retirement or widowhood, but with fewer adult children to provide for their care. Experts agreed that even though middle-aged individuals often lacked numerous siblings to share in the care of the old, most fulfilled their obligations to their aging parents well. Little basis existed, they contended, for the prevailing myth that modern-day individuals had abandoned their parents to substandard nursing homes or inadequate care. "The irony of the myth," wrote gerontologist Elaine Brody, "is that nowadays adult children provide more care and more difficult care to more parents over much longer periods of time than they did in the good old days."[116] Dubbed the "sandwich generation," middle-aged adults often were required to make great sacrifices to provide adequately for their spouses, their children, and their parents.

Such responsibilities, experts concurred, often placed great physical and psychological burdens on the caregiver. Numerous books advised middle-aged adults on how to deal with elderly parents. This literature bore little resemblance to such counsel in past centuries. It spoke little of reciprocal roles, rarely emphasized the particular talents of the aged, and hardly advocated following the "medical model" of disease and irreversible degeneration. Instead, it outlined the most appropriate forms of support and services that might assist both the caregivers and their parents.

Above all else, experts emphasized the advice they had given the old themselves. "Allow your parents to remain independent and autonomous as long as possible," wrote Anne Averyt. "Don't give help where help is not required."[117] Rather than trying to "parent" the parents, middle-aged adults were cautioned that the most effective assistance they could provide was in the form of social and psychological support. Publishing rules for "how to talk to your aging parents" and checklists for the alleviation of intergeneratio-

nal conflicts, writers stressed the importance of allowing the old to determine their requirements and fulfill their desires.[118] "You should not decide
what is best for [your aging parent]," cautioned James Halperin, "where she
should live, what she should eat, or how she should take care of herself.
Often the best way to give help is to make sure that you do not overfunction
for your parent. If you are too helpful your parent may become helpless."[119]
Moreover, middle-aged individuals were advised not to feel guilty if they
could not provide for every aspect of the elderly's care. Instead, writers cautioned, the best assistance they could provide was to help aging parents de-
sign their own future, even if that future entailed planning for the death.[120]
As with advice to the aging parents themselves, experts reiterated that above
all else, children should encourage and support an old age founded on autonomy and independence.

By the 1970s, the advice of experts on old age differed sharply from admonitions in the past. Few writers stressed the importance of divine balance;
they rarely focused on the significance of reciprocal roles and obligations.
Nor did contemporary gerontologists categorize the old according to the
medical model of the late nineteenth century. Old age, they argued, was not
uniformly a time of disease and dependence. Rather, in advice to the elderly,
authorities stressed the possibility of a healthy and economically sound senescence, with continued intimacy and exchange.

To a large degree, such counsel reflected the significant impact Social
Security had on the lives of the old and their relatives. Before the welfare
state, few individuals were secure enough to live independently or to separate
themselves permanently from the labor market and spend their last years in
leisure. Only the extremely wealthy followed this pattern; the middle and
working classes generally remained tied to family and work as bulwarks
against unforeseen disasters. When past experts had cautioned the old on
their appropriate roles or the ways to hide their progressing age, they were
describing the best means for maintaining at least an adequate life-style. The
allocation of Social Security clearly changed these concerns. In freeing the
elderly from work and co-residence, Social Security created the prospect that
for the first time, the majority of elderly individuals might live independent
and autonomous existences.

Social Security also removed the experts' focus from the contest for
power and control that often divided generations.[121] Colonial ministers cautioned the old to relinquish their authority as they aged; late-nineteenth- and
early-twentieth-century analysts admonished society to recognize the increasing powerlessness and dependence of the elderly. With the creation of the
welfare state, the issue of power no longer received central focus. The elderly
were advised to control their own financial, medical, and residential choices.

The establishment of Social Security had an additional impact on advice to the old. With the creation of the welfare state and the growth in the nation's elderly population, aging, as William Graebner, Carroll Estes, and others have noted, has truly become a large-scale enterprise.[122] From medical authorities who trace the health of the old to financial planners who control pensions and estates and even to experts who advise the experts on aging, the elderly have ceaselessly been examined and discussed.[123] In the second half of the twentieth century, the old have become subject to an ever-growing body of expert advice and investigation, all oriented toward the ideal autonomous existence.

In a sense, much of this advice represents both an acceptance of the stereotypes of the past, which continue to portray an inactive old age as repulsive, and an attempt to transform cultural prejudices. While fear of old age still crowds the pages of women's magazine and urges middle-aged men to exercise and to repair retreating hairlines, a universal Social Security system and increasing affluence allows many of the elderly to defy the predictions of a dependent and debilitated last stage. Additional wealth and a guaranteed income also assure the old that they will not have to strike the correct "balance" with the young, whether in the family household or at the place of employment. Armed with vitamins, with magazines that discuss estate planning—as well as fashions—and with scores of advice books, the elderly have been cautioned that the best old age is one that realizes the ideals of independence and autonomy. In the Social Security era, anything less seems to constitute a most obsolete old age.

6

A New History of Old Age

WE HAVE ARGUED that the old have never constituted a single entity, uniformly loved or universally envied, all-powerful or all-impoverished. Rather, the elderly population has always been as complex as other age groups. Class, gender, race, ethnicity, and region have provided these men and women with a wide variety of roles. Yet in tracing their past, we have found that history has had a powerful influence on the elderly as a group, altering their social position and transforming their relationship to children, work, and community. These historical effects can best be explained through the structure of three general periods: the preindustrial, industrial, and Social Security eras. In each period, the elderly's family arrangements, their economic well-being, work, welfare, and advice have displayed unique characteristics. In each, demography, economic conditions, and state policy as well as culture have combined to influence the experience and the meaning of old age.

Important and surprising continuities certainly appear across the whole history. In contrast to an assumption common to both observers in the past and present, the great majority of aged persons have never been impoverished or isolated. For the most part, older people have had sufficient resources and vibrant relationships with their kin. Their economic and familial security demonstrated that they had achieved a major goal in American life.

Nevertheless, a persistent minority of the old remained poverty-stricken, a minority strikingly similar from one period to the next. For many unmarried women, African Americans, and ethnic minorities, the last stage of life was indeed a time of destitution. Old age itself, however, was rarely the sole source of their impoverishment. Poor in young adulthood and middle age, these aged persons simply arrived at old age with few of the assets obtained by their more successful counterparts. Having lost or never having acquired the "useful children" of married peers and having been unable to accumulate the economic reserves of more successful counterparts, they endured the last yeas of life as they had endured the rest. Alone and impoverished, they were considered, at best, the worthy recipients of their communities' benevolence.

Preindustrial America

In early America, the elderly seldom conformed to the long-assumed depiction of preindustrial old age. Rarely presiding over generations of kin, they generally lived out their days in two-generational households. The demographic structure of society largely dictated this arrangement: late age of marriage and childbirth, high infant mortality, and low life expectancy combined to limit the coexistence of numerous generations of kin. Within nuclear households, however, the old often held considerable authority. Through control of valuable farmland, they commanded the activities of children and the profits of their labor. Their continued possession of property even encouraged the respect and obedience of these offspring. Children who desired to inherit valuable property rarely deserted their parents or rebelled from their decrees.

Such power, however, remained severely limited. The relative poverty of preindustrial society allowed few individuals to enjoy their leisure. Most aged individuals worked; only increasing ill health or debility provided them with the justification to end all labor. But such withdrawal from work had negative ramifications. By passing power to the young, aged men removed themselves from their privileged roles of moral authority and economic leadership.

For aged women as well, power in the preindustrial period had exacting restrictions. As a woman's status was generally derived from that of her husband, the death of her spouse brought a marked change in power and property. Even for women who received generous allotments from their husbands' estates, the distribution of family wealth entailed a redefinition of status and authority. Although some women managed to increase the family's estate, most were far less fortunate. Sharing wealth with their offspring or receiving only a "widow's third," they were often deprived of both the assets they had brought into the marriage and the wealth they had helped accumulate after a lifetime of labor. For many, the death of their husbands meant they had to surrender the authority awarded to them as spouse of the household head. In their old age, the traditional family hierarchy was radically altered. No longer sharing control with their husbands and relegated to specific rooms and possessions, they became dependents in their own homes.

For impoverished women as well as destitute men, old age in the preindustrial period hardly represented great power. Although only a minority of the old, such individuals were well represented among the needy who received outdoor assistance, charitable aid, and almshouse shelter. Even in colonial America, welfare policy acknowledged that most impoverished old people deserved consideration and respect. Yet the effect of such recognition was rather limited. If the advanced years of the needy old offered them privilege, it was simply the privilege of a "worthy" dependency.

The acknowledgment of age as a unique time of life, however, permeated advice to and about the old in the preindustrial period. For powerful aged householders as well as dependents in children's homes and even paupers reliant upon the community's good will, the value of old age was clearly determined by more than economics. The elderly's links to family, long years of acquired knowledge and the possession of valued skills all helped to ensure their value, even in the face of declining physical abilities or decreasing prosperity. For ministers and magistrates who spoke about the significance of old age, the importance of the last years of life was not based solely on the wealth the elders possessed. Rather, given the high child and adult mortality of preindustrial society, the individuals' long years of life placed them in a special position. They had survived the ravages of a frontier society, of illness and accidents; they had been fortunate enough to gain knowledge and understanding based on decades of experience.

Yet in describing old age, authorities did not create the image of an all-powerful hierarchy. Rather, they emphasized that the status of the old was determined by well-structured and equally balanced relationships. While the old of the colonial era were often assumed to have gained wisdom and understanding, they were advised that their position was not without its disadvantages. With old age came the need to redefine longstanding social roles and obligations. In increasingly strident tones, early-nineteenth-century ministers argued that the elderly had to accept their place in the life cycle and conform to its limitations. As paragons of longevity, as examples of Christian resignation, even as paupers who allowed the community to express its benevolence, they served well-defined roles in the natural order of the universe.

In preindustrial society, then, the old had certain economic, familial, and cultural advantages, but they could never be secure in their status as unchallenged and independent patriarchs. Even though many possessed greater-than-average assets, few had sufficient wealth to ensure their financial security; most depended on the filial devotion of hard-working sons and daughters. Before industrialization, old age was characterized by continued struggle and interdependence among generations. Old people were advised to strive for balance and harmony in their own lives, with their kin, and in their communities.

The Industrial Era

With industrialization, old age assumed new parameters. Traditionally, the change has been described as a sharp decline in power and status. According to early-twentieth-century advocates for the old, the preindustrial economy provided the greatest support for the elderly: the farm guaranteed their economic survival, while dependent and subservient kin relied upon their elders' experience and knowledge. By the end of the industrial era, however, the dominant role of the old had been transformed. Impoverished by an economy that provided wages based on speed and deserted by children who found better opportunities elsewhere, the old were left in fragmented households, struggling to survive and destined ultimately to become paupers in the almshouse's wards.

We have offered a very different critique of industrialization's effect upon the elderly and the formation of their families. Traditional views assume that the factory denigrated the older worker and forced the elderly into both destitution and isolation from their families. We have found, however, that industrialization brought with it real gains for most older Americans. For large numbers of unskilled, landless laborers, who in preindustrial America had little access to the ladder of farm ownership or who had fallen off its rungs, industrialization brought significant economic gain. By the first decades of the twentieth century, most older persons possessed wealth and assets that were unattainable to all but a few preindustrial elders.

As industrialization did not impoverish the majority of older Americans, neither did it leave them alone and isolated. In the late nineteenth century, in fact, a higher percentage of elderly resided in complex or extended households than had their preindustrial peers. Rather than depriving the elderly of their family network, urbanization actually increased the tendency of the old to live in extended or complex households. The urban elderly markedly exceeded their farm and especially their village counterparts in presiding over households that included adult children and members of other generations.

The emerging urban-industrial pattern of family organization rested on two central factors. First, nineteenth-century demographic change made complex households possible on a wide scale. Declining child and adult mortality, along with a drop in age of marriage and first birth, raised the possibility that large numbers of three-generational families might exist simultaneously. Where few individuals in the preindustrial era had the opportunity to reside with their children and grandchildren or other kin from different generations, by the early twentieth century, extended and complex families could commonly be formed.

Second, complex households brought measurable benefits to both generations: highly desirable living space could be divided, income could be combined, and risk could be shared. In cities where the elderly were far more likely to own property than the young, adult children could shelter themselves in the homes already established by the older generation. In many ways, complex households represented a "luxury" tied to the rising wealth of the working class. The very poor possessed neither the home nor the resources that could be shared with their dependent kin. For the more prosperous, however, extended households allowed an efficient use of shared assets.

For the old, extended and complex household arrangements provided essential resources. Despite the rise in real income experienced by male workers throughout the industrial period, the wages of the old did not keep pace with the young. By the fifth decade, they were likely to earn less than young workers. The family-based economy, however, directly addressed the relatively diminished economic power of aging household heads. By relying on the wages of their children and adding these to their own earnings, older men and women established a "family fund" over which they had primary control. With this resource, they were often able to amass considerable savings while maintaining a comfortable standard of living. Their command over the wages of other family members allowed individuals who might have experienced a decline in income to remain relatively prosperous and protected from some of the vicissitudes of industrial life. As a result, the fortunes of the majority of the elderly showed marked improvement. Rather than facing isolation and impoverishment, as commonly presumed, older people experienced a significant improvement in their standard of living and well-being.

Yet, while assuring a surprising level of economic success among the older population, intrafamilial strategies did not engender harmony. The family economy demanded numerous sacrifices from family members. To support aging kin, children cut short their education, entered the labor market, and postponed their marriages; generations found themselves unhappily obliged to reside together. By the end of the industrial era, therefore, a new pattern of family life began to emerge. With increasing affluence, working-class families moved to combine households, wealth, and resources; in contrast, even wealthier, middle-class families moved away from such complex arrangements. Encouraged by social commentators who praised the private, two-generational home, relatively prosperous elders and their children sought to establish separate households. This pattern, however, was a reflection neither of the disruption of industrialization nor of its denigration of old age. Rather, it was based on the growing prosperity of Americans and the ability of some to realize a long-preferred model of independent households. By the 1920s, the most affluent of the elderly no longer needed to rely on the continued labor of their children. Able to sustain independent households for each generation, they clearly profited from the industrial growth of the nation.

Despite the improvement in economic well-being and the creation of autonomous households among the prosperous middle class, industrialization also brought great insecurity to many of the old. Land in less-productive agricultural regions lost much of its economic and familial value. Children, eager to escape the "bondage of the farm," no longer remained with the old but migrated to factory jobs. For these rural elderly individuals, industrialization devalued the greatest source of wealth and security.[1]

For the urban elderly as well, industrialization often brought uncertainty. While the wages of the working class rose and many individuals received far more income than could be earned in farming, such wages offered none of the assurances of the family farm. Accidents, illnesses, or economic decline could threaten their ability or the ability of their children to earn accustomed income. And even for the most successful workers, old age could bring diminished economic power as new technologies and managerial policies made earlier learned skills and experiences obsolete. The rise of semiskilled production systems undermined the authority once natural to aging skilled workers. Dependent on the assessment of management, they were apt to suffer from negative evaluations of their speed and productivity and from a belief—even when no measurement was made—that aging workers were less capable. Although labor force activity among the old remained relatively stable throughout the industrial period and some elderly workers benefited from the establishment of seniority systems, aged workers had good reason to fear the unemployment spells characteristic of the industrial era. Aging job seekers faced daunting obstacles to obtaining new employment.

Such insecurity was further exacerbated by the established tenets of the public welfare system. While Americans had always judged the elderly to be deserving recipients of public and private charity, during the nineteenth century hostility to outdoor relief placed the almshouse at the center of most public welfare systems. In an effort to control the poor and reduce the numbers applying for relief, welfare authorities had eliminated most traditional public alternatives to institutionalization. In many locales, outdoor assistance was ended or curtailed; if individuals wanted aid they had little choice but to submit to the public asylum. Without sufficient resources or appropriate kin, the impoverished elderly faced the prospect of ending their lives in the punitive almshouse.

This policy had a chilling effect upon the old and their families. The horror of the almshouse was overwhelming; few individuals, whether young or old, voluntarily submitted to confinement. As a result, relatives made strenuous and costly efforts to keep their aged family members from such a dire fate. Rooms were divided and youngsters sent into the labor market in order to save impoverished aged relatives from the shame of almshouse residency. The dread of the almshouse even reached beyond those who made sacrifices for their relatives or feared their own incarceration. In the late nineteenth century, the distribution of Civil War pensions—and the rapid expansion of acceptable recipients—was tied to the long reach of the ominous almshouse. Without a widely applicable pension system, advocates claimed, the nation would be responsible for sending brave veterans to end their lives in the almshouse. Equating age with need, they argued that pensions would rescue the deserving elderly.

The long shadow of the almshouse was also instrumental in the establishment of numerous old-age homes. For urban elites who founded these asylums and devised their rules and regulations, the almshouse seemed an unjust end for hard-working, although impoverished, elders. In committing both their finances and their time, the founders of old-age homes expressed the belief that the almshouse posed a real threat to dignified old age. The inmate population of such asylums, however, was specifically limited to "worthy" individuals who possessed the same ethnic background as the founders. By requiring high entrance fees and certificates of correct moral standing, the developers of private homes intentionally excluded the "less deserving" of the needy elderly.

For those most likely to be impoverished, therefore, these alternatives had little meaning. The most desperate of the aged poor had no family to rescue them from destitution; nor could they rely upon the compassion of native-born elites, their own savings, or even their war experience. For single and widowed women without children, immigrants who had arrived in the United States since the Civil War, and impoverished African Americans who had gained no property as slaves and little as sharecroppers, the almshouse was indeed a valid threat and, for many, a harsh reality. Once they were placed in the institution, their records of admission testified to "failure" in old age. Almost in unison, the impoverished old declared they had no living relatives, tangible assets, or usable income.

As almshouses came to be dominated by the old, advocates for the elderly argued that impoverishment and institutionalization had become the likely fate of all older people in the industrial era. From the late nineteenth century to the 1920s, however, the proportion of the elderly who were institutionalized remained relatively stable; as in the past, about 2 percent of the old were confined to almshouses and other asylums. Throughout American history, most aged persons had above average wealth; the economic growth engendered by industrialization clearly reduced poverty in this age group. In large part, the increasingly dominant presence of the old in the almshouse was the result not of growing poverty but of national programs that removed younger—and, assumedly, more redeemable—inmates from the poorhouses. As a result, where once only a quarter of the inmates were elderly, by the turn of the twentieth century, the majority of almshouse residence were of advanced age. In the eyes of welfare advocates, the old had become the "natural class" of almshouse residents.

Advocates of state pensions for the elderly seized upon the almshouse statistics to justify government relief. Arguing that an increasing proportion of the elderly population suffered institutionalization and that nearly all the aged had reason to fear that the almshouse would be their fate, they maintained that an honorable society had to provide assistance to the aged in their own homes. While pension advocates overstated the degree of institutionalization among the old, their rhetoric reflected the public's fear of the almshouse and its antipathy to the central role it played in the welfare system. Although public officials tried to mollify this aversion by changing the name of the asylums or decorating them with flowers and books, the reality of the debasing institution remained. For families who struggled to keep their relatives from the poorhouse door, for the elderly who lived in its shadow, and for critics who visited its wards and mounted a persuasive campaign to provide the old with pensions, the poorhouse loomed far larger than its small inmate population warranted.

By the early twentieth century, the institution had become not just an object of horror for the extremely poor; it had also evolved into a symbol of the supposedly inevitable fate of all older Americans. While the rate of incarceration did not rise, the heavy preponderance of the aged in the poorhouse led welfare experts to conclude that the elderly themselves had become increasingly impoverished. The rise in aged inmates, these critics argued, was a sure sign of the irreversibly expanding dependency of the elderly in industrial society. With time, they assumed, all aged individuals, whether presently institutionalized or not, would face impoverishment and isolation. Subject to incurable illness, likely to experience a diminished capacity for work, or dependent on the earnings of children, they could not escape their increasing weaknesses and ultimate obsolescence.

Pension advocates were not alone in this negative characterization of old age or in calls for professional intervention. Joined by doctors, businessmen, and social scientists, numerous experts and professionals portrayed the old as the most needy and debilitated of all persons. Their characterization of old age bore no resemblance to that of the preindustrial clerics who emphasized the interdependence of generations and the divine balance of the universe. For the early-twentieth-century authorities, old age appeared as an incurable disease and a useless appendage to the business of life. Fortunate old people could strive to hide the wrinkles and gray hair; all others had little choice but to accept the ravages of time. Although clearly ageist in tone, these appeals were intended to assist the old in attaining support and assistance. Through their publications, however, experts and advocates for the old revealed the worst consequence of industrialization for the elderly; a developing professional culture concluded that the aged were incapable of living like other Americans in modern society. As a result, an unlikely chorus of efficiency experts, trade union leaders and progressive reformers pronounced the old as impoverished and in need of crucial and far-reaching age-based assistance.

Such characterizations of the last stage of life clearly endowed the pension movement with a moral imperative. State annuities, advocates charged, were the only means of saving the old from impoverishment and widespread institutionalization. Pension authorities claimed that the national acceptance of old-age relief was nothing less than a yardstick of society's compassion.[2] These appeals, however, obscured other highly significant forces in the creation of the welfare state for the aged. The majority of elderly people, after all, were not impoverished. In the course of the industrial era, most had improved their standard of living; the family economy allowed a much broader range of the elderly population to amass considerable wealth. The most prosperous of the old had reached an economic status that supported retirement and separate households.

In their call for age- (rather than need-) based pensions, advocates appealed even to the more fortunate among the elderly—and to their adult children. In the twentieth century, falling birthrates and greater life expectancy meant that middle-aged persons faced higher probabilities of having to support their parents. Industrial labor markets and seniority systems made it more difficult for aging unemployed men to find jobs; economic uncertainties threatened the savings and investments of even the successful elderly. And despite growing abundance, poverty persisted among a minority of the elderly. Without a pension system, the old and their kin had few alternatives but to rely upon a family economy that often limited the autonomy of the old and compelled younger people to forfeit their own ambitions and preferences.

The broad demand and, ultimately, the acceptance of pensions cannot be explained simply by focusing on the minority of the old who were poverty-stricken. Rather, the popular call for Social Security must be understood in terms of the growing prosperity of a large proportion of society. By the 1920s, the ability of the old and their children to establish separate households, amass considerable savings, and maintain high levels of expenditures shaped the expectations of the old in the United States. The Depression of the 1930s challenged these assumptions and exacerbated many of the unsolved problems of industrial employment. Homes that had been so important to the household economy were forfeited; private pensions that had supported the retirement of the middle class went bankrupt; banks that housed a family's lifetime of savings were closed. For the poor and working class, the economic crisis challenged the ability of the family fund to meet basic needs. For the middle class, it proved the incapacity of the private market to guarantee autonomy in old age. Such circumstances help explain the paradox of a welfare state erected around an age-based segment of society which, in large part, was neither increasingly impoverished nor deserted by their kin. The Depression of the 1930s did not simply hurt the poor or the destitute aged. It struck all classes and forged a coalition that demanded that the government ensure a respectable old age—without a continued reliance on the sacrifices of family members.

The Social Security Era

Even in its old-age provisions, therefore, Social Security was not simply a response to the needs of the impoverished elderly. It directly addressed the desire of the American people—both young and old—for a secure and independent senescence. The aged never represented a large or powerful enough coalition to have compelled taxation of the young. Rather, numerous generations shared in the desire to escape the internal pressure of family strategies. This aspiration existed well before the creation of the welfare state. It was apparent in the small villages of nineteenth-century America; it gained recognition through the economic decisions and literary declarations of both young and old Americans. Social Security's appeal and effect reached far beyond individuals in the almshouse or on outdoor relief. In its two-tier system of insurance and assistance, it not only offered welfare to the most impoverished but replaced widely used intrafamily strategies with intergenerational ones. Abandoning private decisions that revolved around the family economy and interdependence of kinship members, it established public programs that stressed autonomy and independence across classes and generations.

For the old, Social Security's impact has been dramatic. Its enactment and expansion has affected every aspect of the elderly's existence. Before Social Security, autonomous households were limited to the prosperous; many aged individuals, and especially widowed and single women, faced the prospect of ending their days in extended—and often tension-filled—households. In recent decades, Social Security has allowed the majority of elderly individuals to reside with their spouse or to dwell alone. Generally, such arrangements have not deprived the old or the young of vibrant family relations; they have simply supported the desire for "intimacy at a distance."

Social Security has also created radically new work patterns for the majority of old. In preindustrial America, few individuals retired; in a climate of general scarcity, most had little choice but to contribute to the family enterprise. In the industrial era, a much greater proportion of men were able to retire. Wealthy farmers, the recipients of Civil War pensions, and middle- and upper-class Americans had access to regular incomes outside of work and could choose to leave the labor force. But the majority of men and women—even those who had achieved considerable financial success through family economic strategies—lacked a guaranteed income that would have supported a secure retirement. Without such a resource and without a clear prediction of their own longevity, they had no choice but to remain working people. Women continued to labor as essential figures in the family enterprise. Men in skilled positions or employed by firms that honored seniority maintained good jobs; others used assets to establish their own small businesses and shifted to self-employment. Less-privileged workers fell into lower-status occupations or into protracted unemployment, searching for jobs in labor markets hostile to the elderly. With Social Security and the growth of private pensions, however, retirement has become the norm for the old. Although some individuals are pushed out of the labor market by employment restrictions and find it difficult to get new jobs, the great majority voluntarily retire, assured of economic support through Social Security and private pensions.

Social Security has also directly affected the well-being of the aged. In the industrial era, most elderly workers earned lower wages than younger persons, but reliance on the labor of children provided many aging men and women with high household incomes and greater than average savings. After the enactment of Social Security, large numbers of older workers withdrew from the labor market. At the same time, the family economy fell into disuse. Nonetheless, since 1970, the rising generosity of public transfers and the extension of private pensions have allowed most of the retired aged to maintain adequate income, and welfare formulae have reduced poverty among the least affluent. As was the case in previous eras, older people command large shares of wealth. Given these conditions, the vast majority of the aged cannot be viewed as impoverished. While a stubborn problem of poverty remains (concentrated among elderly women, African Americans, and other minority groups), Social Security has provided a degree of assistance and security that clearly did not exist before.

One tangible sign of Social Security's impact upon the poor has been the eradication of the centuries-long symbol of impoverishment: the almshouse. The formulators of New Deal welfare consciously set out to destroy the institution; it served only too well as a visible remainder of the nation's supposed disregard for its impoverished elders. In devising state pensions, therefore, they mandated that no almshouse resident could receive government support. Almost immediately, almshouses across the nation closed. Yet as officials such as Homer Folks warned, not all old people could live on their own. Large numbers were dependent not simply because they were poor but also because they were physically unable to provide for themselves and lacked the necessary family members. Local and state officials rapidly transferred these individuals into private asylums and boarding houses where they could receive public annuities. Social Security closed the almshouse; both its early stipulations and its later expanded provisions promoted the growth of the private nursing home industry. These institutions affect a far greater number of elderly men and women than did the almshouse in the preindustrial and industrial eras.

Contemporary cultural admonitions about old age, however, generally have little meaning for the dependent or institutionalized elderly. While the impoverished and sickly old are still classified as worthy of relief (and, as such, receive Medicare and Medicaid), few experts focus on the lessons they can teach their community or their role in the order of the universe. Instead, contemporary analysts generally stress that the old should strive for activity and autonomy in the final stage of existence. With the enactment of Social Security, economic dependence on children no longer seems a proper ideal; with the establishment of Medicare, the diseases of old age are enemies to be attacked and eradicated. From financial independence to residential autonomy, the best old age is one of complete health, financial independence, and self-reliance.

Yet not all individuals fulfill these ideals or experience an affluent old age. As in the past, a minority of impoverished elderly exist. Often excluded from Social Security and private pensions by past employment or family patterns, they have not shared in the prosperity of most aged persons. Unmarried women, African Americans, and members of certain ethnic groups still find their old age to be a time of poverty. For them, the middle-class provisions of Social Security devised to support a withdrawal from work or residential autonomy have little application. Failure to find sufficient employment remains an enduring problem; care in public nursing homes, like the almshouse of old, is often substandard in quality. Nor does modern-day culture offer great support for those who do not live up to ideals of independence and autonomy. A passive senescence is often judged "unsuccessful"; only through continued activity can elderly individuals appear to be living a worthwhile old age.

Social Security has affected the modern-day old in one other crucial way: it has recast the debate over power and wealth in society. In the preindustrial era, the elderly often retained land and assets to ensure their status in society. Both political and religious leaders, however, cautioned the old to recognize that this strategy carried with it problems. While such behavior guaranteed continued support, it often led to generational conflict. The old were reminded to recognize their limitations and know when to pass their authority to the next generation. In the industrial era, this conflict was often exacerbated by demographic realities that led to the coexistence of numerous generations. The old found themselves competing with the young for jobs, dictating the distribution of family wealth, and exacting numerous sacrifices from their children.

Social Security has largely removed this contest for power from the private sphere and placed it in the public arena. In the past, families negotiated the exchange of needed resources within the household. Decisions about medical care, work force participation, and schooling demanded sacrifices from related family members. Within the domain of the welfare state, however, discussions about the distribution of wealth have been transformed from a controversy among individuals, kinship members, or competing employees into a debate about the rights and needs of disparate age groups. The political impact of this transformation is apparent in age-based lobbies, such as the American Association of Retired People, and in voting patterns that reflect conflicting generational interests. In areas with a high proportion of elderly people, for example, school bonds are far less likely to pass; issues of property taxes, medical care, and Social Security take precedence.

The realignment of kinship negotiation into generational lobbies has led to recent criticisms of the aged. With the federal budget deficit, growing homelessness among the nation's poor, and an increasing proportion of children impoverished, critics of age-based entitlements argue that benefits for the old should be reapportioned to other needy groups. In terms of federal programs and medical expenditures, the aged are portrayed as "greedy geezers"; once again, they are being accused of controlling more than their fair share.[3]

To some degree, this debate reflects the sudden impact of the welfare state in transforming the family economy; in work, residential patterns, and even advice, the elderly are treated—and, at times, act—as a generation apart. Although families are still the most important source of intergenerational exchange of resources, bumper stickers that proclaim "I'm spending my children's inheritance," do little to modify the image of a selfish and self-centered older generation.

But the resentment to elderly entitlements is based not only on unwise bumper stickers. The controversy also reflects the continued influence of the arguments of early-twentieth-century pension advocates. In justifying the need for pensions, they inaccurately stressed the poverty of all old people; only state support, they argued, would save all elderly persons from almshouse residency and certain impoverishment. Given this conviction, entitlements to the middle-class elderly now appear to be unfair and misguided. The old who are not really "needy" but still receive government benefits are cited as evidence of the inordinate greed of an entire generation.

As we have seen, however, the old never comprised a totally impoverished segment of society. Their central role in the creation of the welfare state was based on persistent and broadly based problems in the laissez-faire economy that reached beyond the middle-class elderly and their children. Throughout the industrial era, the private market could neither guarantee a secure and independent old age to all nor cure the poverty of a significant minority of older people. Aging job seekers, especially widows and women without families, faced labor markets with little promise. Individuals who did not retire appeared to suppress the wage structure and to diminish the prospects of the young and middle-aged through the developing seniority systems. And perhaps most important, without a perpetual annuity, the family remained the foundation of support in old age, either by pressure on children to contribute to parental income, by co-residence in households, or by outright support of the dependent.

The broad acceptance of Social Security, therefore, was never based simply on the need to save the old from destitution. Despite the characterization of welfare advocates, a majority of the elderly were neither impoverished nor increasingly neglected. Rather, age-based state pensions promised a wide variety of elderly people, and their families, a secure old age apart from the conflicts of work and kin. The road to security turned away from family and work, and toward the state. In its appeal, Social Security cut across class, political affiliations, and generations. In its entitlements, it affected both the young and the old; through its allocations, it has written a new chapter in the history of old age, and in turn, of every age, in the United States.

Notes

Introduction

1. See, for example, Ernest W. Burgess, *Aging in Western Society* (Chicago: University of Chicago Press, 1960); Richard C. Crandall, *Gerontology: A Behavioral Science Approach* (Reading, Mass.: Addison-Wesley, 1980); Lowell D. Holmes, "Trends in Anthropological Gerontology: From Simmons to the Seventies," *International Journal of Aging and Development* 7 (1976): 211–20; Jerome Kaplan and G. J. Aldridge, eds., *Social Welfare of the Aging* (New York: Columbia University Press, 1962), p. 350; and Irving Rosow, *Socialization to Old Age* (Berkeley: University of California Press, 1974).

2. D. Cowgill and L. D. Holmes, *Aging and Modernization* (New York: Appleton-Century-Crofts, 1972); M. Clark and B. G. Anderson, *Culture and Aging* (Springfield, Mass.: Charles Thomas, 1967); Leo W. Simmons, "Aging in Preindustrial Societies," in *Handbook of Social Gerontology*, ed. Clark Tibbits (Chicago: University of Chicago Press, 1960), and *The Role of the Aged in Primitive Society* (New Haven, Conn.: Yale University Press, 1945).

3. For a critique of this argument, see W. Andrew Achenbaum and Peter N. Stearns, "Modernization and the History of Old Age," *Gerontologist* 18 (1978): 306–13.

4. Crandall, *Gerontology*, p. 25.

5. David Hackett Fischer, *Growing Old in America* (New York: Oxford University Press, 1977), p. 153.

6. Lawrence Stone, *The Family, Sex and Marriage in England 1500–1800* (New York: Harper and Row, 1977); John Demos, *A Little Commonwealth: Family Life in Plymouth Colony* (New York: Oxford University Press, 1970); Peter Laslett, ed., *Household and Family in Past Time* (Cambridge: Cambridge University Press, 1972); Peter Laslett, *Family Life and Illicit Love in Earlier Generations: Essays in Historical Sociology* (Cambridge: Cambridge University Press, 1977), pp. 174–213. Family relationships extend beyond the physical household, as we show subsequently.

7. Laslett, *Household and Family*, pp. 41–42.

8. John Demos, "Old Age in Early New England," in Michael Gordon, ed., *The American Family in Social-Historical Perspective*, 2d ed. (New York: St. Martin's Press, 1978), pp. 220–56.

9. Philip J. Greven, Jr., *Four Generations: Population, Land and Family in Colonial Andover* (Ithaca, N.Y.: Cornell University Press, 1970). See also John J. Waters, "Patrimony, Succession, and Social Stability: Guilford, Connecticut, in the Eighteenth Century," *Perspectives in American History* 10 (1976): 131–60.

10. William Bridge, *A Word to the Aged* (Boston: John Foster, 1679), p. 5; cited by Demos, "Old Age in Early New England," p. 223.

11. On the position of the aging minister, see Maris Vinovskis, " 'Aged Ministers of the Lord': Changes in Status and Treatment of Elderly Ministers in Colonial America," unpublished paper.

12. Demos, "Old Age in Early New England," p. 250.

13. Daniel Scott Smith, "Old Age and the 'Great Transformation': A New England Case Study," in *Aging and the Elderly*, ed. Stuart F. Spicker, Kathleen M. Woodward, and David D. Van Tassel (Atlantic Highlands, N.J.: Humanities Press, 1978), pp. 285–302.

14. Smith, "Old Age and the 'Great Transformation,'" p. 296.

15. See Carole Haber, *Beyond Sixty-Five: The Dilemma of Old Age in America's Past* (New York: Cambridge University Press, 1983), chap. 1, and Peter N. Stearns, ed., *Old Age in Preindustrial Society* (New York: Holmes and Meier, 1982). For England, see Laslett, *Family Life and Illicit Love*, chap. 5; Peter Laslett, "The Traditional English Family and the Aged in Our Society," in *Aging, Death and the Completion of Being*, ed. David D. Van Tassel (Philadelphia: University of Pennsylvania Press, 1979), pp. 97–113; and Keith Thomas, *Age and Authority in Early Modern England* (London: British Academy, 1976).

16. One historian, Lawrence Stone, disagreed, stating that sentiments about old age "are not so different today from those of Shakespeare's." "Walking over Grandma," *New York Review of Books* 24, no. 8 (May 1977).

17. For a critique of Fischer's argument, see Stone, "Walking over Grandma," p. 15; for Fischer's response, see "Growing Old: An Exchange," *New York Review of Books* 24, no. 14 (September 1977): 48.

18. W. Andrew Achenbaum, *Old Age in the New Land* (Baltimore: Johns Hopkins University Press, 1978), p. 86.

19. Thomas R. Cole, " 'Putting Off the Old': Middle-Class Morality, Antebellum Protestantism, and the Origins of Ageism," in David D. Van Tassel and Peter N. Stearns, eds., *Old Age in a Bureaucratic Society* (Westport, Conn.: Greenwood Press, 1986), p. 61; *The Journey of Life: A Cultural History of Aging in America* (New York: Cambridge University Press, 1992); and "Past Meridian: Aging and the Northern Middle Class" (Ph.D. diss. University of Rochester, 1980).

20. Achenbaum, *Old Age in the New Land*, p. 86.

21. Michel Dahlin, "From Poorhouse to Pension: The Changing View of Old Age in America, 1890–1929" (Ph. D diss. Stanford University, 1983).

22. For the beliefs of these influential writers, see Dahlin, "From Poorhouse to Pension," and Haber, *Beyond Sixty-Five*.

23. On the establishment of asylums for the old in the late nineteenth century, see Arthur E. Anderson, "The Institutional Path of Old Age" (Ph.D. diss., University of Virginia, 1983); Astreda I. Butners, "Institutional Altruism for the Aged" (Ph.D. diss., Columbia University, 1980); Brian Gratton, *Urban Elders: Family, Work and Welfare among Boston's Aged, 1890–1950* (Philadelphia: Temple University Press, 1986), chaps. 4 and 5; Haber, *Beyond Sixty-Five*, chap. 5; Michael B. Katz, "Poorhouses and the Origins of the Public Old Age Home," *Milbank Memorial Fund Quarterly/Health and Society* 62, no. 1 (1984): 110–40; and Ethel McClure, *More than Just a Roof: The Development of Minnesota Poor Farms and Homes for the Aged* (St. Paul: Minnesota Historical Society, 1968).

24. Carole Haber and Brian Gratton, "Old Age, Public Welfare and Race: The Case of Charleston, South Carolina, 1800–1949," *Journal of Social History* 21 (Winter 1987): 263–79.

25. Howard P. Chudacoff and Tamara K. Hareven, "Family Transition into Old Age," in *Transitions: The Family and the Life Course in Historical Perspectives*, ed. Tamara K. Hareven (New York: Academic Press, 1978), pp. 217–43, and "From Empty Nest to Family Dissolution: Life Course Transition into Old Age," *Journal of Family History* 4, no. 1 (Spring 1979): 69–83; and Tamara K. Hareven, "Family Time and Historical Time," in *The Family*, ed. Alice S. Rossi, Jerome Kagan, and Hareven (New York: Norton, 1978), pp. 58–70; "The Last Stage: Historical Adulthood and Old Age," *Daedalus* 105, no. 4 (Fall

1976): 13–23; and "Life Course Transitions and Kin Assistance in Old Age: A Cohort Comparison," in Van Tassel and Stearns, eds., *Old Age in a Bureaucratic Society*, pp. 110–25.

26. Michael Anderson, *Family Structure in Nineteenth-Century Lancashire* (Cambridge: Cambridge Univ. Press, 1971); Steven Ruggles, *Prolonged Connections: The Rise of the Extended Family in Nineteenth-Century England and America* (Madison: Univ. of Wisconsin Press, 1987); N. Sue Weiler, "Family Security or Social Security? The Family and the Elderly in New York State during the 1920s," *Journal of Family History* 11, no. 1 (1986): 77–95.

27. Daniel Scott Smith, "Accounting for Change in the Families of the Elderly in the United States, 1900–Present," in Van Tassel and Stearns, eds., *Old Age in a Bureaucratic Society*, and "Life Course, Norms, and the Family System of Older Americans in 1900," *Journal of Family History* 4, no. 2 (1979): 285–98.

28. Thomas A. Arcury, "Rural Elderly Household Life-Course Transitions, 1900 and 1980 Compared," *Journal of Family History* 11, no. 1 (1986): 55–76; Hal S. Barron, *Those Who Stayed Behind: Rural Society in Nineteenth-Century New England* (New York: Cambridge Univ. Press, 1984); Weiler, "Family Security or Social Security?"; Brian Gratton, "Familism among the Black and Mexican-American Elderly," *Journal of Aging Studies* 1 (Spring 1987): 19–32; Haber and Gratton, "Old Age, Public Welfare and Race"; D. S. Smith, M. Dahlin, and M. Friedberger, "The Family Structure of the Old Black Population in the American South in 1880 and 1900," *Sociology and Social Research* 63 (April 1979): 544–49.

29. Fischer, *Growing Old in America*, pp. 80–82, 101.

30. Achenbaum, *Old Age in the New Land*, p. 95.

31. William Graebner, *A History of Retirement: The Meaning and Functions of an American Institution, 1885–1978* (New Haven, Conn.: Yale University Press, 1980).

32. Roger L. Ransom and Richard Sutch, "The Labor of Older Americans: Retirement of Men on and off the Job, 1870–1937," *Journal of Economic History* 46, no. 1 (March 1986): 1–30.

33. On the possible impact of Civil War pensions, see Maris A. Vinovskis, "Have Social Historians Lost the Civil War? Some Preliminary Demographic Speculations," *Journal of American History* 76 (June 1989): 50–56.

34. Haber, *Beyond Sixty-Five*, chap. 1; Jill Quadagno, "From Poor Laws to Pensions," *Milbank Memorial Fund Quarterly* 62, no. 3 (1984): 417–46; David Rothman, *The Discovery of the Asylum: Social Order and Disorder in the New Republic* (Boston: Scott, Foresman, 1971), chap. 1; Michael Zimmerman, "Old Age Poverty in Pre-industrial New York City," in *Growing Old in America*, ed. Beth Hess (New Brunswick, N.J.: Transaction Books, 1976), pp. 81–104.

35. See the work of Anderson, Dahlin, Gratton, and Haber.

36. W. Andrew Achenbaum, *Shades of Gray* (Boston: Little, Brown, 1978), and *Social Security: Visions and Revisions* (Cambridge: Cambridge University Press, 1986). See also Achenbaum, "The Elderly's Social Security Entitlements as a Measure of Modern American Life," and "Two Roads Diverged: A Rejoinder," in Van Tassel and Stearns, eds., *Old Age in a Bureaucratic Society*.

37. Graebner, *A History of Retirement*. See also Graebner, "A Comment: The Social Security Crisis in Perspective," in Van Tassel and Stearns, eds., *Old Age in a Bureaucratic Society*.

38. Jill Quadagno, *The Transformation of Old Age Security: Class and Politics in the American Welfare State* (Chicago: University of Chicago Press, 1988).

39. For one history that focuses on the elderly's interpretation of their own existence, see Terri L. Premo, *Winter Friends: Women Growing Old in the New Republic, 1785–1835* (Urbana: University of Illinois Press, 1990).

40. See Theda Skocpol, *Proecting Soldiers and Mothers: The Political Origins of Social Policy in the United States* (Cambridge: Harvard Univ. Press, 1992).

1. The Families of the Old

1. In 1886, for example, the directors of Boston's public institutions complained that "the people of to-day are too prone to wish to get rid of the old father or mother . . . when they become helpless in their old age"; see the Twenty-Ninth Annual Report of the Board of Directors for Public Institutions, *Documents of the City of Boston* (DCB) 1, no. 16, p. 34.

2. In this discussion, the term *extended* will be confined to households that include three generations in a family; *complex* will denote these and other household arrangements such as the inclusion of siblings, cousins, fictive kin, or nonkin, as well as households in which older persons retain headship but adult children reside. The classical family and traditional theory can be found in William J. Goode, *World Revolution and Family Patterns* (New York: Free Press, 1963).

3. This is the famous contention of the Laslett school. See *Household and Family in Past Time*, ed. Peter Laslett (Cambridge: Cambridge University Press, 1972).

4. Lillian E. Troll, in "The Family of Later Life: A Decade Review," *Journal of Marriage and the Family* 33 (May 1971), claimed that the fundamental achievement in social gerontology in the 1960s was the recognition of the centrality of the "modified extended family structure" (p. 264). In an influential collaborative work, Ethel Shanas maintained that "the modified extended family, rather than the nuclear, conjugal family, has emerged as the ideal type in present-day Western society." See Ethel Shanas, Peter Townsend, D. Wedderburn, H. Friees, P. Milhoj, and J. Stehouwer, *Old People in Three Industrial Societies* (New York: Atherton Press, 1968), p. 227. For a recent summary, see Marvin B. Sussman, "The Family Life of Old People," in *Handbook of Aging and the Social Sciences*, ed. Robert H. Binstock and Ethel Shanas, (New York: Van Nostrand Reinhold, 1985).

5. A convincing history of the family faces the imposing difficulty of characterizing the *family* relationships of the old, while the historical evidence almost invariably simply reflects *household* conditions. The "family" is rarely confined to those who live in the same residence; the kinship network, in its emotional and functional aspects, ranges well beyond the dwelling. In addition, our evidence is usually drawn from one moment in time—rarely does it trace families and households across time. See David I. Kertzer, "Future Directions in Historical Household Studies," *Journal of Family History* (Spring 1985): 98–105.

6. According to Tamara Hareven, "The predominance of nuclear residence reflects an overall commitment in American society to the separation of the family of orientation from the family of procreation"; see her *Family Time and Industrial Time: The Relationship between the Family and Work in a New England Community* (Cambridge: Cambridge University Press, 1982), p. 165.

7. John Demos, *A Little Commonwealth: Family Life in Plymouth Colony* (New York: Oxford University Press, 1970); Edmund S. Morgan, *The Puritan Family: Religion and Domestic Relations in Seventeenth-Century New England* (New York: Harper and Row, 1944).

8. David Hackett Fischer, *Growing Old in America* (New York: Oxford University Press, 1977), appendix, table VI, p. 228; Robert V. Wells, "Demographic Change and the Life Cycle of American Families," in *The Family in History*, ed. Theodore K. Rabb and Robert I. Rotberg, (New York: Harper and Row, 1971), p. 87; Carole Haber, *Beyond Sixty-Five: The Dilemma of Old Age in America's Past* (New York: Cambridge University Press, 1983), pp. 10–11.

9. Steven Ruggles, *Prolonged Connections: The Rise of the Extended Family in Nine-teenth-Century England and America* (Madison: University of Wisconsin Press, 1987), p. 4.

10. Demos, *A Little Commonwealth*, pp. 101–3; Morgan, *The Puritan Family*, p. 78.

11. *A Report of the Record Commissioners of the City of Boston containing Miscellaneous Papers*, City Document 150, 3 May 1692 (Boston: Rockwell & Churchill, 1886), p. 62.

12. Samuel Willard, *A Compleat Body of Divinity*, Sermon 64, p. 608.

13. John Demos, "Old Age in Early New England," in Michael Gordon, ed., *The American Family in Social-Historical Perspective*, 2d ed. (New York: St. Martin's Press, 1978), pp. 220–56; Philip J. Greven, Jr., *Four Generations: Population, Land, and Family in Colonial Andover* (Ithaca, N.Y.: Cornell University Press, 1970); Daniel Scott Smith, "Old Age and the 'Great Transformation,'" in *Aging and the Elderly*, ed. Stuart F. Spicker, Kathleen M. Woodward, and David D. Van Tassel (Atlantic Highlands, N.J.: Humanities Press, 1978), pp. 294–95; John J. Waters, "Patrimony, Succession and Social Stability: Guilford, Connecticut, in the Eighteenth Century," *Perspectives in American History* 10 (1976): 157–58.

14. Joseph Abbot of Andover, Massachusetts, was chosen to inherit the family residence upon the death of his father. The elder Abbot did not die until 1731, at the advanced age of seventy-three. Until that time, his son remained a "child" in the family home. Only after his father's demise did Joseph, at age forty-five, marry and inherit the house. See Greven, *Four Generations*, p. 142. See also J. H. Plumb, "The Great Change in Children," in *Rethinking Childhood*, ed. Arlene Skolnick (Boston: Little, Brown, 1976), p. 205.

15. Demos, *A Little Commonwealth*, p. 238; Haber, *Beyond Sixty-Five*, p. 20; Alexander Keyssar, "Widowhood in Eighteenth-Century Massachusetts: A Problem in the History of the Family," *Perspectives in American History* 8 (1974): 108.

16. Carole Shammas, Marylynn Salmon, and Michel Dahlin, *Inheritance in America: From Colonial Times to the Present* (New Brunswick, N.J.: Rutgers University Press, 1987), pp. 51–55.

17. Ibid., pp. 55–60.

18. Robert V. Wells, *The Population of the British Colonies of America before 1776: A Survey of Census Data* (Princeton, N.J.: Princeton University Press, 1975), p. 132.

19. Haber, *Beyond Sixty-Five*, pp. 23–24; *A Report of the Record Commissioners of the City of Boston containing Records of the Boston Selectmen 1701–1715* (Boston: Rockwell & Churchill, 1884), p. 68: Laurel Thatcher Ulrich, *A Midwife's Tale: The Life of Martha Ballard, Based on Her Diary, 1785–1812* (New York: Vintage, 1991), p. 263.

20. Morgan, *The Puritan Family*, pp. 145–46.

21. *Report of the Record Commissioners of the City of Boston containing Miscellaneous Papers* (1707), p. 177.

22. Demos, *A Little Commonwealth*, p. 192; Allan Kulikoff, *Tobacco and Slaves: The Development of Southern Culture in the Chesapeake, 1680–1800* (Chapel Hill: University of North Carolina Press, 1986), chap. 5; Greven, *Four Generations*, p. 229.

23. Greven, *Four Generations*, chaps. 7 and 8.

24. Shammas et al., *Inheritance in America*, pp. 55–60.

25. David J. Rothman, *The Discovery of the Asylum: Social Order and Disorder in the New Republic* (Boston: Little, Brown, 1971), pp. 36, 38–39; Gary B. Nash, "Poverty and Poor Relief in Pre-Revolutionary Philadelphia," *William and Mary Quarterly* 33, 3d ser. (January 1977), pp. 6, 9; Charles Lawrence, *History of the Philadelphia Almshouses and Hospitals*, (Philadelphia: Charles Lawrence, 1905), pp. 39–40.

26. Ruggles, *Prolonged Connections*, pp. 60–83.

27. Unless otherwise indicated, findings presented in the text are based on our analysis of the Public Use Sample of the 1900 United States Census (Center for Studies in Demography and Ecology, University of Washington, Seattle, 1980). For somewhat differ-

ent calculations, see Daniel Scott Smith, "Accounting for Change in Families of the Elderly in the United States, 1900–Present," in David D. Van Tassel and Peter N. Stearns, eds., *Old Age in a Bureaucratic Society* (Westport, Conn.: Greenwood Press, 1986): 87–110. The distributions varied sharply by sex: 61 percent of females lived as spouse or household head, 32 percent lived as "dependents," and 7 percent lived outside the family. For men, the corresponding percentages were 78, 13, and 9.

28. For a useful introduction to different propensities to include single or married kin, see Steven Ruggles, "Availability of Kin and the Demography of Historical Family Structure," *Historical Methods* 19 (Summer 1986): 93–102.

29. Thomas A. Arcury, "Rural Elderly Household Life-Course Transitions, 1900 and 1980 Compared," *Journal of Family History* 11, no 1 (1986): 55–76.

30. Ruggles, *Prolonged Connections*, p. 40.

31. According to Smith ("Accounting for Change," p. 103), 29 percent of all old farmers lived with their son or sons; only 18 percent resided with a daughter. In middle-class urban neighborhoods, however, 35 percent of older persons lived with a daughter, while only 18 percent lived with a son.

32. The interchange of power and the reciprocity of relations between generations are certainly underestimated by household data, since intergenerational exchange in farming families most often occurred outside the household sphere. See Jill Quadagno and J. M. Janzen, "Old Age Security and the Family Life Course: A Case Study of Nineteenth-Century Mennonite Immigrants to Kansas," *Journal of Aging Studies* 1 (Spring 1987): 33–49.

33. Hal S. Barron, *Those Who Stayed Behind: Rural Society in Nineteenth-Century New England* (New York: Cambridge University Press, 1984), p. 95.

34. Elizabeth H. Pleck, "Challenges to Traditional Authority in Immigrant Families," in Michael Gordon, ed., *The American Family in Social-Historical Perspective*, 3d ed. (New York: St. Martin's Press, 1983), pp. 514–15. In *Family Time and Industrial Time* (p. 180), Hareven argues that while economic factors contributed to this pattern among the foreign born, so also did "the strong sense of familial solidarity that stemmed from premigration traditions."

35. In native-born white households, about one-quarter were extended down; among the foreign-born, approximately 15 percent. Such extension rates, however, did not include the common practice, especially among the foreign-born, of an adult child remaining in the household. For different reasons, downward extension also distinguishes African-American families in our own time, in particular the extension of older females' households to grandchildren. See Brian Gratton, "Familism among the Black and Mexican-American Elderly: Myth or Reality?" *Journal of Aging Studies* 1 (Spring 1987): 19–32.

36. Only 5 percent of African-American elderly males lived as parent to the household head, in contrast to 12 percent of the native-born white and 16 percent of the foreign-born white male. On this point, see Daniel Scott Smith, Michel Dahlin, and Mark Friedberger, "The Family Structure of the Older Black Population in the American South in 1880 and 1900," *Sociology and Social Research* 63 (April 1979): 544–49. On the African-American family in the South, see also Jacqueline Jones, *Labor of Love, Labor of Sorrow* (New York: Basic Books, 1985), pp. 81–95, 340–41, and Orville Vernon Burton, *In My Father's House Are Many Mansions: Family and Community in Edgefield, South Carolina* (Chapel Hill: University of North Carolina Press, 1985), pp. 230, 260–311, 409.

37. Brian Gratton, "The Labor Force Participation of Older Men, 1890–1940," *Journal of Social History* 20 (Summer 1987): 689–710. See also Stewart A. Tolnay, "Family Economy and the Black American Fertility Transition," *Journal of Family History* (1986): 269. The lack of adult children in black elders' households and the presence of more distant kin

appear almost immediately in the postbellum period. See Burton, *In My Father's House*, figs. 7–1, 7–3; table 7–1; and pp. 263–83.

38. According to Arcury's study of a rural county in Kentucky ("Rural Elderly Household Life-Course Transition"), only 29 percent of women aged sixty-five to seventy-four lived with a spouse in a nuclear family. Forty-eight percent resided in complex families, while 24 percent lived in a nonfamily setting.

39. Shammas et al., *Inheritance in America*, pp. 106–108.

40. Jon R. Moen, "Rural, Nonfarm Households: A New View of the Labor Force Participation Rate of Men 65 and Older, 1869–1980," *Social Science History* (in press).

41. The rare historical evidence that surveys households in proximity to one another shows that family contact and household structure were not equivalent. Kin often lived close to older persons' homes, especially in rural and farm areas. In rural North Carolina in the mid–nineteenth century, 24 percent of men over seventy who headed their own households "resided just next door to someone with the same surname as their own," and many more lived near kin with a different surname. In 1900, more than 15 percent of the elderly heads of households had same-surname kin living in close proximity. See Robert C. Kenzer, *Kinship and Neighborhood in a Southern Community: Orange County, North Carolina, 1849–1881* (Knoxville: University of Tennessee Press, 1987), p. 20. See also Daniel Scott Smith, "Life Course, Norms, and the Family System of Older Americans in 1900," *Journal of Family History* 4, no. 2 (1979): 285–98. Smith, however, finds that "kin propensity declined across the nineteenth century"; see his " 'All in Some Degree Related to Each Other': A Demographic and Comparative Resolution of the Anomaly of New England Kinship," *American Historical Review* 94 (February 1989): 44–79.

42. Michael Anderson first stressed the role urbanization played in increasing rather than decreasing the tendency toward complex households; see his *Family Structure in Nineteenth-Century Lancashire* (London: Cambridge University Press, 1971). In Salem, Lawrence, and Lynn, 64 percent of men and 61 percent of women aged fifty-five and over lived with children; in nonurban areas of Essex County, the corresponding proportions were 47 and 35 percent. These figures, we presume, combine both rural towns and farms into one rural configuration. As we have argued, such a formulation may hide the rather substantial differences between farm and village families. See Howard P. Chudacoff and Tamara K. Hareven, "Family Transitions into Old Age," in *Transitions: The Family and the Life Course in Historical Perspective*, ed. Tamara K. Hareven (New York: Academic Press, 1978), pp. 217–43, and "From the Empty Nest to Family Dissolution: Life Course Transition into Old Age," *Journal of Family History* 4, no. 1 (Spring, 1979): 69–83; Tamara K. Hareven, "Life Course Transitions and Kin Assistance," in Van Tassel and Stearns, eds., *Old Age in a Bureaucratic Society*, pp. 110–25; and N. Sue Weiler, "Family Security or Social Security? The Family and the Elderly in New York State during the 1920s," *Journal of Family History* 11, no. 1 (1986): 77–95.

43. Smith, "Accounting for Change," pp. 87–109.

44. As an example, in 1880, 79 percent of all urban African-American women aged fifty-five and over were widows. In rural areas, the proportion was only 60 percent—surely a product of the movement of African-American rural widows to the cities. See Janice L. Reiff, Michel R. Dahlin, and Daniel Scott Smith, "Rural Push and Urban Pull: Work and Family Experiences of Older Black Women in Southern Cities, 1880–1900," in Sharon Hurley, ed., *The Urban Experiences of Afro-American Woman* (Boston: G. B. Hall, 1981).

45. John Modell and Tamara K. Hareven, "Urbanization and the Malleable Household: An Examination of Boarding and Lodging in American Families," in Gordon, ed., *The American Family in Social-Historical Perspective*, 2d ed., pp. 51–68. For the very old in

the city, boarding houses played another essential role. In chap. 4, we show that many such establishments were de facto nursing homes for the elderly; some even specialized in taking in older residents. Settled into a boarding house, the elderly person without kin became part of a complex household. In the 1900 sample, about 4 percent of those sixty and older lived as boarders.

46. In middle-class urban neighborhoods, 17 percent of persons over fifty-five lived with unmarried daughters; 15 percent lived with a married daughter. The combined figure of 32 percent greatly exceeded the 18 percent who lived with sons. As already discussed, the proportions were far different on the farm. See Smith, "Accounting for Change," p. 103.

47. "Report on Farms and Homes: Proprietorship and Indebtedness," *Eleventh Census of the United States (1890): Housing* (Washington D.C.: Government Printing Office, 1895); Anderson, *Family Structure in Nineteenth-Century Lancashire.*

48. Smith, "Life Course, Norms, and the Family System," pp. 285–98, and "Historical Change in the Household Structure of the Elderly in Economically Developed Societies," in Peter N. Stearns, ed., *Old Age in Preindustrial Society* (New York: Holmes and Meier, 1982), 248–73.

49. Smith, "Accounting for Change," p. 101. Smith confirms the presence of a third locale: in cities with a population less than 25,000, only 56 percent had a child in their homes.

50. Ruggles, *Prolonged Connections*, pp. 30–59.

51. In 1900, only about 4 percent of Americans fifty-five and over lived alone; 29 percent of the married lived with a spouse in an empty nest. See Michel Dahlin, "Perspectives on the Family Life of the Elderly in 1900," *Gerontologist* 20, no. 1 (1980): 99–107. See also Smith, "Life Course, Norms, and the Family System." A declining age of last childbirth strongly influenced whether a period of life without children would occur. Among eighteenth-century Quakers, the median age at which women bore their last child was thirty-eight; in a cohort of women from the 1920s, the median age was 30.5. The age at which the last child married and left home was determined by the child's age and by the propensity to leave home. Robert V. Wells estimates that the empty-nest period for Quakers began at age sixty, for an 1880–89 cohort at fifty-six, and for a 1920 cohort at fifty-two; see his "Demographic Change and the Life Cycle," p. 93.

52. According to Ruggles, *Prolonged Connections* (p. 35), in Erie County in 1880, 41 percent of all families with servants lived with extended kin; by 1915 the proportion was only 20.2 percent.

53. Smith, "Historical Change in the Household Structure of the Elderly," p. 266.

54. Ruggles, *Prolonged Connections*, p. 44. For some scholars, the shift away from providing household shelter to kin outside the nuclear unit shows that cultural norms, largely lost today, strongly influenced behavior. See Smith, "Life Course, Norms, and the Family System," p. 294. For a more moderate position, however, see Smith, " 'All in Some Degree Related to Each Other.' "

55. For the relative poverty of the working class in 1900, see Brian Gratton, *Urban Elders: Family, Work and Welfare among Boston's Aged, 1890—1950* (Philadelphia: Temple University Press, 1986), pp. 55–60. On their ability to accumulate wealth in the twentieth century, see chap. 3 of the present study.

56. Ruggles, *Prolonged Connections*, pp. 43–45.

57. Carl Deglar, *At Odds: Women and the Family in America from the Revolution to the Present* (New York: Oxford University Press, 1980), chap. 5.

58. Tamara K. Hareven and Randolph Langenback, *Amoskeog: Life and Work in an American Factory City* (New York: Pantheon, 1978).

59. On such tensions, see chap. 3. See also the work of John Bodnar: *Workers' World: Kinship, Community, and Protest in an Industrial Society, 1900–1940* (Baltimore: Johns Hopkins University Press, 1982), and *The Transplanted: A History of Immigrants in Urban America* (Bloomington: Indiana University Press, 1985). In *Family Time and Industrial Time*, Hareven notes (p. 185) that disputes between generations over the dual ideals of assistance and autonomy "often generated conflicts of interests within the family."

60. Mary Ryan, *Cradle of the Middle Class* (Cambridge: Cambridge University Press, 1981), pp. 38–39, 91. For another family history contrary to the "sentimental image of several generations living harmoniously under one roof," see Emily K. Abel, "Parental Dependence and Filial Responsibility in the Nineteenth Century: Hial Hawley and Emily Hawley Gillespie, 1884–1885," *Gerontologist* 32, no. 4 (1992): 519–26.

61. Tamara K. Hareven, "Life Course Transitions and Kin Assistance in Old Age: A Cohort Comparison," in Van Tassel and Stearns, eds., *Old Age in a Bureaucratic Society*, pp. 110–25.

62. Ellen A. Kramarow, "Living Arrangements of the Elderly, U.S., 1910: Explorations of Demographic Influence," paper presented at the annual meeting of the Population Association of America, Washington, D.C., March 1991.

63. Gratton, *Urban Elders*, pp. 58–59. On recognition of this problem in the first decades of the twentieth century, seek I. M. Rubinow, *The Care of the Aged* (1930), reprinted in *The Aged and the Depression*, ed. David J. Rothman (New York: Arno, 1972), pp. 8–9.

64. Anonymous, "Old Age Intestate," *Harper's*, May 1931, p. 715. The cultural preference was shared by others; see Tim B. Heaton and Caroline Hoppe, "Widowed and Married: Comparative Change in Living Arrangements, 1900–1980," *Social Science History* 11 (Fall 1987): 261–80.

65. Peter Laslett, *Family Life and Illicit Love in Earlier Generations: Essays in Historical Sociology* (Cambridge: Cambridge University Press, 1977), pp. 212–13.

66. Samuel Butler, *Note-Books* (ca. 1885), cited by Ruggles, *Prolonged Connections*, p. 3.

67. Abraham Epstein, *The Challenge of the Aged* (New York: Arno, 1976 [originally published 1928]), p. 147.

68. Cited by Modell and Hareven, "Urbanization and the Malleable Household," p. 53.

69. Epstein, *The Challenge of the Aged*, pp. 147, 210.

70. "I Am the Mother-in-Law in the Home," *Reader's Digest*, November 1937, pp. 11–14.

71. Steven Mintz and Susan Kellogg, *Domestic Revolutions: A Social History of American Family Life* (New York: Free Press, 1988), p. 135.

72. By 1934, more than half of all homeowners in Indianapolis and Birmingham had defaulted on their loans; ibid., p. 135.

73. Ibid., p. 136.

74. Ibid., p. 137; Julia Kirk Blackwelder, *Women of the Depression: Caste and Culture in San Antonio, 1929–1939* (College Station: Texas A & M University Press, 1984), p. 50.

75. Alvin L. Schorr, *Filial Responsibility in the Modern American Family* (Washington, D.C.: Government Printing Office, 1958), pp. 19–20.

76. Smith, "Historical Change in the Household Structure of the Elderly," p. 260.

77. Frances E. Kobrin, "The Fall in Household Size and the Rise of the Primary Individual in the United States," *Demography* 13 (February 1976): 127, 138; Charles H. Mindel, "Multigenerational Family Households: Recent Trends and Implications for the Future," *Gerontologist* 19 (1979): 461.

78. On modern-day role exits, see Zena Smith Blau, *Old Age in a Changing Society*

(New York: Franklin Watts, 1973), p. 155. For the notion of continuity in the lives of the nineteenth-century old, see Chudacoff and Hareven, "From the Empty Nest to Family Dissolution."

79. Patricia L. Kasschau, *Aging and Social Policy* (New York: Praeger, 1978), pp. 183–84. The study noted, however, a significant difference among Mexican Americans. As a group, they were far more likely to assume that they would eventually live with offspring (32 percent) and that such arrangements would be satisfactory (51 percent). See also Leopold Rosenmayr and Eva Kockeis, "Propositions for a Sociological Theory of Aging and the Family," *International Social Science Journal* 15 (1963): 410–26, and Ethel Shanas, "Social Myth as Hypothesis: The Case of the Family Relations of Old People," *Gerontologist* 19 (1979): 3–9.

80. Victor G. Cicirelli, *Helping Elderly Parents: The Role of Adult Children* (Boston: Auburn House 1981), pp. 3–4.

81. Currently, only the poorest elderly in the population live in three-generation households. In these, however, assistance usually passes from the elderly to the children and grandchildren. The households of elderly African-American women thus exhibit high rates of extension to subfamilies of unmarried daughters and their children. See Gratton, "Familism among the Black and Mexican-American Elderly."

82. Judith Treas, "Family Support Systems for the Aged," *Gerontologist* 16, no. 6 (1977): 486–91. A recent study finds that gender differences in caregiving have been exaggerated; female caregivers were, however, more likely than males to carry out personal care and household tasks. Baila Miller and Lynda Cafasso, "Gender Differences in Caregiving: Fact or Artifact?" *Gerontologist* 32, n.4 (1992): 498–507.

2. Wealth and Poverty

1. Helvering vs. Davis, 1937; U.S. Social Security Board, *Economic Insecurity in Old Age* (Washington, D.C.: Government Printing Office, 1937), pp. 3, 33. In the 1920s, pension advocate Abraham Epstein claimed that "the average weekly wages earned by the great masses of workers in this country are hardly sufficient for the basic immediate needs"; see his *Challenge of the Aged* (New York: Vanguard Press, 1928), p. 89.

2. Finding them too rich today, Michael D. Hurd thinks they were too poor yesterday; see his "Economic Status of the Elderly," *Science* 12 (May 1989): 663. Robert Binstock perceptively criticizes this impoverishment model as fundamentally ageist in "The Aged as Scapegoat," *Gerontologist* 23 (1983): 136.

3. Thomas J. Espenshade and Rachel Eisenberg Braun review various difficulties in assessing well-being in "Economic Aspects of an Aging Population and the Material Well-Being of Older Persons," *Aging in Society: Selected Reviews of Recent Research* (Hillsdale, N.J.: Lawrence Erlbaum Associates, 1983). Deficiencies in historical evidence compound current problems. In particular, cross-sectional data, used to infer life-course characteristics, actually reflect differences among individuals of different ages at a single moment of time.

4. Alice Hanson Jones, *Wealth of a Nation to Be: The American Colonies on the Eve of the Revolution* (New York: Columbia University Press, 1980), p. 214; Jeffrey G. Williamson and Peter H. Lindert, *American Inequality: A Macroeconomic Inquiry* (New York: Academic Press, 1980), p. 26; Mary M. Schweitzer, *Custom and Contract: Household, Government, and the Economy in Colonial Pennsylvania* (New York: Columbia University Press, 1987), pp. 26–29; Jackson Turner Main, *Society and Economy in Colonial Connecticut* (Princeton, N.J.: Princeton University Press, 1985). Main's earlier works focused on poverty in this period, but in *Society and Economy* he finds that the life cycle explained most poverty

in seventeenth- and eighteenth-century Connecticut: "Thus the large number of poor . . . were for the most part not truly poor" (p. 146).

5. Historians have taken two very different views of the early American culture which sponsored seniority privileges. For the argument that emphasizes a static, non-acquisitive culture with high familial values, see James A. Henretta, "Families and Farms: Mentalité in Preindustrial America," *William and Mary Quarterly* 35, no. 2 (January 1978): 3–32; for the "entrepreneurial" school, which emphasizes the impact of the market on behavior, see the essays in *Work and Labor in Early America*, ed. Stephen Innes (Chapel Hill, N. C.: Institute of Early American History and Culture, 1988). Anthropological studies show that the circumstances of the aged vary sharply among preindustrial societies; those in which old persons control valued resources tend to accord the elderly high status. See P. T. Amoss and S. Harrell, "Introduction: An Anthropological Perspective on Aging," in *Others Ways of Growing Old*, ed. P. T. Amoss and S. Harrell (Palo Alto, Calif.: Stanford University Press, 1981).

6. Laurel Thatcher Ulrich, *Good Wives: Image and Reality in the Lives of Women in Northern New England 1650–1750* (New York: Oxford University Press, 1980), and *A Midwife's Tale: The Life of Martha Ballard, Based on Her Diary, 1785–1812* (New York: Alfred A. Knopf, 1990).

7. Lisa Wilson, *A Death in the Family* (Philadelphia: Temple University Press, 1991).

8. Bettye Hobbs Pruitt, "Self-Sufficiency and the Agricultural Economy of Eighteenth-Century Massachusetts," *William and Mary Quarterly*, 41, no. 3 (July 1984): 333–64; Gary Nash, "Poverty and Poor Relief in Pre-Revolutionary Philadelphia," *William and Mary Quarterly* 33, (January 1977): 6, 9; Billie G. Smith, "The Vicissitudes of Fortune: The Careers of Laboring Men in Philadelphia, 1750–1800," in Innes, ed., *Work and Labor*; Robert Fogel, "Nutrition and the Decline in Mortality since 1700: Some Preliminary Findings," in *Long-Term Factors in American Economic Growth*, ed. Stanley L. Engerman and Robert E. Gallman (Chicago: University of Chicago Press, 1986). Main estimates that one-third of Connecticut's male population aged seventy and over had no land during the depressed years of 1730–50; see his *Society and Economy*.

9. Main, *Society and Economy*, p. 142.

10. Lee Soltow, *Men and Wealth in the United States, 1850–1870* (New Haven, Conn.: Yale University Press, 1975), pp. 27–36, 50–57, 70–71, 83–85, 180. Numerous studies confirm the positive influence of age on assets in the early nineteenth century; as examples, see Stuart M. Blumin, "Age and Inequality in Antebellum America," *Social Science History* 6 (Summer 1982): 369–79, and Jeremy Atack and Fred Bateman, *To Their Own Soil: Agriculture in the Antebellum North* (Ames: Iowa State University Press, 1987).

11. Soltow, *Men and Wealth*, pp. 53, 106. Inheritance practices undoubtedly perpetuated inequality, since bequests from rich parents to their children led to substantial increases in wealth.

12. Atack and Bateman, *To Their Own Soil*, p. 98; Carole Haber and Brian Gratton, "Old Age, Public Welfare and Race: The Case of Charleston, South Carolina, 1800–1949," *Journal of Social History* 20 (Summer 1987): 689–710; J. Thomas May, "A Nineteenth-Century Medical Care Program for Blacks: The Case of the Freedman's Bureau," *Anthropological Quarterly* 46 (July 1973): 160–71; Howard N. Rabinowitz, "From Exclusion to Segregation: Health and Welfare Services for Southern Blacks, 1865–1890," *Social Service Review* 48 (September 1974): 327–54; Alan Raphael, "Health and Social Welfare of Kentucky Black People, 1865–1870, *Societas* 2 (Spring 1972): 143–57; Elizabeth Wisner, *Social Welfare in the South from Colonial Times to World War I* (Baton Rouge: Louisiana State University Press, 1970). See also chap. 3 of the present work.

13. As an example of the prevalence of the aged on public relief rolls, see *Documents*

of the City of Boston, 1835, no. 7, p. 10; we discuss institutional relief in chap. 4. On women and poor relief, see Carole Haber, *Beyond Sixty-Five: The Dilemma of Old Age in America's Past* (New York: Cambridge University Press, 1983), and Jill S. Quadagno, "From Poor Relief to Pensions: The Evolution of Economic Support for the Aged in England and America," *Milbank Memorial Fund Quarterly* 62 (Summer 1984).

14. Carole Shammas, Marylynn Salmon, and Michel Dahlin, *Inheritance in America: From Colonial Times to the Present* (New Brunswick, N.J.: Rutgers University Press, 1987), pt. 1. For maintenance contracts in the nineteenth and twentieth centuries, see Hal Barron, *Those Who Stayed Behind: Rural Society in Nineteenth-Century New England* (New York: Cambridge University Press, 1984), and Mark Friedberger, *Farm Families and Change in Twentieth-Century America* (Lexington: University Press of Kentucky, 1988). We discuss the retirement function of maintenance contracts in chap. 3.

15. David Thomson claims that "a majority of all elderly persons" in England and Wales received public support during the mid–nineteenth century; see his "Decline of Social Welfare: Falling State Support for the Elderly since Early Victorian Times," *Ageing and Society* 4 (December 1984): 468. See also Quadagno, "From Poor Relief to Pensions."

16. Quadagno, "From Poor Relief to Pensions"; Haber, *Beyond Sixty-Five;* Gratton, *Urban Elders: Family, Work, and Welfare Among Boston's Aged, 1890–1950* (Philadelphia: Temple University Press, 1986); Marcus Wilson Jernegan, *Laboring and Dependent Classes in Colonial America, 1607–1783* (New York: Ungar, 1965 [1931]), p. 196.

17. James W. Oberly argues that the Old Soldiers Act of 1855 "must be understood as a pension program," instituted in part because "a group of older men formed a pressure group to demand pecuniary benefits from the federal government." Perhaps 10 percent of free adults aged sixty and over received a land grant; most sold their warrants for cash. See Oberly, *Sixty Million Acres: American Veterans and the Public Lands before the Civil War* (Kent, Ohio: Kent State University Press, 1990), pp. 54, 159, 163. See also William Glasson, *Federal Military Pensions* (New York: Oxford University Press, 1918), and Haber, *Beyond Sixty-Five*, p. 110.

18. Soltow, *Men and Wealth*, p. 70.

19. *Report of the Commissioners of Pensions for 1904* (Washington, D.C., 1905). In the first year that age proved incapacitation, 47,090 Civil War pensioners were added to the rolls; see Glasson, *Federal Military Pensions*, pp. 246–47. Hace Tishler estimated that two-thirds of the aged native white population received assistance through Civil War pensions; see *Self-Reliance and Social Security, 1870–1917* (Port Washington, N.Y.: Kennikat Press, 1971), p. 89. Civil War pensions have only recently begun to receive the attention they deserve in studies of the origins of the U.S. welfare state. In assessing the program's influence on U.S. social welfare policy, Ann Orloff and Theda Skocpol estimate that 30 percent of all males sixty-five and over received Civil War pensions in 1910. Individual states in both the North and the South also offered pensions to veterans, suggesting that about one-third received benefits of one kind or another. See their "Why Not Equal Protection? Explaining the Politics of Public Social Spending in Britain, 1900–1911, and the United States, 1880s–1920," *American Sociological Review* 49 (1984): 726–50. For further discussion, see chap. 3.

20. The data for *Cost of Living of Industrial Workers in the United States and Europe, 1888–1890* and *Cost of Living in the United States, 1917–1919* can be accessed in machine-readable format from the Inter-University Consortium for Political and Social Research in Ann Arbor, Mich. For a detailed analysis of the surveys, see Brian Gratton and Frances M. Rotondo, "Industrialization, the Family Economy, and the Economic Status of the American Elderly," *Social Science History* 15 (Fall 1991): 337–62.

21. As an example of potential bias, men forty-five and over made up 32 percent of

all males twenty-five and over in the 1889–90 study; such men constituted 38 percent of the male population aged twenty-five and over in the United States in 1890. In the second study, older men made up only 20 percent of adult males surveyed, versus 38 percent in the population as a whole. The criteria for each study tended to exclude both the affluent and the impoverished aged.

22. The next chapter points out the dangers in inferring life-cycle events from cross-sectional data such as these.

23. John Bodnar has been instrumental in opening up this "family-centered world," as has Ewa Morawksa, in her insightful study of eastern European immigrants. See Bodner, *Workers' World: Kinship, Community, and Protest in an Industrial Society, 1900–1940* (Baltimore: Johns Hopkins University Press, 1982), and *The Transplanted: A History of Immigrants in Urban America* (Bloomington: Indiana University Press, 1985); and Morawska, *For Bread with Butter: The Life-Worlds of East Central Europeans in Johnstown, Pennsylvania, 1900–1940* (Cambridge: Cambridge University Press, 1985). Other examinations of the family economy include Cathy L. McHugh, *Mill Family: The Labor System in the Southern Cotton Textile Industry, 1880–1915* (New York: Oxford University Press, 1988); Jacquelyn Dowd Hall et al., *Like a Family* (Chapel Hill: University of North Carolina Press, 1988); Tamara K. Hareven, *Family Time and Industrial Time* (Cambridge: Cambridge University Press, 1982); Louise Lamphere, *From Working Daughters to Working Mothers: Immigrant Women in a New England Industrial Community* (Ithaca, N.Y.: Cornell University Press, 1987); and Mark Stern, *Society and Family Strategy: Erie County, New York, 1850–1920* (Albany: State University of New York Press, 1987).

24. Ruth Cowan, "Women's Work, Housework, and History: The Historical Roots of Inequality in Work-Force Participation," in *Families and Work*, ed. Naomi Gerstel and Harriet Gross (Philadelphia: Temple University Press, 1987); John Modell and Tamara K. Hareven, "Urbanization and the Malleable Household: An Examination of Boarding and Lodging in American Families," *Journal of Marriage and the Family* 35 (1973): 467–79; Lamphere, *From Working Daughters*; Morawska, *For Bread with Butter*; Susan J. Kleinberg, "Technology and Women's Work: The Lives of Working Class Women in Pittsburgh, 1870–1900," *Labor History* 17 (Winter 1976): 72. While it depended on women, the family economy may have inordinately profited men. For discussions of unequal distributions among members, see "Family Strategy: A Dialogue," *Historical Methods* 20, no. 3 (Summer 1987): 113–25.

25. This is Stern's conclusion in *Society and Family Strategy*, p. 15. Most parents, however, did not receive a return equal to the investment they had made in their sons and daughters. See Gratton and Rotondo, "Industrialization," and Clark Nardinelli, *Child Labor and the Industrial Revolution* (Bloomington: Indiana University Press, 1990). For other observations on the usefulness of children, see Michael R. Haines, "The Life Cycle, Savings, and Demographic Adaptation: Some Historical Evidence for the United States and Europe," in *Gender and the Life Course*, ed. Alice S. Rossi (New York: Aldine, 1985), and Viviana Zelizer, *Pricing the Priceless Child: The Changing Social Value of Children* (New York: Basic Books, 1985), p. 58.

26. Bodnar, *The Transplanted*, p. 73, and *Workers' World*, pp. 22, 165–66, 176, 180.

27. Caroline F. Ware Papers, Franklin Delano Roosevelt Library, Hyde Park, N.Y., boxes 51–55, "Greenwich Village Study: Handling Family Funds."

28. Bodnar, *Workers' World*, p. 180; Stern, *Society and Family Strategy*, p. 41.

29. Morawska, *For Bread with Butter*, p. 117; Caroline F. Ware, *Greenwich Village, 1920–1930* (Boston: Houghton Mifflin, 1935), pp. 66, 73–74.

30. Michael Haines, "Industrial Work and the Family Life Cycle, 1889–1890," *Research in Economic History* 4 (1979): 302.

31. All but the oldest cohort of households met the ideal in which the male's earnings constituted a "family wage," sufficient to support children in school and wife at home; see Ron Rothbart, " 'Homes Are What Any Strike Is About:' Immigrant Labor and the Family Wage," *Journal of Social History* 23 (Winter 1989): 267–84. Patrick M. Horan and Peggy G. Hargis show that higher male earnings (and lower demands on it) reduced the number of working children in families in the 1889–90 survey; see their "Children's Work and School-ing in the Late Nineteenth-Century Family Economy," *American Sociological Review* 56 (Oc-tober 1991): 583–96.

32. Reviewing the 1889–90 study just after its completion, E. R. L. Gould concluded that "if a surplus is to be built up, it must be at the expense of some of the children"; see his "Social Condition of Labor," in *Labor, Slavery, and Self-Government*, vol. 9, ed. H. B. Adams (Baltimore: Johns Hopkins University Press, 1893), p. 31.

33. Higher per capita expenditure in middle-aged and older households reflected in part the higher costs of more mature children. On these and other points regarding con-sumption and expenditure, see Frances M. Rotondo, "Work and Well-being: The American Elderly in the Industrial Era," master's thesis, 1991, Arizona State University.

34. Haines finds that the proportion of savers and the savings rate also increased by age of household head ("Life Cycle, Savings, and Demographic Adaptation," p. 51).

35. Ware Papers.

36. Elyce Rotella and George Alter mention the compounding effect of annual sur-pluses in the 1889–90 study in "Working Class Debt in the Late Nineteenth Century," Indiana University Economic History Workshop, 1989.

37. Certain polling districts in each study were chosen as "typical" or "representative," rather than by lot; see *Report on Old-Age Pensions* (Boston: Commonwealth of Massachu-setts, 1925), p. 9, and *Extent of Old Age Dependency* (New York: National Civic Federation, 1928). Each study excluded institutionalized persons as well as recipients of military pen-sions. Using National Civic Federation and other data for New York State, N. Sue Weiler finds that the elderly enjoyed relatively good economic conditions in the 1920s; see her "Industrial Scrap Heap: Employment Patterns and Change for the Aged in the 1920s," *Social Science History* 13 (Spring 1989): 65–88. Published reports from these surveys failed to distinguish between or divide the assets of married couples; thus if a couple reported $4,000 in assets, both were placed in that wealth category. We assume, therefore, that all assets were to be shared by two persons; this is equivalent to our household accumulation measurement. Contemporary studies commonly correct for underreporting among older wealthholders; see John L. Palmer, Timothy Smeeding, and Christopher Jencks, "The Uses and Limits of Income Comparisons," and Daphne T. Greenwood and Edward N. Wolff, "Relative Wealth Holdings of Children and the Elderly in the United States, 1962–83," in *The Vulnerable*, ed. John L. Palmer, Timothy Smeeding, and Barbara Boyle Torrey (Wash-ington, D.C.: Urban Institute Press, 1988).

38. Certainties never exist for length of life and other variables in the calculation, and the assets of the aged may not be readily converted into income, but we should recognize savings as rational, with one of its goals to provide resources in old age. For current use of the annuity approach, see Marilyn Moon, *The Measurement of Economic Welfare: Its Application to the Aged Poor* (New York: Academic Press, 1977), pp. 29–40. For the annuity calculations used here, see Gratton and Rotondo, "Industrialization."

39. Soltow, *Men and Wealth*, p. 106. In 1900–1902, men sixty-five and over had an average of 11.5 years of life expectancy and women, 12.2; see Jacob S. Siegel, *Demographic Aspects of Aging and the Older Population in the United States*, Current Population Reports, Special Studies (Washington, U.S.: Government Printing Office, 1976), p. 26.

40. Michael R. Haines and Allen C. Goodman, "A Home of One's Own: Aging and

Home Ownership in the United States in the Late Nineteenth and Early Twentieth Centuries," paper delivered at the Breckenridge Conference on the Historical Demography of Aging, Bowdoin College, 1990.

41. The basic sources for these calculations are table 4 in *Extent of Old Age Dependency*, p. 34, and table 7 in *Report on Old-Age Pensions*, p. 54. An "adequate" budget for an elderly person was judged to be $7 per week (*Report*, pp. 14, 45, 61); we estimate a couple required $10 a week, or $520 per year, for subsistence.

42. Shammas et al., *Inheritance in America*, pp. 83–86; Susan Grigg, "Women and Family Property: A Review of U.S. Inheritance Studies," *Historical Methods* 22, no. 3 (Summer 1989); 116–22; Helen S. Carter, "Legal Aspects of Widowhood and Aging," in *Widows and Widowhood in the American Southwest: 1848–1939*, ed. Arlene Scadron (Urbana: University of Illinois Press, 1988).

43. Modell and Hareven, "Urbanization and the Malleable Household"; Lamphere, *From Working Girl*.

44. For the lack of effect of age on wealth among African Americans, see Atack and Bateman, *To Their Own Soil*; see also Brian Gratton, "The Labor Force Participation of Older Men: 1890–1950," *Journal of Social History* 20, no. 4 (Summer 1986): 689–710. Blumin reports similar consequences for the foreign-born in the mid–nineteenth century ("Age and Inequality"). For older women's labor market difficulties see Gratton, *Urban Elders*.

45. Christopher Anglim and Brian Gratton, "Organized Labor and Old Age Pensions," *International Journal of Aging and Human Development* 25 (1987): 91–107; Jill Quadagno and Madonna Harrington Meyer, "Organized Labor, State Structures, and Social Policy Development: A Case Study of Old Age Assistance in Ohio, 1916–1940," *Social Problems* 36 (April 1989): 181–96.

46. As an example, by 1934 more than half of all homeowners with mortgages in Indianapolis and Birmingham had defaulted on their loans; see Steven Mintz and Susan Kellogg, *Domestic Revolutions: A Social History of American Family Life* (New York: Free Press, 1988), p. 135. Failure to pay taxes led to repossession of fully owned property. These reverses followed a long trend toward greater home ownership levels. See U.S. Department of Commerce, *1990 Census Housing Highlights*, CH-S-1-1, July 1991.

47. Robert M. Ball, "Social Security across the Generations," in *Social Security and Economic Well-Being across Generations*, ed. John R. Gist (Public Policy Institute, American Association of Retired Persons, 1988); Edward Berkowitz, "The First Advisory Council and the 1939 Amendments," in *Social Security after 50: Successes and Failures*, ed. Edward Berkowitz (Westport, Conn.: Greenwood Press, 1987); Mark H. Leff, "Speculating in Social Security Futures: The Perils of Payroll Tax Financing, 1939–50," in *Social Security: The First Half-Century*, ed. Gerald D. Nash, Noel H. Pugach, Richard F. Tomasson (Albuquerque: University of New Mexico Press, 1988); Jerry R. Cates, *Insuring Inequality: Administrative Leadership in Social Security, 1935–54* (Ann Arbor: University of Michigan Press, 1983).

48. Binstock, "Aged as Scapegoat," p. 141.

49. In a report to President Roosevelt, Social Security experts proposed welfare legislation for the elderly but admitted that "no even reasonably complete data are available regarding the means of support of aged persons." See *50th Anniversary Edition: The Report of the Committee on Economic Security of 1935* (Washington, D.C.: National Conference on Social Welfare, 1985); p. 24.

50. Thomas Osman, "The Role of Intergenerational Wealth Transfers in the Distribution of Wealth over the Life Cycle: A Preliminary Analysis," in *The Distribution of Economic Well-Being*, ed. F. Thomas Juster (Cambridge, Mass.: National Bureau of Economic Research, 1977), p. 398; Greenwood and Wolff, "Relative Wealth Holdings," p. 137; U.S.

Department of Commerce, *How Much Are We Worth? Household Wealth and Asset Owner-ship*, Bureau of the Census Statistical Brief SB/91–5, February 1991.

51. Greenwood and Wolff, "Relative Wealth Holdings"; Stephen Crystal and Dennis Shea, "Cumulative Advantage, Cumulative Disadvantage, and Inequality Among Elderly People," *Gerontologist* 30, no. 4 (1990): 437–43.

52. Except for a brief period when Civil War pensions were broadly distributed, few older persons in previous eras had wealth of this type.

53. U.S. Department of Commerce, *Money Income of Households, Families and Persons in the United States: 1990*, CPS Consumer Income, Series P-60, no. 174, August 1991, table 8; Bureau of the Census, Current Population Reports, *Money Income and Poverty Status of Families and Persons in the United States: 1981*, series P-60, no. 134, 1983.

54. Alicia Haydock Munnell, *The Effect of Social Security on Personal Saving* (Cambridge, Mass.: Ballinger 1974), pp. 22–29. In the larger Old Age Assistance program, the real value of benefits rose between 1940 and 1950.

55. Peter O. Steiner and Robert Dorfman, *The Economic Status of the Aged* (Berkeley: University of California Press, 1957), p. 84.

56. Stephen Crystal and Dennis Shea, "The Economic Resources of the Elderly," working paper, Institute for Health, Health Care Policy, and Aging Research, Rutgers University, New Brunswick, N.J., n.d., p. 17.

57. In "Cumulative Advantage," Crystal and Shea estimate that before annuitization of assets the corrected income of the elderly is 103 percent of the corrected income of nonelderly and after annuitization reaches 124 percent of the average. See also Sheldon Danziger, Jacques van der Gaag, Eugene Smolensky, and Michael K. Taussig, "Implications of the Relative Economic Status of the Elderly for Transfer Policy," in *Retirement and Economic Behavior*, ed. Henry J. Aaron and Gary Burtless (Washington, D.C.: Brookings Institution, 1984), and "The Relative Economic Status of the Aged," *IRP Focus* 6 (Spring 1983), based on research by Danziger, van der Gaag, and Smolensky.

58. Most scholars agree that "it can be safely said that today the aged are *at least* as well off economically as the rest of us." See Crystal and Shea, "Cumulative Advantage"; Danziger et al., "Implications of the Relative Economic Status of the Elderly"; Hurd, "Economic Status." Even a report designed to counter arguments that the elderly live too well found "the average standard of living—as measured by per capita income adjusted for economies of scale, taxes, and other factors—appears to be almost the same for elderly and nonelderly households." See *The Other Side of Easy Street: A Report of the Villers Foundation* (Washington, D.C.: Villers, 1987), n. 34.

59. Robert L. Clark and J. A. Menefee, "Federal Expenditures for the Elderly: Past and Future," *Gerontologist* 21 (1986): 132–37; Samuel H. Preston, "Children and the Elderly: Divergent Paths for America's Dependents," *Demography* 21 (November 1984): 435–57; Richard A. Easterlin, "The Age Structure of Poverty in America: Permanent or Transient?" *Population and Development Review* 13 (June 1987): 196–97; U.S. Department of Commerce, *Poverty in the United States: 1990*, CPS Consumer Income Series P-60, no. 175, August 1991, table 3.

60. U.S. Department of Commerce, *Measuring the Effect of Benefits and Taxes on Income and Poverty: 1990*, CPS Consumer Income Series P-60, no. 176-RD, August 1991, table 1. Such transfers have much less powerful effects for persons under eighteen years of age. Medicare not only reduces the cost of health insurance for the aged but also means that they rarely experience lapses in insurance. U.S. Department of Commerce, *Health Insurance Coverage: The Haves and Have-Nots*, Bureau of the Census Statistical Brief SB-9-90, September 1990.

61. Michael Hurd notes the persistence of high poverty rates among elderly widows and the fact that a sizable group of the elderly depend solely on public benefits; see his "Economic Status," p. 662. Also see Munnell, *Effect of Social Security*, p. 24; Christine Ross, Sheldon Danziger, and Eugene Smolensky, "The Level and Trend of Poverty, 1939–1979," IRP Discussion Paper no. 790–85 (Madison, Wis.: Institute for Research on Poverty, 1985); Department of Commerce, *Poverty in the United States: 1990*; Madonna Harrington Meyer, "Family Status and Poverty among Older Women: The Gendered Distribution of Retirement Income in the United States," *Social Problems* 37, no. 4 (November 1990): 551–63. According to the Commonwealth Fund Commission on Elderly People Living Alone, *Old, Alone and Poor*, Report Highlights, April 16, 1987, n.p., "The problems facing elderly poor people are to a substantial degree a reflection of widows' poverty" (p. 16). Elderly widows who live alone make up more than 40 percent of the 2.6 million older people with incomes below the poverty line.

62. Peter Uhlenberg and Mary Anne Salmon, "Change in Relative Income of Older Women, 1960–1980," *Gerontologist* 26 (1986): 164–70. Thus Linda Gordon's recent claim that the gendering of welfare policies means that better programs such as Old Age Insurance "disproportionately serve white men" is questionable; see her "Social Insurance and Public Assistance: The Influence of Gender in Welfare Thought in the United States, 1890–1935," *American Historical Review* 97, no. 1 (February 1992): 20. *Given* a gender-differentiated social organization of work and family life, women have been treated more than fairly because of Social Security's adequacy principles. Estimates for 1979 show women paid about 28 percent of taxes to the system but received 54 percent of benefits. See Alicia H. Munnell and Laura E. Stiglin, "Women and a Two-Tier Social Security System," in *A Challenge to Social Security: The Changing Roles of Women and Men in American Society*, ed. Richard V. Burkhauser and Karen C. Holden (New York: Academic Press, 1982). A much more reasonable critique addresses the persistent devaluation of women's household work. Although clearly critical to the family economy of the industrial era, its worth was discounted in both the private and the public spheres. Were childraising and other household tasks valued as highly as market work, women would have earned reasonable incomes and better retirement benefits.

63. Massachusetts, *Report*, p. 50. The film is available from the Metropolitan Museum of Art, Circulating Film Library, in New York.

64. See, for example, Bodnar, *Workers' World*, pp. 175–76. Bodnar de-emphasizes the extent and impact of intergenerational friction, we think unduly. On this point, see Donna Gabaccia, "The Transplanted: Women and Family in Immigrant America," *Social Science History* 12 (Fall 1988): 247–49.

3. Work and Retirement

1. The continued vitality of the paradigm is attested to by the introductory essay, "Industrialization and Retirement: An International Perspective," in Kyriakos S. Markides and Cary L. Cooper, eds., *Retirement in Industrialized Societies* (New York: John Wiley, 1987).

2. Mildred Doering, Susan R. Rhodes, and Michael Schuster, *The Aging Worker: Research and Recommendations* (Beverly Hills, Calif.: Sage, 1983); Martin Lyon Levine, *Age Discrimination and the Mandatory Retirement Controversy* (Baltimore: Johns Hopkins University Press, 1988), chap. 13; Pauline Robinson, "Age, Health, and Job Performance," in *Age, Health, and Employment*, ed. James E. Birren, Pauline K. Robinson, and Judy E. Livingston (Englewood Cliffs, N.J.: Prentice-Hall, 1986). Despite Robinson's rather san-

guine view, the data show productivity losses, especially past age seventy and in jobs with physical demands or high pace. Difficulty or incapacity to perform certain work-related tasks clearly rises with age; see U.S. Department of Health and Human Services, *Aging in the Eighties: Ability to Perform Work-Related Activities*, NCHS Advance Data, no. 136, May 8, 1987. For the better safety records of older pilots, see *Arizona Republic*, 11 November 1991.

3. Daniel Scott Smith, "Old Age and the 'Great Transformation': A New England Case Study," in *Aging and the Elderly: Humanistic Perspectives in Gerontology*, ed. S. F. Spicker, K. M. Woodward, and D. D. Van Tassel (Atlantic Highlands, N.J.: Humanities Press, 1978); John Demos, "Old Age in Early New England," in *The American Family in Social-Historical Perspective*, 2d ed., ed. Michael Gordon (New York: St. Martin's Press, 1978), pp. 220–56; Philip J. Greven, *Four Generations: Population, Land and Family in Colonial Andover, Massachusetts* (Ithaca, N.Y.: Cornell University Press, 1970); David Hackett Fischer, *Growing Old in America*, (New York: Oxford University Press, 1977).

4. Laurel Thatcher Ulrich, *Good Wives: Image and Reality in the Lives of Women in Northern New England 1650–1750* (New York: Oxford University Press, 1980), and "Martha Ballard and Her Girls: Women's Work in Eighteenth-Century Maine," in Stephen Innes, ed., *Work and Labor in Early America* (Chapel Hill: Institute of Early American History and Culture [University of North Carolina Press], 1988).

5. Greven, *Four Generations*, pp. 87–88. The essays in Innes, ed., *Work and Labor in Early America*, emphasize "the surprising importance of family labor" in all the colonies and the benefits which thereby accrued to older property owners (p. 31).

6. By the mid–eighteenth century, new financial alternatives, such as bonds, encouraged very wealthy farmers to retire from work altogether; see Mary M. Schweitzer, *Custom and Contract: Household, Government, and Economy in Colonial Pennsylvania* (New York: Columbia University Press, 1987), pp. 26–34. These financial instruments became more widespread in the nineteenth century.

7. Demos, "Old Age in Early New England"; Fischer, *Growing Old in America*, chap. 1; Carole Haber, *Beyond Sixty-Five* (New York: Cambridge University Press, 1983), chap. 1. Also see chap. 2 of the present work.

8. Lisa Wilson, *Life after Death: Widows in Pennsylvania, 1750–1850* (Philadelphia: Temple University Press, 1992); Terri L. Premo, *Winter Friends: Women Growing Old in the New Republic, 1785–1835* (Urbana: University of Illinois Press, 1990).

9. Carole Shammas, Marylynn Salmon, and Michel Dahlin, *Inheritance in America: From Colonial Times to the Present* (New Brunswick, N.J.: Rutgers University Press, 1987), pt. 1; Randolph B. Campbell, "Slave Hiring in Texas," *American Historical Review* 93 (February 1988): 107–14; J. W. Dean, Jr., "Patterns of Testation: Four Tidewater Counties in Colonial Virginia," *American Journal of Legal History* 16 (1972): 154–76. Shammas et al. argue that maintenance wills denied the widow the right to control her estate (*Inheritance in America*, pp. 51–58). The specificity of the wills suggest, however, that elderly couples who feared desertion used wills to force their children to provide retirement support.

10. Smith, "Old Age."

11. Hal S. Barron, *Those Who Stayed Behind: Rural Society in Nineteenth-Century New England* (New York: Cambridge University Press, 1984), pp. 103, 67–68, 94–95; Anne B. Webb, "Minnesota Women Homesteaders: 1863–1889," *Journal of Social History* 23, no. 1 (Fall 1989): 115–36.

12. Although a smaller proportion of African Americans reached old age than whites, about 15 percent of the slave labor force (excluding children) exceeded the age of fifty. U.S. Bureau of the Census, *Historical Statistics of the United States: Colonial Times to 1970*, pt. 1 (Washington, D.C.: Government Printing Office, 1975), p. 18.

13. *Narrative of the Life of Frederick Douglass* (New York: New American Library, 1968), p. 62. For a proslavery view, see Ulrich Bonnell Phillips, *American Negro Slavery* (Baton Rouge: Louisiana State University Press, 1966).

14. Eugene Genovese, *Roll, Jordan, Roll* (New York: Pantheon Books, 1974), pp. 519, 522–23; Jacqueline Jones, *Labor of Love, Labor of Sorrow: Black Women, Work, and the Family from Slavery to the Present* (New York: Basic Books, 1985), pp. 29–30, 40–41. Neither author provides much direct evidence for older slaves' privileges.

15. Peter Gaillard, Jr., Plantation Book, 1825–1847, South Carolina Historical Society (SCHS); Thomas A. Coffin Plantation Book, Journals for 1813 and 1816, SCHS; Daniel Webb, Plantation Journals, 1817–1850, vol. I and IV, SCHS; Genovese, *Roll, Jordan, Roll*, p. 520; Jones, *Labor of Love*, pp. 29–30. Charles Joyner's study of a single plantation also finds assignment of "jobs particularly suited to the enhanced knowledge and diminished physical capacity of elderly slaves"; see his *Down by the Riverside: A South Carolina Slave Community* (Urbana: University of Illinois Press, 1984), pp. 60–65.

16. "'List Book' of Negroes Sold by Alonzo J. White," SCHS; Coffin Plantation Book, Journal for 1816, SCHS; Dirleton Plantation Book, 1859–1866, SCHS.

17. "'List Book.'" The letter "O" usually meant old, although at times it distinguished the older of two slaves bearing the same name.

18. On one plantation, older slaves "became retired around the age of seventy"; see Joyner, *Down by the Riverside*, p. 63. Cf. Leslie Howard Owens, *This Species of Property: Slave Life and Culture in the Old South* (New York: Oxford University Press, 1976), pp. 47–49.

19. *The Countryside in the Age of Capitalist Transformation: Essays in the Social History of Rural America*, ed. Steven Hahn and Jonathan Prude (Chapel Hill: University of North Carolina Press, 1985). In nineteenth-century Vermont, farmers worked well into old age. Hal Barron considers New England agriculture "stable," but the inability of farmers to retire marks the region as inferior to new agricultural areas; see his *Those Who Stayed Behind*, pp. 67–68, 94–95. Also see Thomas Dublin, "Rural-Urban Migrants in Industrial New England: The Case of Lynn, Massachusetts, in the Mid–Nineteenth Century," *Journal of American History* 73, no. 3 (December 1986): 623–44. For a theoretical treatment of prodigal children, see William A. Sundstrom and Paul A. David, "Old-Age Security Motives, Labor Markets, and Farm Family Fertility in Antebellum America," *Explorations in Economic History* 25, no. 2 (April 1988): 164–97.

20. Kathleen Neils Conzen, "Peasant Pioneers: Generational Succession among German Farmers in Frontier Minnesota," in *The Countryside in the Age of Capitalist Transformation*, ed. Hahn and Prude, p. 275; and Mark Friedberger, "The Farm Family and the Inheritance Process, Evidence from the Corn Belt, 1870–1950," *Agricultural History* 57 (1983): 1–13, and *Farm Families and Change in Twentieth-Centry America* (Lexington: University Press of Kentucky, 1988), esp. pp. 56–87.

21. Jon R. Moen, "Rural, Nonfarm Households: A New View of the Labor Force Participation Rate of Men 65 and Older, 1860–1980," unpublished paper, University of Mississippi, 1991.

22. Brian Gratton, "The Labor Force Participation of Older Men: 1890–1950," *Journal of Social History* 20 (Summer 1987): 689–710.

23. For the development of the sharecropping system, see Roger L. Ransom and Richard Sutch, *One Kind of Freedom: The Economic Consequences of Emancipation* (New York: Cambridge University Press, 1977), and *Historical Statistics*, pt. 1, p. 465. David I. Kertzer discusses the family labor unit in *Family Life in Central Italy, 1880–1910: Sharecropping, Wage Labor and Coresidence* (New Brunswick, N.J.: Rutgers University Press, 1984), pp. 18–34.

24. Gratton, "Labor Force Participation." White southerners reported only slightly higher labor-force activity than older men from nonsouthern states. Bureau of the Census, *Fifteenth Census of the United States: 1930 Population*, vol. IV, *Occupations, By States*, table 20; vol. V, *General Report on Occupations*, table 17 (Washington, D.C.: Government Printing Office, 1933).

25. Janice L. Reiff, Michel R. Dahlin, and Daniel Scott Smith, "Rural Push and Urban Pull: Work and Family Experiences of Older Black Women in Southern Cities, 1880–1900," *Journal of Social History* 16 (Summer 1983): 39–48. For white farm widows' fortunes, see Jeremy Atack and Fred Bateman, *To Their Own Soil: Agriculture in the Antebellum North* (Ames: Iowa State University Press, 1987), p. 43.

26. Abraham Epstein, *Facing Old Age* (New York: Alfred A. Knopf, 1922), pp. 20–68. Certainly older than Epstein's remarks, this thesis became formalized as "modernization theory" in the 1950s.

27. As examples in a voluminous literature, see Amos Warner, "The Causes of Poverty Further Considered," *American Statistical Association* 4, no. 27 (September 1894): 46–48; Lee Welling Squier, *Old Age Dependency in the United States* (New York: Macmillan, 1912); and Arthur J. Todd, "Old Age and the Industrial Scrap Heap," *American Statistical Association* 13, no. 110 (June 1915): 550–57.

28. Alan Dawley, *Class and Community: The Industrial Revolution in Lynn* (Cambridge, Mass.: Harvard University Press, 1976); various essays in Charles Stephenson and Robert Asher, eds., *Life and Labor: Dimensions of American Working-Class History* (Albany: State University of New York Press, 1986), esp. Thomas E. Leary, "Industrial Ecology and the Labor Process: The Redefinition of Craft in New England Textile Machinery Shops, 1820–1860," pp. 51–52, and Charles Stephenson, " 'There's Plenty Waitin' at the Gates': Mobility, Opportunity and the American Worker," p. 86; Judith A. McGaw, *Most Wonderful Machine: Mechanization and Social Change in Berkshire Paper Making, 1801–1885* (Princeton, N.J.: Princeton University Press, 1987); Philip Scranton, *Proprietary Capitalism: The Textile Manufacture at Philadelphia, 1800–1885* (New York: Cambridge University Press, 1983); Ileen A. DeVault, *Sons and Daughters of Labor: Class and Clerical Work in Turn-of-the-Century Pittsburgh* (Ithaca, N.Y.: Cornell University Press, 1990). The advantaged status of craftsmen in the twentieth century can be followed in Brian Gratton, *Urban Elders: Family, Work, and Welfare among Boston's Aged* (Philadelphia: Temple University Press, 1986), chap. 3. Montgomery refers to Davis's experience in *Workers' Control*, p. 11 (see n. 30 below). In the 1920s, Davis recalled bias against older workers in steel mills; see his " 'Old Age' at Fifty," *North American Review* (May 1928), reprinted in *Monthly Labor Review* 26, no. 6 (June 1928): 1–6.

29. W. S. Rogers in 1891, quoted by David Montgomery, *The Fall of the House of Labor: The Workplace, the State, and American Labor Activism, 1865–1920* (New York: Cambridge University Press, 1987), p. 184. The propensity of older, presumably wealthier, workers to set up business endeavors is examined in Melanie Archer, "Self-Employment and Occupational Structure in an Industrializing City: Detroit, 1880," *Social Forces* 69, no. 3 (March 1991): 785–809.

30. Leary, "Industrial Ecology," p. 51; Bingham quoted in Dan Clawson, *Bureaucracy and the Labor Process: The Transformation of U.S. Industry, 1860–1920* (New York: Monthly Review Press, 1980), p. 108, and see pp. 104–10. David Montgomery has been the most articulate proponent of this view of nineteenth-century U.S. labor history; see his essays in *Workers' Control in America: Studies in the History of Work, Technology, and Labor Struggles* (New York: Cambridge University Press, 1979).

31. New York State Joint Legislative Commission on Discrimination in Employment

of the Middle Aged, series Loo21, box 119-4, New York State Archives (NYSA); Patricia A. Cooper, *Once a Cigar Maker: Men, Women, and Work Culture in American Cigar Factories, 1900–1919* (Urbana: University of Illinois Press, 1987), p. 64; *Twenty-Third Annual Report of the Commissioner of Labor, 1908* (Washington, D.C.: Government Printing Office, 1909), p. 33.

32. Harris, letter to J. N. A. Griswold, 10 December 1877, Harris Letters, Chicago, Burlington and Quincy papers, Newberry Library, Chicago; Alexander Keyssar, *Out of Work: The First Century of Unemployment in Massachusetts* (New York: Cambridge University Press, 1986), p. 377; Walter Licht, *Working for the Railroad: The Organization of Work in the Nineteenth Century* (Princeton, N.J.: Princeton University Press, 1983), pp. 168–71, 212; Brian Gratton, " 'A Triumph of Modern Philanthropy': Age Criteria in Labor Management: Pennsylvania Railroad, 1900," *Business History Review* 64, no. 4 (Winter 1990): 630–56.

33. Joan M. Jensen, *Loosening the Bonds: Mid-Atlantic Farm Women, 1750–1850* (New Haven, Conn.: Yale University Press, 1986); Ulrich, "Martha Ballard and Her Girls."

34. Nineteenth-century censuses actually recorded housewives as productive workers, a reflection of their vital market and nonmarket contributions. Using such data, Nancy Folbre has explored both the economic and cultural factors that inhibited married women's entry into gainful employment; see her "Unproductive Housewife: Her Evolution in Nineteenth-Century Economic Thought," *Signs* 16 (Spring 1991): 463–84. Also see Gratton, *Urban Elders*, chap. 3; Premo, *Winter Friends*, chap. 1; and Michel R. Dahlin, "No Revolution without Ideology: Aging, Androgyny and Women in Twentieth Century America," paper presented at the meeting of the Pacific Coast branch of the American Historical Association, Hawaii, August 1991. In *Home and Work: Housework, Wages, and the Ideology of Labor in the Early Republic* (New York: Oxford University Press, 1990), Jeanne Boydston argues that patriarchal culture devalued women's work inside and outside the home. See chap. 2 for further discussion of women's contribution to the family economy.

35. For long unemployment, see Keyssar, *Out of Work*, and Roger L. Ransom and Richard Sutch, "The Labor of Older Americans: Retirement of Men on and off the Job, 1870–1937," *Journal of Economic History* 46 (March 1986): 1–30.

36. The classic appraisal of this process is Harry Braverman's *Labor and Monopoly Capital: The Degradation of Work in the Twentieth Century* (New York: Monthly Review Press, 1974). Montgomery and other U.S. labor historians follow Braverman's theory. For a criticism, see William Form, "On the Degradation of Skills," in *Annual Review of Sociology*, vol. 13 (1987), pp. 29–47.

37. Henry Ford claimed that 85 percent of his workers could be trained in less than two weeks; see *My Life and Work* (Garden City, N.Y.: Garden City Publishing, 1922), p. 110, cited in Ely Chinoy, *Automobile Workers and the American Dream* (New York: Doubleday, 1955), p. 19. Chinoy concludes that most jobs in the post–World War II automobile industry required "only a few days or weeks of training." Cooper describes deskilling in a traditional trade in *Once a Cigar Maker*, pp. 31–34.

38. On Taylor, see Sanford M. Jacoby, *Employing Bureaucracy: Managers, Unions, and the Transformation of Work in American Industry, 1900–1945* (New York: Columbia University Press, 1985), pp. 40–46.

39. Brutish physical demands in nineteenth-century work—and their reduction through technological innovation—can be followed in Keith Dix's "Work Relations in the Coal Industry: The Handloading Era, 1880–1930," in *Case Studies on the Labor Process*, ed. Andrew Zimbalist (New York: Monthly Review Press, 1979). Daniel Nelson describes the pace of work in "Mass Production and the U.S. Tire Industry," *Journal of Economic History*

47, no. 2 (June 1987): 329–39. Robinson discusses the effects of physical demands and pace on older workers' productivity in "Age, Health, and Job Performance."

40. The consistently negative effects of rapid technological change can be followed in Elliot Dunlop Smith, "Employment Age Limitations," *Bulletin of the Taylor Society* 19 (October 1929): 223–24; Solomon Barkin, *The Older Worker in Industry: A Study of New York State Manufacturing Industries* (Albany: State of New York, 1933), p. 61; Keyssar, *Out of Work*, pp. 90–96; and Herbert S. Parnes, ed., *Work and Retirement: A Longitudinal Study* (Cambridge, Mass.: MIT Press, 1981). Daniel Nelson discusses the use of public schooling for job qualifications in chap. 5 of *Managers and Workers: Origins of the New Factory System in the United States, 1880–1920* (Madison: University of Wisconsin Press, 1975).

41. Census Bureau, *Historical Statistics*, pt. 1, p. 133; Susan M. Reverby, *Ordered to Care: The Dilemma of American Nursing, 1850–1945* (Cambridge, Mass.: Harvard University Press, 1987), pp. 60, 111, 114–15; Gratton, *Urban Elders*, pp. 87–94; Scranton, *Proprietary Capitalism*, p. 346.

42. Jean Donnison, *Midwives and Medical Men* (New York: Shocken Books, 1977), p. 33; Judy Barrett Litoff, *American Midwives* (Westport, Conn.: Greenwood Press, 1978), pp. 31–32; James Lincoln Huntington, "The Midwife in Massachusetts," *Boston and Surgical Journal* 68 (March 1913): 418–21; and Joseph B. DeLee, "Progress toward Ideal Obstetrics," *Transactions of the American Association for the Study and Prevention of Infant Mortality* 6 (1915): 114–23. Both the Huntington and DeLee essays were reprinted in *The American Midwife Debate*, ed. Judy Barrett Litoff (Westport, Conn.: Greenwood Press, 1986), pp. 110–16, 102–9.

43. Joyce Shaw Peterson quotes Lutz in her discussion of the upgrading of laborers' occupational positions in *American Automobile Workers, 1900–1933* (Albany: State University of New York Press, 1987), p. 39. See also Stephen Meyer III, *The Five Dollar Day* (Albany: State University of New York Press, 1981).

44. At what age they achieved their highest wage cannot be determined. On the distortions in cross-sectional data, see John D. Owen, *Working Lives: The American Work Force since 1920* (Lexington, Mass.: Lexington, 1986), p. 33.

45. Barkin's review of wage studies in the early twentieth century confirms the cost-of-living data: earnings of factory workers increased until their late thirties, then declined, especially when corrected for periods of unemployment; see Barkin, *The Older Worker in Industry*, pp. 339–44. John Owen provides instructive observations on conservative forecasting in *Working Lives*.

46. Brian Gratton, "The Worker's Right to Retire, 1850–1950," *Generations* 13, no. 2 (Spring 1989): 11–14. Barkin discovered that "the higher social classes do not experience as early a decline in earning powers as do the wage earners" and the decline was "not as sharp" (*Older Worker*, p. 345). See also Louis I. Dublin and Alfred J. Lotka, *The Money Value of a Man*, rev. ed. (New York: Ronald Press, 1946), pp. 64–5. In *Old Age Dependency*, Squier reviews civil service and other pensions in the early twentieth century.

47. For the meaning of *retirement*, see the *Oxford English Dictionary* (New York: Oxford University Press, 1971); W. Andrew Achenbaum, *Old Age in the New Land: The American Experience since 1790* (Baltimore: Johns Hopkins University Press, 1978), p. 50; Gordon Streib, "Comment," in Rita Ricardo-Campbell and Edward P. Lazear, eds., *Issues in Contemporary Retirement* (Stanford, Calif.: Hoover Institution Press, 1988), p. 29.

48. Moen, "Rural, Nonfarm Households"; Gratton, *Urban Elders*, chap. 3; Ransom and Sutch, "Labor of Older Americans." Ransom and Sutch argue that retirement occurred quite commonly as early as 1870. Indeed, if high labor force activity in agricultural occupations is discounted, labor force participation appears to increase in the early twentieth century. This interpretation confuses "retirement" with unemployment and labor force

measures and depends on a tendentious reading of census evidence and labor force data. See Jon Moen, "The Labor of Older Men: A Comment," *Journal of Economic History* 47, no. 3 (September 1987): 761–67. Ransom and Sutch reply in "The Trend in the Rate of Labor Force Participation of Older Men, 1870–1930," *Journal of Economic History* 49, no. 1 (March 1989): 170–83. Rotondo finds that the long unemployment used by Ransom and Sutch to proxy retirement fits the occupations and marital status of casual or intermittent workers, age itself having a weak relationship; see "Work and Well Being: The American Elderly in the Industrial Era," master's thesis, Arizona State University, 1991. Robert Margo and Moen have also questioned the usefulness of long-term unemployment in distinguishing "retired" persons from persons with occupational roles. See Margo's "Labor Force Participation of Older Americans in 1900: Further Results," NBER working paper, series on Historical Factors in Long Run Growth, no. 27, 1991, and Moen's "Unemployment and Retirement of Older Men: Further Evidence from the 1900 and 1910 Censuses," December 1991, unpublished paper.

49. Robert Whaples, "The 'Problem of Old Age' in America: Older Men, Retirement, and the Industrial Scrap Heap," paper delivered at the annual meeting of the Social Science History Association, Washington, D.C., 1989; Gratton, "Labor Force Participation." Studies that show the strong effects of veterans' pensions on labor-force activity include Whaples, " 'The Problem of Old Age,' "; Whaples and Jon Moen, "Civil War Veterans and the Retirement of Older Men," unpublished paper, 1991; Larry M. Logue, "Union Veterans and Their Government: The Effect of Public Policies on Private Lives," *Journal of Interdisciplinary History* 22, no. 3 (Winter 1992): 411–34; Maris A. Vinovskis, "Have Social Historians Lost the Civil War? Some Preliminary Demographic Speculations," *Journal of American History* 76 (June 1989): 50–56. Vinovskis finds the "average" Civil War pension equal to about 40 percent of average annual earnings at the turn of the century. For the proportion covered, see n. 19, chap. 2.

50. In "Unemployment and Retirement," Moen suggests that voluntary and temporary withdrawal from work was quite common among older workers at the turn of the century. Also see Ransom and Sutch, "Labor of Older Americans"; Rotondo, "Work and Well Being"; Nancy Brandon Tuma and Gary D. Sandefur, "Trends in the Labor Force Activity of the Elderly in the United States, 1940–1980," in Rita Ricardo-Campbell and Edward P. Lazear, eds., *Issues in Contemporary Retirement* (Stanford, Calif.: Hoover Institution Press, 1988). Ransom and Sutch lay great emphasis on downward mobility, or "retirement on the job," repeating a common theme in previous literature (see, for example, Tamara Hareven in "The Last Stage: Historical Adulthood and Old Age," *Daedalus* 105 [1976]: 20). However, a 1925 sample of aged men and women in Massachusetts raises doubts about its aggregate importance. Comparing present and past occupations, "service" categories increased in number but remained a small part of the labor force. The majority of working older people remained in the same occupation, although we cannot tell if their duties changed. See Commission on Pensions, *Report on Old-Age Pensions* (Boston: Commonwealth of Massachusetts, 1925), pp. 62–63.

51. Accurate statistics on pensions do not exist; if private pensioners are generously estimated at 100,000 and this number is added to those receiving government pensions of some sort, about 11 percent of the population sixty-five and over received pensions in the late 1920s. See U.S. Bureau of Labor Statistics, *Care of Aged Persons in the United States*, Bulletin no. 489 (Washington, D.C.: Government Printing Office, 1929), table 1; see also Samuel H. Williamson, "U.S. Pensions before 1930: A Historical Perspective," in John A. Turner and Daniel J. Beller, eds., *Trends in Pensions* (Washington, D.C.: Department of Labor, 1989).

52. Roy Lubove, *The Struggle for Social Security: 1900–1935* (Cambridge, Mass.: Har-

vard University Press, 1968); William Graebner, *A History of Retirement: The Meaning and Function of an American Institution* (New Haven, Conn.: Yale University Press, 1980), p. 133.

53. Achenbaum, *Old Age in the New Land*, p. 114. This interpretation has appeared in our own work as well. See, for example, Haber, *Beyond Sixty-Five*, chap. 6.

54. Burton J. Hendrick, "The Superannuated Man: Labor Pensions and the Carnegie Foundation," *McClure's* 32, no. 2 (December 1908): 122; Haber *Beyond Sixty-Five*, chap. 6; Graebner, *A History of Retirement*, pt. 1; *Report of the Massachusetts Commission on Old Age Pensions, Annuities, and Insurance* (Boston, 1910), pp. 270–71. In "What Do We Know about Historical Age Discrimination? A Critique and Extension," presented at the Social Science History meetings in November 1991, Robert Whaples shows that by 1880, when asked by census takers, people reported themselves younger than they actually were. According to David Hackett Fischer, this characteristically modern bias is at odds with a prejudice *toward* age in eighteenth-century records; see his *Growing Old in America*, pp. 82–86.

55. Abraham Epstein, *The Problem of Old Age Pensions in Industry* (Harrisburg, Pa.: Pennsylvania Old Age Commission, 1926), pp. 76–77; National Association of Manufacturers, *The Older Worker in Industry* (New York, 1929), p. 12; State of California, Department of Industrial Relations, *Middle-Aged and Older Workers in California*, Special Bulletin no. 2 (San Francisco, 1930); "Hiring and Separation Methods in American Factories," *Monthly Labor Review* 35, no. 5 (November 1932): 1013–18. Firms that profess to have no limits have been shown to hire few or no older applicants; see the report of the secretary of labor, *The Older American Worker: Age Discrimination in Employment* (Washington, D.C.: Government Printing Office, 1965).

56. *Labor Leaf*, 3 December 1884, quoted in Richard Jules Oestreicher, *Solidarity and Fragmentation: Working People and Class Consciousness in Detroit, 1875–1900* (Urbana: University of Illinois Press, 1986), p. 17. See Epstein's *Facing Old Age* for his assumption of inefficiency. Gary Becker argues that discrimination on any basis other than productivity is irrational and costly to the employer; see his *Economics of Discrimination*, 2d ed. (Chicago: University of Chicago Press, 1971); see also Steven H. Sandell, ed., *The Problem Isn't Age: Work and Older Americans* (New York: Praeger, 1987).

57. Commons quoted in Stephenson, " 'There's Plenty Waitin,' " p. 86. Magnus Alexander wrote the seminal analysis of turnover costs, focusing on semiskilled workers: "Hiring and Firing: Its Economic Waste and How to Avoid It," *Annals of the American Academy of Political and Social Sciences* 65 (May 1916): 128–44. See Keyssar, *Out of Work*, pp. 267–71, for management's concern about turnover. Sanford Jacoby maintains that turnover did not entail large costs for employers. He argues that personnel managers used the turnover issue to legitimize their new profession and thinks concern over turnover diminished in the 1920s *(Employing Bureaucracy*, pp. 116–25); also see Montgomery, *House of Labor*, pp. 239–41, 438–59. For a different slant, see David Brody, "The Rise and Decline of Welfare Capitalism," *Workers in Industrial America: Essays on the Twentieth Century Struggle* (New York: Oxford University Press, 1980), and Brian Gratton, "Rewarding Age: Management-Designed Seniority Systems, 1900–1935," paper presented at the Social Science History meetings, Washington, D.C., 1989. Too much evidence exists for management concern about turnover costs and the basic discontent from which it sprang to accept Jacoby's view.

58. Meyer, *Five Dollar Day*; David Gartman, *Auto Slavery: The Labor Process in the American Automobile Industry, 1897–1950* (New Brunswick, N.J.: Rutgers University Press, 1986), pp. 204, 209–13, 234–41; Nelson, *Managers*, pp. 148–51. Eligibility for Ford's five-dollar day required six months of continuous service. Daniel M. G. Raff argues that fear of unions rather than turnover inspired Ford's plan; see Raff's "Wage Determination Theory and the Five-Dollar Day at Ford," *Journal of Economic History* 48, no. 2 (June 1988): 387–99.

59. William A. Sundstrom, "Internal Labor Markets before World War I: On-the-Job Training and Employee Promotion," *Explorations in Economic History* 25 (October 1988): 424–45; "Hiring and Separation Methods in American Factories," *Monthly Labor Review* 35, no. 5; Jacoby, *Employing Bureaucracy*, pp. 116–78, 195–97; Jacoby and Sunil Sharma, "Employment Duration and Industrial Labor Mobility in the United States, 1880–1980," *Journal of Economic History* 52 (March 1992): 161–79. Jacoby and other historians contend that seniority was neither widespread nor strongly upheld by management; their views are contested in Gratton, "Rewarding Age."

60. Ransom and Sutch, "Labor of Older Americans"; Gratton, "Rewarding Age"; N. Sue Weiler, "Family Security or Social Security? The Family and the Elderly in New York during the 1920s," *Journal of Family History* 11 (1986): 77–95.

61. Strong public reaction to age limits prompted employers to explain hiring and retention policies, e.g., in *The Older Worker in Industry*. On educational and language deficiencies, see Joint Legislative Commission, box 119-1, folder "Educational Requirements," NYSA.

62. Edward P. Lazear, "Why Is There Mandatory Retirement?" *Journal of Political Economy* 87 (December 1979): 1261–84, and "Agency, Earnings Profiles, Productivity and Hours Restrictions," *American Economic Review* 71, no. 4 (September 1981): 606–20. Seniority's effects on older employees vs. aging applicants can be compared in *The Older American Worker*, pp. 53–60.

63. For the origins of mandatory retirement, see Carole Haber, "Mandatory Retirement in Nineteenth-Century America: The Conceptual Basis for a New Work Cycle," *Journal of Social History* 12 (1978): 77–96, and Graebner, *History of Retirement*, chap. 1.

64. Gratton, " 'A Triumph of Modern Philanthropy' "; *Twenty-third Annual Report of the Commissioner of Labor (1908): Workman's Insurance and Benefit Funds in the United States* (Washington, D.C.: Government Printing Office, 1909). Mandatory retirement at age fifty-five in Japan arises out of the same conditions. See Toshi Kii, "Retirement in Japan," in Markides and Cooper, *Retirement*.

65. Many aged workers were self-employed as farmers, businessmen, and so forth; employers' labor policies did not affect these individuals. See John D. Durand, *The Labor Force in the United States, 1890–1960* (New York: Social Science Research Council, 1948), pp. 110–13.

66. See a consulting firm's recommendations regarding long-service workers to the management of Hoopes Brothers and Darlington, Inc., box 2, Administrative, Hagley Museum and Library (Hagley).

67. Barkin, *Older Worker*, pp. 61, 143–57, 289–305, 327–35, and chaps. 9–13; E. B. Mittelman, "The Displacement of Workers, 45–64 Years of Age," *American Economic Review* 26 (March 1936): 81–83; Lucille Eaves, "Discrimination in the Employment of Older Workers in Massachusetts," *Monthly Labor Review* 44, no. 6 (June 1937): 1359–86; State of New York, Final Report of Joint Legislative Committee on Discrimination in Employment of the Middle-Aged, Legislative Document (1940) no. 80 (Albany, 1940).

68. State Emergency Welfare Relief Commission, *Michigan Census of Population and Unemployment*, no. 1 (Lansing: State of Michigan, 1936); Eaves, "Discrimination." By 1940 the pattern of moderate increases in unemployment by age and then declines after age sixty-five had returned. See Durand, *The Labor Force*, pp. 113–14, and Bureau of the Census, *Sixteenth Census . . . Population. Estimates of Labor Force, Employment, and Unemployment in the United States, 1940 and 1930* (Washington, D.C.: Government Printing Office, 1944), p. 3.

69. Quotation from preliminary documents for the 1940 Republican platform, Republican Program Committee, Documents 41 & 42, box 96, Post-Presidential Subject Files, Hoover Presidential Library; Abraham Holtzman, *The Townsend Movement: A Political Study*

(New York: Bookman, 1963); Lizabeth Cohen, *Making a New Deal: Industrial Workers in Chicago, 1919–1939* (Cambridge: Cambridge University Press, 1990). Studies of age discrimination, such as those of New York's Joint Legislative Commission, were common in the 1930s. Letters from workers to government officials reflect popular antagonism to the poor treatment of older workers. See *"Slaves of the Depression": Workers' Letters about Life on the Job*, ed. Gerald Markowitz and David Rosner (Ithaca, N.Y.: Cornell University Press, 1987). For one assessment of the political effects of the failure of private-sector guarantees, see Cohen, *Making a New Deal*; Cohen's evaluation of workers' fortunes before the New Deal, especially those of older workers, is not well informed.

70. Graebner, *History of Retirement*. Benjamin Kline Hunnicutt argues that President Roosevelt used such claims largely for political purposes; see his *Work without End: Abandoning Shorter Hours for the Right to Work* (Philadelphia: Temple University Press, 1988).

71. For a summary of the econometric literature, see S. Danziger, R. Haveman, and R. Plotnick, "How Income Transfer Programs Affect Work, Savings, and the Income Distribution: A Critical Review," *Journal of Economic Literature* 19 (1981): 975–1028. Tuma and Sandefur renew the traditional argument that Social Security (i.e., OAI) had little effect before the 1950s in "Trends in the Labor Force Activity of the Elderly."

72. *Social Security Bulletin*, July 1950; Jerry R. Cates, *Insuring Inequality: Administrative Leadership in Social Security, 1935–1954* (Ann Arbor: University of Michigan Press, 1983), pp. 104–35; Domenico Gagliardo, *American Social Insurance* (New York: Harper and Brothers, 1949), p. 67; Patricia M. Randall, *A History of the County Department of Public Welfare, Charleston, South Carolina* (n.d., n. p.; ca. 1961); General Files, City Archives, Charleston, South Carolina; former Massachusetts Commissioner of Public Welfare Robert F. Aut (interview with Brian Gratton, 12 July 1977); U.S. Social Security Administration, *Public Attitudes toward Social Security, 1935–1965*, by Michael E. Schlitz (Washington, D.C.: Government Printing Office, 1970).

73. Gratton, "The Labor Force," pp. 700–702.

74. Brian Gratton, "The New Welfare State: Social Security and Retirement in 1950," *Social Science History* 12 (Summer 1988): 171–96. The average OAA benefit in a state was assigned as a characteristic of men from that state.

75. See Moen, "Rural, Nonfarm Households," and "From Gainful Employment to Labor Force," *Historical Methods* 21, no. 4 (Fall 1988): 149–59.

76. William Bowen and T. Aldrich Finnegan, *The Economics of Labor Force Participation*, (Princeton, N.J.: Princeton University Press, 1969). Private pensions increased in scope and generosity, especially after 1950. Jill Quadagno, *The Transformation of Old Age Security: Class and Politics in the American Welfare State* (Chicago: University of Chicago Press, 1988); Richard E. Barfield and James N. Morgan, *Early Retirement: The Decision and the Experience* (Ann Arbor: University of Michigan Press, 1969); and U.S. Department of Commerce, Bureau of the Census, "Statistical Brief," SB-1-88, January 1988.

77. Danziger, Haveman, and Plotnick, "Income Transfer Programs"; Parnes, *Work and Retirement*.

78. One study, however, found Social Security did not reduce aggregate female labor-force participation in the immediate postwar period: Lee Ohanian, Eileen M. Crimmins, and Richard A. Easterlin, "Changes in Labor Force Participation of Older Men and Women since 1940: A Time Series Analysis," paper presented at the national meetings of the Gerontological Society of America, San Francisco, 1983.

79. Brian Gratton and Marie R. Haug, "Decision and Adaptation: Research on Female Retirement," *Research on Aging* 5, no. 1 (March 1983): 59–76. About half of older female workers have private pension coverage versus 70 percent of men. See "Retirement,

Too, Favors Men," *Arizona Republic*, 10 September 1991. Using the 1917–19 survey, Rotondo shows that the characteristics of a woman's husband and family influenced her decision to work in the industrial era as well. Her husband's age, for example, had stronger effects than her own; see Rotondo, "Work and Well Being."

80. L. K. George and G. L. Maddox, "Subjective Adaptation to Loss of Work Role: A Longitudinal Study," *Journal of Gerontology* 32 (1977): 456–62; Parnes, *Work and Retirement*. Social Security amendments passed in 1983 will gradually shift the full benefit retirement age to 67.

81. Nancy D. Ruggles and Richard Ruggles, "The Anatomy of Earnings Behavior," in *The Distribution of Economic Well-Being*, F. Thomas Juster, ed. (Cambridge, Mass.: NBER, 1977), pp. 123, 129. For earlier data, see Herman P. Miller, *Income Distribution in the United States* (Washington, D.C.: U.S. Department of Commerce, 1966).

82. Gavin Wright, *Old South, New South* (New York: Basic Books, 1986), p. 4; Rotondo, "Work and Well Being"; Bernstein and Bernstein, *Social Security: The System That Works*, pp. 157–58; Leanne M. Tigges, *Changing Fortunes: Industrial Sectors and Workers' Earnings* (Westport, Conn.: Praeger, 1987), p. 87; Ruggles and Ruggles, "The Anatomy of Earnings Behavior"; Herman P. Miller, *Income of the American People* (New York: John Wiley, 1955).

83. Ronald William Schatz, "American Electrical Workers: Work, Struggles, Aspirations, 1930–50," (Ph.D. diss., University of Pittsburgh, 1977), pp. 122–23. Although probably rare, throwing older workers on the "industrial scrap heap" did occur and was rarely forgotten by other workers. For a poignant example, see Stuart Bruce Kaufman, *Challenge and Change: The History of the Tobacco Workers International Union* (Urbana: University of Illinois Press, 1986), p. 67.

84. Chinoy, *Automobile Workers*, p. 83. See also Sidney Fine, *The Automobile under the Blue Eagle* (Ann Arbor: University of Michigan Press, 1963), pp. 364–67; Carl Gersuny and Gladis Kaufman, "Seniority and the Moral Economy of the U.S. Automobile Workers, 1934–46," *Journal of Social History* 18, no. 3 (Spring 1985): 463–76; Gratton, "Rewarding Age." For copious evidence of antagonism to management on this score and the early demand for straight seniority rules, see the collections for United Automobile Worker Locals nos. 9, 51, 212, and 400 at the Archives of Labor and Urban Affairs, Wayne State University.

85. William Heston McPherson traces the origins and expansion of seniority rights in *Labor Relations in the Automobile Industry* (Washington, D.C.: Brookings Institution, 1940), esp. pp. 119–26, 148–49. Ronald Schatz proves seniority's appeal to both management and unions in *The Electrical Workers: A History of Labor at General Electric and Westinghouse, 1923–1960* (Urbana: University of Illinois Press, 1983), chap. 5. See also Steve Jefferys, *Management and Managed: Fifty Years of Crisis at Chrysler* (New York: Cambridge University Press, 1986), pp. 63, 86, 94–124; Jacoby, *Employing Bureaucracy*, pp. 243–48; and *The Older American Worker*, pp. 55–56.

86. Parnes, *Work and Retirement*; Sandell, *The Problem Isn't Age*; *The Older American Worker*. A subsequent report of the secretary of labor, *Labor Market Problems of Older Workers* (Washington, D.C.: Government Printing Office, January 1989), was more optimistic about the chances of older job seekers.

87. Quadagno, *Transformation*, pp. 166–71; "General Motors," Group 10, no. 624–11, Pierre S. du Pont Papers, Hagley; Clarence E. Odell, "The Trend toward Earlier Retirement," in *Age, Work, and Automation*, ed. Paul M. Paillat and Marion E. Bunch (Basel, Switzerland: S. Karger, 1970), p. 34. See also Levine, *Age Discrimination*, esp. chap. 7. For the rush toward early retirement and for the strong inducements often given to older work-

ers by firms seeking to cut labor costs, see *Arizona Republic*, 15 April 1990, 10 October 1990.

4. The Threat of the Almshouse

1. In fact, many persons receiving nursing home care under Medicaid manage to preserve assets for their heirs. See Stephen A. Moses, "The Fallacy of Impoverishment," *Gerontologist* 30, no. 1 (1990), pp. 21–25.

2. See the following articles by Martin Tolchin, in the *New York Times*: "Conferees Agree to Repeal Disputed Medicare Program," 18 November 1989, p. A8; "Senate Spurns Move to Cancel Long-Term Health Care Plan," 20 November 1989, pp. A1, A19; "Conferees Back Major Overhaul in Medicare Fees," 21 November 1989, pp. A1, A21; "Congress Rescinds Long-Term Care Act before Adjourning," 22 November 1989, pp. A1, B6; "Lawyers Tell the Elderly 'Next Year' on Health Care," 23 November 1989, p. A20.

3. In 1980, 1.5 million individuals were in skilled nursing facilities; in 1960, the number had only been one-half million. It is estimated that by 2000, two million elderly individuals will be institutionalized. The proportion of institutionalized elderly individuals rises greatly with age. For those over eighty-five, the proportion is 22 percent. See Michael J. Salamon, *A Basic Guide to Working with Elders* (New York: Springer, 1986), p. 41. See also Frank E. Moss and Val J. Halamandaris, *Too Old, Too Sick, Too Bad: Nursing Homes in America* (Germantown, Md.: Aspen Systems Corp., 1977), pp. 3–8, and Robert N. Butler, *Why Survive?* (New York: Harper and Row, 1975), p. 273.

4. Butler, *Why Survive?*, p. 273.

5. W. Andrew Achenbaum, *Old Age in the New Land* (Baltimore: Johns Hopkins University Press, 1978), p. 80; Brian Gratton, *Urban Elders* (Philadelphia: Temple University Press, 1986), pp. 132–33. An additional, unknown number resided in boarding houses essentially operating as homes for the aged. See Commonwealth of Massachusetts, *Annual Report of the Department of Public Welfare, 1928* (Boston, 1928), and Barbara Bolling Manard et al., *Old-Age Welfare Institutions* (Lexington, Mass.: Lexington Books, 1975), p. 125.

6. *A Report of the Record Commissioners of the City of Boston containing Miscellaneous Papers*, City Document 150 (May 2, 1692), p. 62. See also *A Report of the Record Commissioners of the City of Boston containing Boston Records from 1660–1701*, City Document 68 (1682); *A Report of the Record Commissioners of the City of Boston containing Boston Records from 1700–1728*, City Document 77 (1722); *A Report of the Record Commissioners of the City of Boston Selectmen, 1701–1715*, p. 68; Douglas Lamar Jones, "The Strolling Poor: Transiency in Eighteenth Century Massachusetts," *Journal of Social History* 8 (Spring 1975): 45.

7. *A Report of the Record Commissioners of the City of Boston containing the Records of the Boston Selectmen, 1701–1715*, p. 57. See also Jill Quadagno, "The Transformation of Old Age Security," in David D. Van Tassel and Peter N. Stearns, eds., *Old Age in a Bureaucratic Society* (Westport, Conn.: Greenwood Press, 1986), p. 132.

8. In 1770, for instance, the welfare authorities of Charleston, S.C., listed three groups of individuals who would not be considered for public relief: immigrants from France, Ireland, and Germany, along with migrants from neighboring colonies; Carolinians who had failed to return to their original communities; and women and children left by men who had joined the army. The elderly, though, were not included in the roster of undesirables. As long as they were official inhabitants of the city, they were eligible for municipal support. See J. H. Easterly, "Public Poor Relief in Colonial Charleston," *South Carolina Historical Magazine*, 42, no. 2 (1941): 85–86.

9. Quadagno, "Transformation," pp. 130–31.

10. David Rothman, *The Discovery of the Asylum* (Boston: Little, Brown, 1971), pp. 35–42.

11. Carole Haber and Brian Gratton, "Old Age, Public Welfare, and Race: The Case of Charleston, South Carolina, 1800–1949," *Journal of Social History* 21, no. 2 (Winter 1987): 267.

12. Robert W. Kelso, *A History of Poor Relief in Massachusetts, 1620–1920* (Montclair, N.J.: Patterson Smith, 1969), p. 111.

13. Robert Cray, *Paupers and Poor Relief in New York City and Its Rural Environs* (Philadelphia: Temple University Press, 1988); Priscella Ferguson Clement, *Welfare and the Poor in the Nineteenth-Century City: Philadelphia, 1800–1854* (Rutherford, N.J.: Fairleigh Dickinson University Press, 1985), pp. 20–21, 42–43, 54.

14. Quadagno, "Transformation," p. 135.

15. In Philadelphia, for example, the completion of a large public almshouse in 1835 led city officials to declare that all persons seeking support had to enter the almshouse rather than receive outdoor relief. Although some outdoor aid was reinstated in 1840, the proportion receiving such assistance was quite small. In contrast to the 798 individuals who had obtained outdoor relief before the establishment of the poorhouse, only 123 were supplied with such aid. The great majority of applicants were forced to forgo such relief or agree to institutionalization. See Clement, *Welfare and the Poor*, pp. 179, 299; Rothman, *Discovery of the Asylum*, pp. 165–66.

16. Report of the Committee on the Subject of Pauperism and a House of Industry in the Town of Boston, Town Meeting, March 1821; see the annual reports for 1850–60 of the Boston Society for the Prevention of Pauperism and the Annual Report of the Directors of the House of Industry, in the Documents of the City of Boston (DCB), 1840 through 1860; Brian Gratton, "The Invention of Social Work: Welfare Reform in the Antebellum City," *Urban & Social Change Review* 18, no. 1 (Winter 1985): 3–8.

17. Gratton, "The Invention of Social Work."

18. Report of the Committee on the Subject of Pauperism, Documents of the City of Boston, 1821–1828, p. 7.

19. Stephen A. Klips, "Institutionalizing the Poor: The New York City Almshouse, 1825–1860" (Ph.D. diss., City University of New York, 1980).

20. Clement, *Welfare and the Poor*, p. 110.

21. Keith Thomas, *Age and Authority in Early Modern England* (London: British Academy, 1976), p. 241.

22. Charles E. Rosenberg, *The Care of Strangers: The Rise of America's Hospital System* (New York: Basic Books, 1987), p. 29; Clement, *Welfare and the Poor*, p. 84.

23. In Boston, societies that supported the harsh institutional system nevertheless sought to establish separate wards for the old and to prohibit the separation of aged couples. See *Report of Committee for Erecting a House of Industry*, Boston Town Records, vol. 37, Town Meeting, 22 October 1821, and Boston Prison Society, *Twenty-Sixth Annual Report* (Boston, 1851).

24. Michael B. Katz, *In the Shadow of the Poorhouse: A Social History of Welfare in America* (New York: Basic Books, 1986), p. 29; Barbara G. Rosenkrantz and Maris Vinovskis, "The Invisible Lunatics: Old Age and Insanity in Mid-Nineteenth-Century Massachusetts," in *Aging and the Elderly: Humanistic Perspectives in Gerontology*, ed. Stuart F. Spicker, Kathleen M. Woodward, and David D. Van Tassel (Atlantic Highlands, N.J.: Humanities Press, 1978) pp. 112–13.

25. *Majority and Minority Reports of an Investigation of Boston Alms House and Hospital at Long Island* (Boston: Municipal Printing Office, 1904); Rothman, *Discovery of the Asylum*, chap. 11. Inquiries into the condition of public almshouses in this period have a fa-

miliar ring for those familiar with the periodic investigations of nursing homes in our own time.

26. Estelle May Stewart, *The Cost of American Almshouses*, U.S. Bureau of Labor Statistics, Bulletin no. 386, June 1925, p. iii.

27. See, for example, the statements of Homer Folks, who served as commissioner of New York City's charities, in his "Disease and Dependence," *Charities* 10, no. 20 (May 1903), pp. 499–500, 11, no. 14 (October 1903), pp. 297–300.

28. Katz, *In the Shadow*, p. 29.

29. Rothman, *Discovery of the Asylum*, pp 207–10.

30. Charleston's *Poor House Journal*, 15 May 1867, p. 33, located at the Charleston City Archives; Haber and Gratton, "Old Age, Public Welfare, and Race," pp. 267–68.

31. Mary Roberts Smith, "Almshouse Women," *American Statistical Association*, 4, no. 31 (September 1895): 240.

32. Frederick L. Hoffman, "Stare Pensions and Annuities in Old Age," *Journal of the American Statistical Association* 11, n.s. 85 (March 1909), p. 395; Gerald N. Grob, "Explaining Old Age History," in Van Tassel and Stearns, eds., *Old Age in a Bureaucratic Society*, pp. 34–35; Gratton, *Urban Elders*, p. 132.

33. Department of Commerce, Bureau of the Census, *Paupers in Almshouses: 1910* (Washington, D.C.: Government Printing Office, 1915), p. 18.

34. Stewart, *Cost*, p. 5.

35. Folks, "Disease and Dependence," *Charities* 10, p. 500; *Charleston City Year Book for 1913* (Charleston, 1914), p. 311; Edward T. Devine, *The Principles of Relief* (New York: Macmillan, 1910), pp. 131–32.

36. *Charities and the Commons*, "New York City Homes," vol. 17 (August 27, 1900), p. 133. In Charleston, South Carolina, almshouse managers used the same language to characterize the comforts of their asylum. In 1924, they wrote:

> Our city provides the best the markets afford and in abundance. All are comfortably clothed and steam heat provides warmth during day and night . . . We encourage them to read newspapers, magazines, and books, and to attend entertainments and to worship God according to the dictates of their hearts. The welfare of each person as an individual is considered, every effort is made for his or her comfort. (*Charleston City Year Book for 1924* [Charleston, 1925], pp. 163–64)

37. *Charleston City Year Book for 1886* (Charleston, 1887), p. 193.

38. Report of the Visiting Medical Staff, Long Island Hospital, *Seventh Annual Report of the Pauper Institutions Department for the Year ending 1904* (Boston, 1905), p. 15.

39. Smith, "Almshouse Women," p. 223.

40. New York Association to Improve the Condition of the Poor, *Tenth Annual Report* (New York, 1853), pp. 66–67; Haber, *Beyond Sixty-Five*, pp. 37–40.

41. Grob, "Explaining Old Age History," p. 34.

42. Barbara G. Rosenkrantz and Maris Vinovskis, "The Invisible Lunatics: Old Age and Insanity in Mid-Nineteenth-Century Massachusetts," in Stuart F. Spicker, Kathleen M. Woodward, and David D. Van Tassel, eds., *Aging and the Elderly* (Atlantic Highlands, N.J.: Humanities Press, 1978), p. 98.

43. Ibid., pp. 98–100.

44. *Majority and Minority Reports*, p. 1730.

45. By the early twentieth century, large numbers of elderly persons did begin to fill insane asylums. Their presence, however, reflected the fact that mental institutions, like almshouses, had assumed primarily a custodial function. The superintendents of public

insane asylums held out little hope for the insane of any age. They no longer assumed that they could cure or reform them; they simply warehoused all patients, including the elderly, and prepared them for death. Grob, "Explaining Old Age History," pp. 38, 41–42.

46. St. Luke's Hospital, *Eighth Annual Report* (Chicago, 1866), p. 9.

47. Morris Vogel, "Boston's Hospitals 1870–1930: A Social History" (Ph.D. diss., University of Chicago, 1974), p. 138, and *The Invention of the Modern Hospital* (Chicago: University of Chicago Press, 1980), pp. 73–74.

48. *Majority and Minority Reports*, p. 1146.

49. Folks, "Disease and Dependence," *Charities* II, p. 298.

50. *Majority and Minority Reports*, p. 1730.

51. Charles Booth, *The Aged Poor in England and Wales* (London: Macmillan, 1894); Booth, *Pauperism and the Endowment of Old Age* (London: Macmillan, 1892). On the significance of Booth, see T. S. Simey and M. B. Simey, *Charles Booth: Social Scientist* (London: Oxford University Press, 1960). Abraham Epstein, *The Challenge of the Aged* (New York: Vanguard Press, 1929), p. 35.

52. Haber, *Beyond Sixty-Five*, chaps. 5–6.

53. Epstein, *Challenge of the Aged*, p. 60.

54. Will M. Carleton, "Over the Hill to the Poorhouse" (1871), published in Gordon and Walter Moss, ed., *Growing Old* (New York: Pocket Books, 1975), pp. 224–29. I would like to thank David Van Tassel for drawing my attention to this version.

55. "Over the Hill to the Poor House," music by David Braham, lyrics by George L. Catlin, 1874, reprinted in Donald M. Scott and Bernard Wishy, eds., *America's Families: A Documentary History* (New York: Harper and Row, 1982), p. 282.

56. This film is available from the Metropolitan Museum of Art, Circulating Film Library, in New York.

57. Gratton, *Urban Elders*, chap. 4; Haber, *Beyond Sixty-Five*, chap. 5.

58. Zimmerman, *Old Age Poverty*, p. 96. For similar origins in the Midwest, see Ethel McClure, *More than a Roof: The Development of Minnesota Poor Farms and Homes for the Aged* (St. Paul: Minnesota Historical Society, 1968).

59. Home for Aged Women, *Thirtieth Annual Report* (Boston, 1880), pp. 5–6; Gratton, *Urban Elders*, pp. 100–101.

60. "Charitable Needs in New York," *Charities* I, no. 7 (June 1898), p. 1; repeated in vol. I, no. 8 (July 1898), p. 1; vol. I, no. 9 (August 1898), p. 9; vol. I, no. 10 (September 1898), p. 10; vol I, no. 11 (October 1898), p. 8.

61. *Twenty-Eighth Annual Report of the Indigent Widows' and Single Women's Society for the Year 1844* (Philadelphia, 1845), p. 3.

62. Henry B. Rogers, *Remarks before the Association for Aged Indigent Females at the Opening of Their Home* (Boston, 1850), pp. 7–8.

63. On the later development of old-age homes by specific religious and ethnic groups see Carole Haber, "The Old Folks at Home: The Development of Institutional Care for the Aged in Nineteenth-Century Philadelphia," *Pennsylvania Magazine of History and Biography* 110, no. 2 (April 1977): 240–57.

64. Such lack of concern was not due to an absence of immigrant almshouse residents. In 1893, in Charleston, S. C., a majority of the inmates in the almshouse were from Ireland; only 33 percent were natives of the state. *Poor House Records*, Charleston, S. C. (samples taken from the year 1893). On Boston's attempts to separate native-born from immigrants, · see *Report of the Directors of the House of Industry* (Boston, 1827).

65. *Poor House Journal*, Charleston, S. C., July 1866, p. 429.

66. Ibid., April 1878, p. 309.

67. *Charleston City Year Book for the Year 1924* (Charleston, 1925), pp. 163–64.

68. Isaac M. Rubinow, "The Modern Problem of the Care of the Aged," *Social Service Review* 4 (1930): 178.

69. *Report of the Pennsylvania Commission on Old Age Pensions* (Harrisburg: J. L. L. Kuhn, 1919).

70. See, for example, Edward T. Devine, *Economics* (New York: Macmillan, 1898), *The Principles of Relief* (New York: Macmillan, 1904), and *Misery and Its Causes* (New York: Macmillan, 1909); Abraham Epstein, *Facing Old Age: A Study of Old Age Dependency in the United States and the Old Age Pension* (New York: Alfred A. Knopf, 1922), and *The Problem of Old Age Pensions in Industry* (Harrisburg,: Pennsylvania Old Age Commission, 1929); I. M. Rubinow, *Social Insurance* (New York: Henry Holt, 1913), and *The Quest for Security* (New York: Henry Holt, 1934); Lee Welling Squier, *Old Age Dependency in the United States* (New York: Macmillan, 1912); Arthur J. Todd, "Old Age and the Industrial Scrap Heap," *American Statistical Association* 14, no. 110 (June 1915): 550–57; and Amos Warner, "The Causes of Poverty Further Considered," *American Statistical Association* 4, no. 27 (September 1879): 46–48. On the vast collection of late-nineteenth- and early-twentieth-century writers on old age and industrialization, see Michel Dahlin, "From Poorhouse to Pension" (Ph.D. diss., Stanford University, 1983), and Haber, *Beyond Sixty-Five.* chap. 2.

71. Rubinow, *Social Insurance*, p. 302; Todd, "Old Age and the Industrial Scrap Heap," pp. 550–57.

72. Director's Preface, *Aged Clients of Boston's Social Agencies* (Boston: Women's Educational and Industrial Union, 1925), p. 3.

73. Epstein, *Challenge of the Aged*, p. 128.

74. In 1888, for example, the Republican national platform denounced the possibility that an honorable veteran might became "an inmate of an almshouse." See William Henry Glasson, *History of Military Pension Legislation in the United States* (New York: Columbia University Press, 1900).

75. Harry C. Evans, *The American Poor Farm and Its Inmates*, p. 5, cited by Epstein, *Challenge of the Aged*, p. 128.

76. *Eagle Magazine*, June 1925, p. 10; reprinted in Quadagno, *Transformation of Old Age Security*, opposite p. 1.

77. DCB 1897 (Boston 1898), no. 14; Marshall proposed that a public pension be provided to old people.

78. This study surveyed 86,000 inmates, 90 percent of the nation's total. Of those surveyed, 80 percent were over fifty years of age. U.S. Bureau of the Census, *Paupers in the Almshouses: 1923* (Washington, D.C.: Government Printing Office, 1925); Stewart, *The Cost of American Almshouses.*

79. *Majority and Minority Reports.*

80. See chapter 2 of this work; Gratton, *Urban Elders*, pp. 161–62; Massachusetts Commission on Pensions, *Report on Old-Age Pensions* (Boston: Commonwealth of Massachusetts, 1925).

81. Illinois State Federation of Labor, *Weekly News Letter*, 17 March 1923, cited by Quadagno, *Transformation of Old Age Security*, pp. 94–95.

82. *Eagle Magazine*, 1920–28, passim.

83. *Boston Globe*, 9 November 1923.

84. Epstein, *Challenge of the Aged*, pp. 144–48. Also see material on this theme in the papers of Franklin Delano Roosevelt, New York State Archives and Record Administration (NYS Archives), Albany, New York, Papers of New York State Governor, Central Subject and Correspondence Files, box 124, folder "Legislation: Old Age Pensions."

85. Mabel Nassau, *Old Age Poverty in Greenwich Village*, cited by Roy Lubove, *The*

Struggle for Social Security 1900–1935 (Cambridge, Mass.: Harvard University Press, 1968), p. 133.

86. Paul H. Douglas, Curtice N. Hitchcock, and Willard E. Atkins, eds., *The Worker in Industrial Society* (Chicago: University of Chicago Press, 1923), p. 465. As our analysis of the family economy suggests, this argument had considerable validity.

87. *American Labor Legislation Review* 18, no. 3 (September 1927): 224.

88. Papers of Franklin Delano Roosevelt, Franklin D. Roosevelt Library, Hyde Park, New York, Campaign of 1928, box 16: "Campaign Speeches, October–November 1928"; and NYS Archives, folder "Legislation: Old Age Pensions." See Smith's 7 March 1928 message to the legislature and Roosevelt's messages of 18 January and 28 February 1929.

89. NYS Archives, folder "Legislation: Old Age Pensions"; Louis McHenry Howe Papers, FDR Library, box 41, Correspondence 1928–32.

90. NYS Archives, folder "Legislation: Old Age Pensions."

91. Howe Papers, FDR Library, box 46, folder "State Campaign 1930. Campaign Strategy. Publicity and Campaign Issues."

92. Social Security Administration, National Archives, Washington, D.C., Central Files, 1935–1947, box 57, folder "050–1937."

93. See, for example, the *Report of the Commission on Old Age Pensions, Annuities and Insurance* (Boston: Wright and Potter, 1910), and the *Report of the Pennsylvania Commission on Old Age Pensions.*

94. DCB, 1923, no. 1, (Boston, 1924); *Boston Globe,* 9 November 1923. For further evidence of support by O'Conor and the archdiocese, see "Report of the CCB for the Year 1926," 31 January 1927, Archdiocese Archives, Chancery of the Archdiocese of Boston, Catholic Charitable Bureau Files.

95. FDR Library, "Campaign Speeches, October–November 1928."

96. NYS Archives, "Legislation–Old Age Pensions."

97. See the statements of James J. Davis, Herbert Hoover's secretary of labor, in the Pittsburgh Press, 1927 June 26, cited by Epstein, *Challenge of the Aged,* pp. 130–31.

98. Abraham Epstein, *Facing Old Age* and *The Problem of Old Age Pensions in Industry;* Rubinow, *Social Insurance* and *The Quest for Security;* Lee Welling Squier, *Old Age Dependency in the United States.*

99. Helvering vs. Davis, 1937; U.S. Social Security Board, *Economic Insecurity in Old Age.*

100. U.S. House of Representatives, 81st Congress, 1st Session, 1949, *Hearings on H. R. 2892,* p. 17; cited by William Thomas, Jr., *Nursing Homes and Public Policy* (Ithaca, N.Y.: Cornell University Press, 1969), p. 97.

101. Violet M. Fischer, "Kansas County Homes after the Social Security Act," *Social Service Review* 17, no. 4 (December 1943): 442–65. The practice came to an end when federal investigators declared the homes public institutions.

102. *Charleston City Year Book for 1938* (Charleston, 1939), p. 237.

103. *Charleston City Year Book for 1948* (Charleston, 1949), pp. 324–25.

104. Manard et al., *Old Age Institutions,* p. 125.

105. Homer Folks, New York State Commission on Old Age Security, *Hearings, 1929–1930,* cited by Thomas, *Nursing Homes and Public Policy, p.* 40.

106. Clyde F. Snider, "The Fading Almshouse," *National Municipal Review* (February 1956): 45, 60–65.

107. Moss and Halamandaris, *Too Old, Too Bad, Too Sick,* p. 6; Thomas, *Nursing Homes and Public Policy,* p. 54.

108. Thomas, *Nursing Homes and Public Policy,* pp. 17–18.

109. Moss and Halamandaris, *Too Old, Too Sick, Too Bad*, pp. 76–78.

110. Ibid., chap. 1.

111. See, for example, Claire Townsend, *Old Age: The Last Segregation* (New York: Grossman, 1971).

5. Advice to the Old

1. Old age, we believe, contrasts greatly with other stages of life, such as childhood or adolescence, which, many scholars contend, were "discovered" as distinct periods in specific historical eras. See, for example, Philippe Ariès, *Centuries of Childhood: A Social History of Family Life* (New York: Vintage Books, 1962), and Joseph Kett, *Rites of Passage: Adolescence in America, 1790 to the Present* (New York: Basic Books, 1977).

2. For a somewhat different view, see David Hackett Fischer, *Growing Old in America* (New York: Oxford University Press, 1977), and W. Andrew Achenbaum, "The Obsolescence of Old Age in America, 1865–1914," *Journal of Social History* 8 (Fall 1974): 48–62, and *Old Age in the New Land* (Baltimore: Johns Hopkins University Press, 1978). For the debate over the "golden age," see Lawrence Stone, "Walking over Grandma," *New York Review of Books* 24, no. 8 (May 1977), and David Hackett Fischer, "Growing Old: An Exchange," *New York Review of Books* 24, no. 14 (September 1977).

3. Increase Mather, *Dignity and Duty of Aged Servants of the Lord* (Boston: B. Green, 1716), p. 52.

4. Cotton Mather, *The Angel of Bethesda*, ed. Gordon W. Jones (Boston: American Antiquarian Society, 1972), p. 315.

5. Samuel Willard, *A Compleat Body of Divinity in Two Hundred and Fifty Expository Lectures of the Assembly's Sorter Catechism* (Boston: B. Eliot and D. Henchman, 1726), Sermon 180, p. 617.

6. Edward Morgan, *The Puritan Family: Religion and Domestic Relations in Seventeenth-Century New England* (New York: Harper and Row, 1966), pp. 17–28.

7. Cotton Mather, *Addresses to Old Men and Young Men and Little Children* (Boston: R. Pierce, 1690); Willard, *Compleat Body*, Sermon 180, pp. 617, 689.

8. Mather, *Addresses*, p. 40.

9. Willard, *Compleat Body*, Sermon 180, p. 689.

10. Cotton Mather, *Diary of Cotton Mather*, vol. 2 (Boston: Massachusetts Historical Society, 1912), p. 240.

11. On the tendency for the old to retire from work or fail to be first-time political leaders, see John Demos, "Old Age in Early New England," in Michael Gordon, ed., *The American Family in Social-Historical Perspective*, 2d ed. (New York: St. Martin's Press, 1978), pp. 240–44, and *A Little Commonwealth* (New York: Oxford University Press, 1970), pp. 173–74.

12. Cotton Mather, *A Brief Essay on the Glory of Aged Piety* (Boston: S. Kneeland and T. Freed, 1726), p. 28.

13. Samuel Sewall repeatedly examined his health for signs of decline, in order to know when he should retire. At age seventy-five, he finally judged himself unable to continue as a Supreme Court justice. See *The Diary of Samuel Sewall, 1674–1729* (Boston: Massachusetts Historical Society, 1878), pp. 168, 359–60, 382. Not all elderly individuals found the transition from active adult to "resigned" ancient either easy or fulfilling. In his advanced age, Increase Mather repeatedly complained that his importance to the community and his authority among the young had greatly diminished. Upon retiring from his role as minister, time weighed heavily on his hands. He comforted himself with the notion

that such transitions in power were "God's will" and that "His Holy will must be humbly and patiently submitted to." See his *Two Discourses* (Boston: B. Green, 1716), p. 134. Also see Cotton Mather, *Diary*, vol. 2, p. 617.

14. Cited by Philip Greven, *The Protestant Temperament* (New York: Alfred A. Knopf, 1977), p. 27. See also Robert Ashton, ed., *Works of John Robinson*, vol. 1 (Boston: Doctrinal Tract and Book Society, 1851), p. 246.

15. Such a perception was shared by other professional men as well. Judge Sewall, for example, congratulated a fellow judge for recognizing the weaknesses that came with age and resigning from the bench; see his *Diary*, p. 358; see also p. 8.

16. Mather, *Addresses*, p. 224.

17. Nicholas Noyes, "An Essay against Periwigs," in *Remarkable Provinces*, ed. John Demos (New York: George Braziller, 1972), p. 215.

18. William Bridge, *A Word to the Aged* (Boston: John Foster, 1679), pp. 3–4.

19. Mather, *Two Discourses*, p. 105; see also Gay (cited in n. 30 below).

20. Willard, *Compleat Body*, Sermon 97, pp. 363–64.

21. Increase Mather, *Solemn Advice to Young Men* (Boston: B. Green, 1695), p. 20.

22. Mather, *Two Discourses*, pp. 98–99.

23. Willard, *Compleat Body*, Sermon 177, p. 608.

24. Cotton Mather, *The Widow of Nain* (Boston, 1728), pp. 10–11; see also Alexander Keyssar, "Widowhood in Eighteenth-Century Massachusetts: A Problem in the History of the Family," *Perspectives in American History* 8 (1974): 99.

25. Mather, *Diary*, vol. 2, p. 208; see also pp. 42, 44–45, 145–46, 152, 160, 228, 247, 253, 257, 272, 277, 344, 348, 364, 576, 606, 676, and 763.

26. Jill S. Quadagno, "From Poor Law to Pensions," *Milbank Memorial Fund Quarterly* 62, n. 3 (Summer 1984): 417–46; John S. Williamson, "Old Age Relief Policies in the New Land, 1650–1900," in *Growing Old In America*, 3d ed., ed. Beth B. Hess and Elizabeth W. Markson (New Brunswick, N.J.: Transactions Books, 1985), pp. 56–70; Haber, *Beyond Sixty-Five*, chap. 1.

27. Willard, *Compleat Body*, Sermon 180, p. 689.

28. Mather, *Solemn Advice to Young Men*, p. 20.

29. See, for example, *A Report of the Record Commissioners of the City of Boston containing Miscellaneous Papers* (Boston: Rockwell & Churchill, 1886), City Document 150 (3 May 1692), p. 62; *A Report of the Record Commissioners of the City of Boston containing Boston Records from 1660–1701* (Boston: Rockwell & Churchill, 1881), City Document 68 (1682); and *A Report of the Record Commissioners of the City of Boston containing Boston Records from 1700–1728* (Boston: Rockwell & Churchill, 1882), City Document 77 (1722).

30. Ebenezer Gay, *The Old Man's Calendar: A Discourse on Joshua XIV. 10 delivered in the First Parish of Hingham on the Lord's Day, August 26, 1781* (Boston, 1781; Hingham: Jedidiah Farmer, 1846); cited by Daniel Scott Smith, "Old Age and the 'Great Transformation': A New England Case Study," in *Aging and the Elderly*, ed. Stuart F. Spicker, Kathleen M. Woodward, and David Van Tassel (Atlantic Highlands, N.J.: Humanities Press, 1978), p. 288.

31. Although our interpretation of the sermons of northern evangelical ministers differs slightly from that of Thomas R. Cole, it relies on his research and explication. See his "Past Meridian: Aging and the Northern Middle Class, 1830–1930" (Ph.D. diss., University of Rochester, 1980), and *The Journey of Life: A Cultural History of Aging in America* (New York: Cambridge University Press, 1992).

32. Charles Finney, "Traditions of the Elders," *Lectures on Revivals of Religion* (New York, 1835), p. 88; cited by Thomas R. Cole, " 'Putting Off the Old': Middle-Class Morality,

Antebellum Protestantism, and the Origins of Ageism," in *Old Age in a Bureaucratic Society*, ed. David Van Tassel and Peter N. Stearns (New York: Greenwood Press, 1986), pp. 49, 56.

33. Jacob Knapp, *The Autobiography of Jacob Knapp* (New York, 1858), p. 88; cited by Cole, " 'Putting Off the Old,' " pp. 55–56. Peter Cartwright, *The Autobiography of Peter Cartwright*, (New York, 1834), p. 43; cited by Cole, " 'Putting Off the Old,' " p. 56.

34. Albert Barnes, *Life at Three-score and Ten* (Philadelphia, 1859), p. 28; cited by Cole, "Past Meridian," p. 91.

35. Parker, "The Aged," *The Works of Theodore Parker* (Boston, 1910–13) pp. 195–96; cited by Cole, "Past Meridian," p. 117.

36. Beecher, "Old Age," *Forty Six Sermons*, (London, 1885), p. 237; cited by Cole, "Past Meridian," p. 142.

37. Cortlandt Van Rensselaer, *Old Age a Funeral Sermon* (Washington, D.C., 1841) p. 6; cited by Cole, "Past Meridian," p. 89.

38. C. D. Hemphill, "Manners For Americans" (Ph.D. diss., Brandeis University, 1988).

39. Adams to Jefferson, 2 December 1822, in *The Adams-Jefferson Letters*, ed. Lester J. Cappon (Chapel Hill: University of North Carolina Press, 1959), pp. 585–86.

40. Jefferson to Adams, 7 October 1818, in ibid., p. 528.

41. Jefferson to Adams, 1 June 1822, and Adams to Jefferson, 11 June 1822, in ibid., pp. 577–78. See also Adams to Jefferson, 2 March 1816, p. 464; Adams to Jefferson, 3 May 1816, pp. 469–71; and Jefferson to Adams, 1 August 1816, pp. 483–484.

42. For a study of the values and beliefs of elderly women in the period after the Revolution, see Terri Premo, *Winter Friends* (Urbana: University of Illinois Press, 1990).

43. Cited by Premo, *Winter Friends*, p. 144.

44. Ibid., p. 143.

45. Ibid., p. 33.

46. Benjamin Rush, "An Account of the Body and Mind in Old Age and Observations upon its Diseases and their Remedies," *Medical Inquiries and Observations* (Philadelphia: Thomas Dobson, 1797).

47. Ibid., p. 451.

48. On the effect of romanticization, see Ann Douglas, *The Feminization of American Culture* (New York: Alfred A. Knopf, 1977).

49. Horace Bushnell, "How to Make a Right and Ripe Old Age," *Hours at Home* 4 (December 1866): 106–12, cited by Cole, "Past Meridian," p. 119; Bushnell, "The Power of the Endless Life," *Sermons for a New Life* (New York, 1865), p. 308; cited by Cole, "Past Meridian," p. 134.

50. *Second Annual Report of the Old Man's Home for 1866* (Philadelphia, 1867), p. 8.

51. Perhaps not surprisingly, Protestant ministers and their affiliated groups of women volunteers played a large role in creating the first homes for aged women. In calls for financial support, the benevolent societies echoed the ministers' characterization of the impoverished widow. The elderly women for whom the institutions were erected were portrayed as needing society's sympathy and compassion; they were the most fragile and needy of life's unfortunate outcasts. Having lost their financial and emotional supports, they required the charity and kindness of more prosperous Americans. The organizers of the first such institution in Philadelphia, the Indigent Widows' and Single Women's Society, declared at its founding in 1817 that "Providence has sanctioned the endeavor to rescue from suffering a class of fellow being, who without the attractions of infancy are equally helpless and dependent; who surviving all those endearing ties which give a value to existence, have

no resources, no hope, but in a principle of benevolence." See the *Annual Report of the Managers of the Indigent Widows and Single Women's Society for 1817* (Philadelphia, 1818), p. 6.

52. Carole Haber, *Beyond Sixty-Five*.

53. Isaac Ray, *A Treatise on the Medical Jurisprudence of Insanity* (1838), ed. Winfred Overholse (Cambridge, Mass.: Belknap Press, 1962), pp. 206–7.

54. Ibid., p. 16.

55. Ibid., p. 336.

56. Ibid., pp. 212, 336.

57. Ibid., p. 338.

58. Margaret K. Krasik, "The Lights of Science and Experience: Historical Perspectives on Legal Attitudes toward the Role of Medical Expertise in Guardianship of the Elderly," *American Journal of Legal History* 33, no. 3 (July 1989): 201–40.

59. In re Beaumont, 1 Whart. 52 (Pa. 1836); cited by Krasik, "Lights of Science," pp. 207–10.

60. M'Elroy's Case, 6 Watts & Serg. (1943); cited ibid., pp. 220–23.

61. Ibid.

62. Ibid., p. 224.

63. See, for example, John S. Holme, *Light at Eventide*, 1871; S. G. Lathrop, *Fifty Years and Beyond*, 1881; Cora Nourse, *Sunset Hours of Life*, 1875; and Lydia Sigourney, *Past Meridian*, 1856. The authors would like to thank Tom Cole for these references.

64. On the development of the medical model, see Haber, *Beyond Sixty-Five*, chaps. 3 and 4.

65. I. L. Nascher, "Pathology of Old Age," *Medical Council* 15 (March 1910): 94. Numerous other doctors agreed. "The weight of evidence," wrote W. H. Curtis, "seems to establish the fact that old age is never physiological but pathological, at least its visible and appreciable evidences are pathological ones." See his "Disease in the Aged," *Illinois Medical Journal* 10, no. 4 (October 1906): 401. See also Frederick N. Brown, "Some Observations upon Old Age and Its Consequences," *Providence Medical Journal* 10, no. 1 (January 1909): 91; W. C. Bunce, "Some of the Influences That Determine Age," *Ohio State Medical Journal* 1 (April 1906): 467; W. C. Goodno, "Senility, with especial reference to the Changes Developing in the Circulatory Organs, their Exciting Causes, and Symptoms," *Transactions of the Thirty-Third Session of the Homeopathic Medical Society of the State of Pennsylvania* 33 (1897): 244; William Kinnear, "Postponing Old Age," *Medical Age* 17, no. 2 (January 1899): 49; E. N. Leake, "At What Period Does Old Age Begin?" *Medical Examiner* 25 (October 1894): 757; Charles G. Stockton, "The Delay of Old Age and the Alleviation of Senility," *Buffalo Medical Journal* 61, no. 1 (August 1905): 3; J. Madison Taylor, "The Conservation of Energy in Those Advancing in Years," *Popular Science Monthly* 64 (March 1904): 407; and William Gilman Thompson, *Practical Dietetics* (New York: D. Appleton, 1906), p. 312.

66. I. L. Nascher, "The Treatment of Senility," *Medical Record* 76, no. 24 (December 1909), p. 988; see also George E. Day, *A Practical Treatise on the Domestic Management and Most Important Diseases of Advanced Life* (London: T. and W. Boone, 1849), pp. 52–53.

67. I. L. Nascher, "Hygiene and Regimen in Old Age," *Medical Council* 15: 166. See also Samuel G. Dorr, "Care and Treatment of Old People," *Buffalo Medical Journal* 35, no. 1 (August 1895): 147.

68. A. Loomis, "Climate and Environment Best Suited to Old Age in Health and Disease," *Transactions of the Fifth Climatological Association* (1888), pp. 8–9.

69. Gutheie Rankin, "Old Age," *Practitioner* 72 (May 1904): 703–704. See also Taylor, "Conservation of Energy," p. 345; Daniel Maclachlan, *A Practical Treatise on the Diseases*

and Infirmities of Advanced Life (London: John Churchill, 1863), p. 58; and W. M. Gibson, "Some Considerations of Senescence," *New York State Journal of Medicine* 9, no. 9 (September 1909): 385.

70. Taylor, "Conservation of Energy," p. 345.

71. Thompson, *Practical Dietetics*, pp. 312–13. See also John Bell, *On Regimen and Longevity* (Philadelphia: Haswell & Johnson, 1842), p. 85; S. W. Caldwell, *Thoughts on the Effects of Age on the Human Constitution* (Louisville: John C. Noble, 1846), p. 16; Day, *Practical Treatise on the Diseases of Advanced Life*, pp. 24–32; Dorr, "Care and Treatment of Old People," p. 147; Henry Holland, *Medical Notes and Reflections* (Philadelphia: Haswell, Barrington and Haswell, 1839), p. 177; George Hawson Keyworth, "Notes on Disease in Advanced Life," *British Medical Journal* 1 (31 January 1903): 240; Arnold Lorand, *Old Age Deferred* (Philadelphia: F. A. Davis, 1910), pp. 280–367; I. N. Love, "The Needs and Rights of Old Age," *Journal of the American Medical Association* 24, no. 21 (20 November 1897): 1036; Maclachlan, *Practical Treatise*, p. 59; I. L. Nascher, "Hygiene and Regimen in Old Age," *Medical Council* 25, no. 5: 166; Marvin E. Nuchols, "Old Age and the Modifications in the Course of the Ordinary Diseases When They Attack the Aged," *Maryland Medical Journal* 42, no. 15 (7 October 1899): 199; Richard Webb Wilcox, "The Therapeutics of Old Age," *American Medicine* 4, no. 4 (April 1909): 182.

72. Fernand Lagrange, "Exercise for Elderly People," *Popular Science Monthly* 39 (1891): 771–78. See also Loomis, "The Climate and Environment Best Suited to Old Age," p. 4; Maclachlan, *Practical Treatise*, p. 60; Stewart Skinner, "The Effects of Age on the Vascular System," *Maritime Medical News* 9, no. 11 (November 1897): 373; J. Madison Taylor, "How to Postpone the Degenerative Effects of Old Age," *Transactions of the American Climatological Association* 19 (1903): 237.

73. Taylor, "How to Postpone," p. 223.

74. On the ideas of longevity experts before the nineteenth century, see Gerald A. Gruman, *History of Ideas about the Prolongation of Life* (Philadelphia: American Philosophical Society, 1966), and "The Rise and Fall of Prolongevity Hygiene," *Bulletin of the History of Medicine* 35 (1961): 221–27.

75. Rankin, "Old Age," p. 703.

76. For exceptions, see the British physician George M. Humphrey, "Centenarians," *British Medical Journal* (5 March 1887): 502–4, and *Old Age* (Cambridge: Macmillan, 1885), and the American psychologist G. Stanley Hall, *Senescence: The Last Half of Life* (New York: D. Appleton, 1923), pp. 3–31.

77. George M. Beard, *Legal Responsibility in Old Age Based on Researches in the Relation of Age to Work* (New York: Russells' American Stead, 1873).

78. Sir William Osler, "The Fixed Period," *Scientific American* 25 (March 1905).

79. Hall, *Senescence*, pp. 3–31; E. G. Dexter, in *Popular Scientific Monthly* (July 1902); *Baltimore American*, 24 February 1905, p. 13; *Baltimore Sun*, 25 February 1905, p. 8; *Harper's Weekly*, 11 March 1905, p. 347; *New York Times*, 25 February 1905, p. 8, 23 October 1905, p. 8; *Washington Evening Star*, 25 February 1905, pt. 1, p. 4.

80. Osler, "The Fixed Period."

81. On Osler's reaction to the response, see William Graebner, *A History of Retirement: The Meaning and Function of an American Institution, 1885–1978* (New Haven, Conn.: Yale University Press, 1980), pp. 3–10.

82. We disagree with Leslie Hannah, who has argued that doctors only reflected "the dotty prejudices of their age in all their splendid variety" and did not influence policy. As is obvious, no absolute uniformity of opinion on old age exists in any era, but the new medical model of aging clearly had a social influence beyond the medical texts. Moreover,

we believe that although there was variety of opinion among the physicians, the over-whelming majority spoke of the aged in new terms that emphasized their increasing de-bility and declining mental states. The one example Hannah gives of a positive view of aging is that of G. Stanley Hall. Writing late in life, Hall had his own agenda. His work does not negate the opinions of scores of physicians who published and prescribed accord-ing to a negative medical model of senescence. See Hannah, *Inventing Retirement: The Development of Occupational Pensions in Britain* (Cambridge: Cambridge University Press, 1986), pp. 123–24, and Hall, *Senescence.*

83. Francis A. Walker, *The Wages Question* (New York: Henry Holt, 1876), pp. 414–15.

84. I. M. Rubinow, *Social Insurance* (New York: Henry Holt, 1913), p. 302.

85. Burton J. Hendrick, "The Superannuated Man," *McClure's* 32 (December 1908): 117; Ohio Commission on Old Age, p. 223; Pennsylvania Health Insurance Commission Report, pp. 31–32; *American Labor Legislation Review* (December 1920): 232; all cited by Abraham Epstein, *Facing Old Age* (New York: Alfred A. Knopf, 1922), pp. 68–84; Con-necticut Public Welfare Commission, cited by Epstein, *The Challenge of the Aged* (New York: Macy-Masius, 1928), pp. 66–68; *Report of the Massachusetts Commission on Old Age Pensions, Annuities, and Insurance*, pp. 270–71; Graebner, *History of Retirement*, chap. 2.

86. *Report of the Commissioners of Pensions for 1900* (Washington, D.C., 1901), p. 26; *Report of the Commissioners of Pensions for 1904* (Washington, D.C., 1905); Bureau of Pen-sions, *Instructions to Examining Surgeons* (Washington, D.C.: Government Printing Office, 1913), p. 20. See also "The Pensions Inquiry," *Nation* 78, no. 2021 (March 1904): 224.

87. Quoted in Elias S. Cohen and Anna L. Kruschwitz, "Old Age in America Rep-resented in Nineteenth and Twentieth Century Popular Sheet Music," *Gerontologist* 30, no. 3 (June 1990): 345–54.

88. Della T. Lutes, "Why I Don't Tell My Age," *Forum* 97, no. 5 (April 1937): 244–48; Richard LeGallienne, "The Art of Not Growing Old," *Harper's Magazine* 142 (April 1921): 655–60; Francis G. Peabody, "On Keeping Young," *Atlantic Monthly* 145 (June 1930): 820–24; "Let's Stay Young," *Colliers* 83 (13 April 1929); Martha Cutler, "How to Remain Young," *Harper's Bazaar* 43 (September 1909): 131; *Good Housekeeping*, "What Makes A Woman Old?" (January 1924): 23, 186; Ruth F. Wadsworth, "Let's Stay Young Together," *Colliers* 83 (3 April 1929): 22, 61.

89. LeGallienne, "The Art of Not Growing Old," p. 660.

90. Genevieve Grandcourt, "Eternal Youth as Scientific Theory," *Scientific American* (15 November 1919): 482, 490, 500; Jerome Lachenbruch, "The Fight to Conquer Old Age," *Scientific American* 128, no. 1 (January 1923): 22; "Old Age Can be Deferred—An Interview with Dr. Serge Voronoff," *Scientific American* 133, no. 4 (October 1925): 226–27.

91. Paula Fass, *The Damned and the Beautiful: American Youth in the 1920s* (New York: Oxford University Press, 1977); Howard P. Chudacoff, *How Old Are You? Age Consciousness in American Culture* (Princeton, N.J.: Princeton University Press, 1989).

92. According to Alice Hamilton, a new problem arose in modern society: "the prob-lem of premature old age, of the forced idleness of men and women still in the prime of life, of the establishment of a dead line at forty years, after which one is classified as unfit for work." See her "State Pensions or Charity?" *Atlantic Monthly* 145 (1930): 684; see also Rubinow, *Social Insurance*, p. 304.

93. Lutes, "Why I Don't Tell My Age," p. 246.

94. I. L. Nascher, "Geriatrics," *New York Medical Journal* 90 (21 August 1909): 358–59.

95. On the problems that confronted the establishment of geriatrics in the early twen-tieth century, see Carole Haber, "Geriatrics: A Specialty in Search of Specialists," in *Old Age in a Bureaucratic Society*, pp. 66–84.

96. Despite the increased optimism and interest in old age, geriatrics still has developed slowly. In 1977, only 317 physicians listed their primary interest as geriatrics; another 312 identified the specialty as their secondary or tertiary concern. These 629 practitioners made up only 0.2 percent of the profession. See Robert L. Kane et al., *Geriatrics in the United States* (Lexington, Mass: Lexington, 1981), p. 83. See also Haber, "Geriatrics."

97. Edward Stieglitz, *Geriatric Medicine* (Philadelphia: W. B. Saunders, 1943), pp. 11, 49.

98. Many of the writers in Stieglitz's *Geriatric Medicine* attempted to define the "normal" aspects of aging. See, for example, Anton J. Carlson, "Principal Physiologic Changes with Normal Aging," pp. 51–71; Jean Oliver, "Principal Anatomic Changes with Normal Aging," pp. 72–98; and Walter R. Miles and Catharine C. Miles, "Principal Mental Changes with Normal Aging," pp. 99–117.

99. Nathan Shock, *Trends in Gerontology* (Stanford, Calif.: Stanford University Press, 1951; 2d ed. 1957).

100. The debate over "disengagement" versus activity theory that existed in the 1960s and 1970s was one example of the academic attempt to prescribe social and psychological norms for senescence. See Elaine Cummings and William E. Henry, *Growing Old* (New York: Basic Books, 1961), and Arlie Russell Hochschild, "Disengagement Theory: A Critique and Proposal," *American Sociological Review* 40 (October 1975): 553–69.

101. Robert C. Atchley, *Social Forces and Aging* (Belmont, Calif.: Wadsworth, 1988); Robert H. Binstock and Ethel Shanas, eds., *Handbook of Aging and the Social Sciences* (New York: Van Nostrand Reinhold, 1976); *Growing Old In America*, ed. Beth B. Hess and Elizabeth W. Markson; Bernice Neugarten, ed., *Middle Age and Aging* (Chicago: University of Chicago Press, 1968); Matilda Riley and Anne Foner, *Aging and Society: A Sociology of Age Stratification* (New York: Russell Sage Foundation, 1972); Leo W. Simmons, *The Role of the Aged in Primitive Society* (New Haven, Conn.: Yale University Press, 1945).

102. Robert N. Butler, *Why Survive? Being Old in America* (New York: Harper and Row, 1975).

103. Robert Butler, "Age-ism: Another Form of Bigotry," *Gerontologist* 9 (1969): 243–46.

104. One notable exception to this rule can be found in the work of Jean Beaven Abernathy. In *Old Is Not a Four-Letter Word*, (Nashville, Tenn.: Abingdon Press, 1975), p. 37, she wrote, "Older people gradually develop, quite inadvertently, a very important, necessary, and even productive role for themselves, namely, that of teaching others how to grow old."

105. Abernathy, *Old Is Not a Four-Letter Word*, and *Older and Wiser: Wit, Wisdom and Spirited Advice for the Older Generation* (New York: Walker and Walker, 1986); Margaret Hellie Huyck, *Growing Older: Things You Need to Know about Aging* (Englewood Cliffs, N.J.: Prentice-Hall, 1974); Jack Levin and William C. Levin, *Ageism: Prejudice and Discrimination against the Elderly* (Belmont, Calif.: Wadsworth, 1980); Charles H. Russell, *Good News about Aging* (New York: John Wiley, 1989).

106. Anne C. Averyt, *Successful Aging: A Sourcebook for Older People and Their Families* (New York: Ballantine Books, 1987); Leopold Bellak, *The Best Years of Your Life: A Guide to the Art and Science of Aging* (New York: Atheneum, 1975); Janet K. Belsky, *Here Tomorrow: Making the Most of Life after Fifty* (Baltimore: Johns Hopkins University Press, 1988); Paula Brown Doress and Diana Laskin Siegal, *Ourselves, Growing Older* (New York: Simon and Schuster, 1987); Art Linkletter, *Old Age Is Not for Sissies: Choices for Senior Americans* (New York: Viking, 1988).

107. Haber, *Beyond Sixty-Five*, chap. 6.

108. Fred Best, *Flexible Life Scheduling* (New York: Praeger, 1980); Joseph C. Buckley, *The Retirement Handbook* (New York: Harper and Row, 1977); Helen Dennis, ed., *Retirement Preparation* (Lexington, Mass.: D. C. Heath, 1984); Max Kaplan, *Leisure: Lifestyle and Lifespan* (Philadelphia: W. B. Saunders, 1979); Gordon F. Streib and Clement J. Schneider, *Retirement in American Society* (Ithaca, N.Y.: Cornell University Press, 1971).

109. David A. Tombs, *Growing Old: A Handbook for You and Your Aging Parent* (New York: Viking, 1984), pp. 55–56. See also Barbara Silverstone and Helen Kandel Hyman, *You and Your Aging Parent* (New York: Pantheon, 1989), p. 149.

110. Marshall B. Kapp and Arthur Bigot, *Geriatrics and the Law* (New York: Springer, 1985).

111. Teresa Schwab Myers, *How to Keep Control of Your Life after Sixty* (Lexington, Mass.: D. C. Heath, 1989), p. xv.

112. Joan Ader, *The Retirement Book* (New York: Morrow, 1975); Averyt, *Successful Aging*; Lorin A. Baumhover and Joan Dechow Jones, eds., *Handbook of American Aging Programs* (Westport, Conn.: Greenwood Press, 1987); Wesley J. Smith, *The Senior Citizens' Handbook* (Los Angeles: Price Stern Sloan, 1989); Tombs, *Growing Old*, pp. 66–68.

113. "Old Age Intestate," *Harper's Monthly* 162 (May 1931): 712–14; "I Am the Mother-In-Law in the Home," *Reader's Digest* 31 (November 1937): 11–14.

114. Bellak, *Best Years of Your Life*, p. 28; Silverstone and Hyman, *You and Your Aging Parent*, p. 149; Tombs, *Growing Old*, pp. 55–56.

115. Avis Jane Ball, *Caring for an Aging Parent: Have I Done All I Can?* (Buffalo, N.Y.: Prometheus Ball, 1986); Victor G. Cicirelli, *Helping Elderly Parents: The Role of Adult Children* (Boston: Auburn House, 1981).

116. Elaine Brody, cited by Averyt, *Successful Aging*, p. 370. See also Elaine M. Brody, "Women in the Middle and Family Help to Older People," *Gerontologist* 21 (1981): 471–80, and "Parent Care as a Normative Family Stress," *Gerontologist* 25 (1985): 19–29. Brody does not consider the financial contributions made by working children to the family fund in the preindustrial and industrial eras.

117. Averyt, *Successful Aging*, p. 376.

118. Mark A. Edinberg, *Talking with Your Aging Parents* (Boston: Shambhala, 1987); Lissy Jarvik and Gary Small, *Parentcare: A Commonsense Guide for Adult Children* (New York: Crown, 1988); Linkletter, *Old Age Is Not for Sissies*.

119. James Halperin, *Helping Your Aging Parents: A Practical Guide for Adult Children* (New York: McGraw-Hill, 1987), p. 53.

120. Silverstone and Hyman, *You and Your Aging Parent*, p. 142.

121. To some extent, as we discuss in the final chapter, this debate has reappeared in the 1980s as a struggle between age groups over entitlements rather than as an intrafamily conflict over resources and provisions. See Daniel Callahan, *Setting Limits: Medical Goals in an Aging Society* (New York: Simon and Schuster, 1987), and Phillip Longman, *Born to Pay: The New Politics of Aging in America* (Boston: Houghton Mifflin, 1987).

122. Graebner, *History of Retirement*; Carroll Estes, *The Aging Enterprise* (San Francisco: Jossey-Bass, 1979). See also Laura Katz Olsen, *The Political Economy of Aging* (New York: Columbia University Press, 1982).

123. For some examples of advice to the advisers, see R. Adelson et al., "Behavioral Ratings of Health Professionals' Interactions with the Geriatric Patient," *Gerontologist* 22 (1982): 227–81; Patricia K. Alpaugh and Margaret Haney, *Counseling the Older Adult: A Training Manual for Paraprofessionals and Beginning Counselors* (Los Angeles: University of Southern California Press, 1978); Phillip Ash, "Pre-retirement Counseling," *Gerontologist* 6 (1966): 97–99, 127–28; and Kapp and Bigot, *Geriatrics and the Law*.

6. A New History of Old Age

1. Robert M. Fogelson, *The Fragmented Metropolis: Los Angeles, 1850–1930* (Cambridge: Harvard University Press, 1967), p. 69.

2. See, for example, Abraham Epstein, *Facing Old Age: A Study of Old Age Dependency in the United States and Old Age Pensions* (New York: Alfred A. Knopf, 1922), and *The Challenge of the Aged* (New York: Vanguard Press, 1929); and I. M. Rubinow, *Social Insurance* (New York: Henry Holt, 1913), and *The Quest for Security* (New York: Henry Holt, 1934).

3. H. Fairlie, "Talkin' 'bout My Generation," *New Republic* 198, no. 13 (1988): 19–22; Daniel Callahan, *Setting Limits: Medical Goals in an Aging Society* (New York: Simon and Schuster, 1987), and Phillip Longman, *Born to Pay: The New Politics of Aging in America* (Boston: Houghton Mifflin, 1987).

Sources Used in Preparing the Figures

Figure 2.1 Alice Hanson Jones, *Wealth of a Nation To Be: The American Colonies on the Eve of the Revolution* (New York: Columbia University Press, 1980); Lee Soltow, *Men and Wealth in the United States, 1850–1870* (New Haven: Yale University Press, 1975); and Daphne T. Greenwood and Edward N. Wolff, "Relative Wealth Holdings of Children and the Elderly in the United States, 1962–83," in *The Vulnerable*, ed. John L. Palmer, Timothy Smeeding, and Barbara Boyle Torrey (Washington: Urban Institute Press, 1988).

Figures 2.2, 2.3, 2.4, 3.1. *Cost of Living of Industrial Workers in the United States and Europe, 1888–1890* and *Cost of Living in the United States, 1917–1919* can be accessed in machine-readable format from the Inter-university Consortium for Political and Social Research in Ann Arbor, Michigan.

Figure 3.2. U.S. Department of Commerce, *Money Income of Households, Families, and Persons in the United States: 1988 and 1989*. CPS Consumer Income, Series P-60, No. 172, July 1991.

Index

Carole Haber is Professor of History at the University of North Carolina in Charlotte and author of *Beyond Sixty-Five: The Dilemma of Old Age in America's Past*.

Brian Gratton is Associate Professor of History at Arizona State University and author of *Urban Elders: Family, Work, and Welfare Among Boston's Aged, 1890–1950*.